Unmaking Contact

Unmaking Contact

Choreographing South Asian Touch

ROYONA MITRA

with

AKILA
DIYA NAIDU
NAHID SIDDIQUI
LAWHORE VAGISTAN

OXFORD
UNIVERSITY PRESS

Oxford University Press is a department of the University of Oxford.
It furthers the University's objective of excellence in research, scholarship,
and education by publishing worldwide. Oxford is a registered trade mark of
Oxford University Press in the UK and certain other countries.

Published in the United States of America by Oxford University Press
198 Madison Avenue, New York, NY 10016, United States of America.

© Oxford University Press 2025

All rights reserved. No part of this publication may be reproduced, stored in a retrieval system, transmitted, used for text and data mining, or used for training artificial intelligence, in any form or by any means, without the prior permission in writing of Oxford University Press, or as expressly permitted by law, by license or under terms agreed with the appropriate reprographics rights organization. Inquiries concerning reproduction outside the scope of the above should be sent to the Rights Department, Oxford University Press, at the address above.

You must not circulate this work in any other form
and you must impose this same condition on any acquirer

CIP data is on file at the Library of Congress

ISBN 978-0-19-762777-8 (pbk.)
ISBN 978-0-19-762776-1 (hbk.)

DOI: 10.1093/oso/9780197627761.001.0001

To *Gega*

Whose Healing Touch Empowers

Contents

Acknowledgments   ix
Preface   xiii

Introduction: Unmaking Contact   1

1. Contact as Caste Justice: *Theenda Theenda* (2018) by Akila and the Touch of Death   64

2. Contact as Reframing Sociality: *Rorschach Touch* (2018) by Diya Naidu and "Normalizing Touch"   103

3. Contact as Ecological Relationality: *Mirror Within* (2022) by Nahid Siddiqui and Shakila Maan and Touch without Tactility   140

4. Contact as *Adda*: Critical Encounters in *#KaateNahinKatte* Instareel (2020) by LaWhore Vagistan and Digital Touching   184

Afterwords: Against Conclusions   234

Notes   247
Index   251

Acknowledgments

This book has taken the best part of a decade to come into being, and I hope and feel that it is by far more sincere a quest for this slowness. In a profession that demands of us both haste and volume at once, I am thankful to my academic mentor and friend Janet O'Shea for encouraging me to embrace the value of slow research.

To my editor at Oxford University Press, Norman Hirschy, thank you for your patience and unwavering support in enabling its slowness to emerge, shapeshift, and materialize since our first conversation in 2015. Your encouragement has been steadfast and invaluable.

My deep gratitude to the anonymous reviewers of my proposal and manuscript—you modeled critical friendship through your questions, suggestions, and commentaries, and my book is undoubtedly stronger for your interventions.

I am grateful too for the caring and critical eyes of my scholar-siblings Anurima Banerji, Kareem Khubchandani, Sharanya Murali, Brahma Prakash, and Arabella Stanger for strengthening my chapters with loving critique.

At the heart of this book project is so much good faith, founded on deep and sustained dialogues between many dance artists and myself.

My deepest gratitude to all my generous interlocutor-artists whose words and works permeate every page. Thank you Akila, Chandiran, Diya Naidu, Nahid Siddiqui, Shakila Maan, and LaWhore Vagistan for trusting me with your sustained creative and critical sharings, your vulnerabilities, your visions, and your open hearts. Thank you too for trusting my instincts and encouraging me to find new ways to author. In writing about each of you, I have written with each of you—and this has been a gift of togetherness.

Nrithya Pillai—your unwavering commitment to dismantling Indian dance's caste supremacist foundations is an inspiration. I learn from you every day. I am indebted to your words and work, and I am grateful to be held to account by them.

I have learned from Shaista Patel the art of critical generosity, vulnerability, and accountability in and through your scholarship. You model these with so much care.

My beautiful conversations over the years with Pia Bunglowala, Akram Khan, Hari Krishnan, Masoom Parmar, Lionel Popkin, Asha Ponikiewska, Mandeep Raikhy, and Anishaa Tavag have informed my thinking in crucial ways. Thank you for giving so generously of your time and reflections and learnings, and for believing in my project. You are all present in my thinking.

It is undeniable that my February 2016 Skype with the late Steve Paxton laid the foundations to this project—and for this and your generosity to a complete stranger, I shall forever remain grateful.

Working closely with my oldest friends Rukminee Guha Thakurta and Nityan Unnikrishnan, listening to them ideate together a book cover-design that speaks so deeply to its interiorities, and receiving Rukminee's gift of its beautiful materialization, a labor of love and vision, have been nothing short of sheer joy and privilege.

The stunning images that accompany this book and enable my writing to come alive for my readers are integral to this project. Thank you to photographers Sridhar Balasubramaniyam, Dannilla Correya, Nabila Mujassam Maan, Shakila Taranum Maan, and Kareem Khubchandani for your permissions so that my words can live in and through your images. Thank you also to all the performers in these images for lending me your permissions to use these photos in the book: Akila, Chandiran, Kareem Khubchandani, Diya Naidu, Dayita Nereyeth, Priyabrata Panigrahi, Masoom Parmar, Nihal Pasha, Asha Joanna Grażyna Ponikiewska Ranjan, Nahid Siddiqui, Anishaa Tavag, and LaWhore Vagistan.

There are several structural opportunities that have scaffolded the evolution of this book. I am grateful to Brunel University of London's BRIEF Award in 2015 which enabled me a year's sabbatical and research funds; it is during this year that the kernels of this project were sown. In 2016 the opportunity to share my initial research ideas at Brunel Theatre's Research Seminar Series was valuable, as was the invitation to present at Kingston University's Postgraduate Research Seminar Series. In 2018, publishing my conversation with Steve Paxton as an interview-essay in *Dance Research Journal* crystallized the multiple intersecting questions of power in the movement practice of contact improvisation. In 2019, an invitation to deliver a keynote at the University of Malta's School of Performing Arts Annual Conference was an invaluable opportunity to share the intellectual premise of this book. In 2021, this went on to become my article "Unmaking Contact: Choreographic Touch at the Intersections of Race, Caste, and Gender" published in *Dance Research Journal*. Thank you to *Dance Research Journal* for publishing my article in Volume 53, Issue 3, and allowing me to reprint revised sections of it, distributed across the Preface and Introduction to this book. And finally, in 2022, Brunel University London awarded me a short sabbatical to work on this book. All these opportunities have structurally enabled this book to be birthed in a sustained manner, and for this, I am grateful.

Universities quell coalitional and resistive politics. Working in them while seeking joy in collective resistance is thus a survival instinct. For bringing this joy and critical friendship to my work life at Brunel University of London—Shafeena Anas, Imarn Ayton, Filipa Baptista, Sara De Benedictis, Sandra Eyakware, Asress Gikay, Ivan Girina, Victor Ladron de Guevara, Surya Haldania, Balbir Kaur, Sharon Lockyer, Geeta Ludhra, Claire Lynch, Sarita Malik, Sharanya Murali, Beatrice Otudeko, Maninder Panaser, Rohini Rai, Tina Ramkalawan, Rachel Stuart, and Gavin Thatcher—thank you.

To all my scholar-siblings who sustain me with love and nourishment, and who inspire me with courage—Mojisola Adebayo, Roaa Ali, Anurima Banerji, Melissa Blanco Borelli, Broderick Chow, Clare Croft, Lennox Goddard, Claire Hampton, Rachel Hann, Nesreen Hussein, Jasmine Johnson, Anusha Kedhar, Kareem Khubchandani, Sharanya Murali, Justine Nakase, Adelina Ong, Ella Parry-Davies, Brahma Prakash, Prarthana Purkayastha, Rajni Shah, Arabella Stanger, Munjulika R. Tarah, Hannah Thuraisingam Robbins, and Tia-Monique Uzor—I am so fortunate to be un/learning with you all in our shared endeavors to create more just futures for dance, theater, and performance studies. Thank you for your critical friendships, and for modeling how to be audacious and vulnerable in your work—I learn from you all to do better by dance, theater, and performance studies every day.

To Maya—I can never thank you enough for literally being my weighted comfort blanket, through rain and shine that accompanied the writing of this book, but especially when comfort was impossible to find.

Nothing has been more clarifying in my life than experiencing the scale and depth of responsibility in nurturing a human in and for this broken world. To my sparkling diamond daughter Heera—I hope I can equip you in my lifetime with the imaginaries, the will, and the know-how to unmake this world you have inherited, toward more emancipatory futures.

To my life partner Colin—your unwavering love and radical hope for humanity teaches me, against all odds, that such worlds are not only critical, but also possible. Thank you for being my light.

To Ma, Baba, Dada, and Luna—thank you for letting me go and for letting go of me. And for embracing me back into the fold of home—where I started this journey—and where I return fundamentally changed.

And finally to Gega—to whom this book is dedicated—for loving me unconditionally and for teaching me that touch can indeed heal and emancipate—I shall never be able to adequately express how foundational you are to my book, my life, my being.

Preface

Her arms are flung to the sides, palms facing up, eyes closed, back arched, head thrown back, her body open and receptive, as her rhythmic musicality and larger-than-life aura radiates through the screen and touches me.

She is alone. And she is enough.

In the summer of 1988, my cousins and I were spending sultry afternoons sprawled on cool tiled living room floors, desperate for some respite from the oppressive Kolkata heat. One afternoon we sat down to watch the Bollywood blockbuster *Mr India* starring the late Sridevi as journalist Seema Sohni, and Anil Kapoor as Arun Verma, a philanthropist-violinist. Verma's fortunes turn overnight when he inherits an invisibility cloak, and henceforth becomes the savior of the people, "Mr India." Its storyline had no impact on me whatsoever. But my impressionable ten-year-old heart was set on fire by Sridevi (and I suppose Kapoor's) love-dance. The same love-dance that generations later remains iconic and formative, for so many of us Indian and Indian heritage women and people of minoritized genders, across so many social positions, vis-à-vis our relationships to desire, touch, womanhood, femininity, and (self)fulfillment.

A prelude in Hindi between a coy Sridevi and Kapoor, who remains invisible to her, frames this love-dance. I share it in translation here.

Sridevi: Mr India? How much love do you hold in your heart for the people?
Kapoor: Only for the people? Not for you?
Sridevi: How would I know? You have never told me how you feel....
Kapoor: Not every word needs to be spelt out, does it?
Sridevi: No... some words are exchanged when eyes meet. But in our case, even that isn't possible.
Kapoor: Ok then—those words that you are yet to hear, that you are yet to see. Those words—I am going to share with you up close, very, very close. I shall touch you with my words. I shall let my words envelope

you in my arms. And I shall speak those words in such a way, that you will hear them—not through your ears—but through your lips.

As Kapoor concludes this cryptic and luring promise, we see Sridevi's lips quiver, suppressed by an invisible kiss, as she absorbs his words into her skin.

Prising open this brief prelude between Sridevi and Kapoor decades later is like being handed a treasure trove of realizations. Their dialogue necessitates a fundamental reconsideration of the words "contact" and "touch," beyond the materiality of bodies, and beyond physical, skin-to-skin communication. In this prelude, touch is conjured as a meta-physical act; contact is promised at ocular dimensions; aurality moves bodies to pleasure; and a kiss transpires without skin-to-skin tactility.

Sridevi and Kapoor's words implicate every sense in our (the audiences') bodies in truly expansive ways, to create a nexus through which we can reimagine all the different ways in which touch may transpire, and all the different ways in which contact may be made between people. And their love-dance that follows continues these expansive meditations. Sridevi dances her pleasure alone, willing Kapoor's physical absence into being through her imagination. At times we see him even as he is invisible to her. At other times, he is invisible to us all. In these moments, we sense his presence through the ways in which her dancing body responds to his words, his breath, his imagined proximity, his invisible corporeality.

She is alone. And she is enough.

She extends her arms and locks her wrists around thin air, as though she is returning his embrace. As her eyes shift focus around the outdoor location, desperately trying to locate him, they reveal that she really has no way of finding his physical presence in relation to her own. In these moments, while her lyrics address him—her bodily movements exist alone, on her own terms.

She wraps herself languidly around a spiral staircase and hauls herself up, one step at a time. She slides up and down a tall red pole, using it for support.

She is free, self-fulfilled, taking up space.

She writhes on a haybale—twitching her spine and giving into pleasure, as though being kissed all along its length, from the base of her spine to the back of her neck.

As torrential rain comes down on them, their love-dance conjures the classic Bollywood trope of the wet-sari dance sequence. Sridevi's electric blue chiffon sari clings to her breasts and her hips, accentuating her bodily form.

The wet fabric is the closest thing to her skin.
It embraces her in a way he cannot.

The present materiality of this non-human object stands in for the absent materiality of his human body. This shape-shifting choreography between images of deriving pleasure on her own, and images of deriving pleasure from his imagined presence, expands meditations of touch and contact in choreography, and the world at large, in truly generative ways.

She is alone, and she is enough.

Years later, through performance studies scholar Kareem Khubchandani's thrilling theorization of Sridevi's "danced gesture" in *Nagina* (1986) as a "diva's appeal," I will come to understand further the stakes of "risking her body on screen ... [to make] legible an Indian womanhood that defies dominant dichotomies of wife and whore" (2020, 145). I shall consider too, with greater nuance, how Sridevi's alone-ness creates a necessary critical imaginary for Indian womanhood to exist outside of this constrained dichotomy, conjuring the woman ascetic, detached from and queering (hetero)normativity. In this, I shall also think with Sandra Chatterjee and Cynthia Ling Lee's call to conceptualize "lack as a mode of exceeding dominant boundaries" that creates "the possibility of queer desire" (2017, 46). A call echoed in film and media studies scholar Usha Iyer's powerful analyses of how Sridevi's danced corporeality, "quivering with sensuousness, boldly libidinous," transforms Kapoor into a "side show, a stunned, mute spectator to their danced expressions of sexual appetite," championing instead "intimate dialogues between choreographer [Saroj Khan] and the dancing heroine" (2020, 182).

She is alone, and she is enough.

But "danced-gesture" of whose emancipation?

Perhaps this is why, in that summer of 1988, my ten-year-old self is blown away by the multiple possibilities presented to me through the make-believe in this choreography; the possibilities of who one can become through self-determination. And subsequently, years on, navigating my way through my own youth, desiring desire, and in search of (self)fulfillment, I find myself in my Ma's chiffon saris dancing under the shower, remembering and reliving the visceral imprints left on my own body by Sridevi's "danced gesture." I don't need anyone to dance with me. Like Sridevi, I am alone, and I am enough. I evolve in and through my childhood memories of my own encounters with Sridevi's cinematic materiality that I have replayed over and over in my own body.

Communication Studies scholar Jennifer M. Barker argues that the experience of cinema is one of tactility, enabling an exchange that "gets beneath the skin, and reverberates in the body" (2009, Book Cover).[1] While Barker's focus is on the tacit tactility of the cinema as a medium and an art form in and of itself, my dwelling on Sridevi's danced presence and absence of touch on screen thus presents an opportunity to considers cinema's tactility as a compounded phenomenon. Moreover, three decades on, I have come to realize that Sridevi's "danced gesture" on screen haptically and viscerally revealed to me as a child, and subsequently through endless replays in my own body, the myriad liberatory ways in which touch and contact *could* manifest in our lives, **if only we had the imagination and/or the will to build such emancipatory worlds.**

Ideologically, the impetus for this book is born out of the urge to build such emancipatory worlds.

But whose emancipation?

Politically, it is born out of the need to critique myriad interlocking power regimes in dance(making) that inflict social harm and violence, despite the art form's overriding reputation as an intrinsically liberatory language, urged by dance scholar Arabella Stanger's gentle but firm and compelling call to our field (2021).

But how am I implicated in this interlocked power-grid?

Temporally, it is born in a very specific moment that stands out as transformative and lies at the heart of many embodied intercultural tensions in my movement training during my undergraduate studies in the UK. It is the moment when, during my first contact improvisation (CI) workshop in 1998, I was first touched by another body in the context of performance training. This touch, unlike the kinds of touch I had previously experienced during my kathak dance training in India, was not instructional.

This touch did not correct my posture, redirect my gaze, or accentuate my *mudra* (hand gestures), for example. Instead, this touch felt free, exploratory, and consequently, even threatening. This touch was, of course, mutual—by virtue of being touched, I too was touching my partner's body. But from where I moved, my reciprocating touch felt

    clinical,

           mechanistic,

                  functional.

While it allowed us to explore shifting points of physical contacts, so that we could be responsible for each other's balance and weight, it made me hyperconscious about how I moved. And yet, I could see from my tutor's demonstrations earlier, that the quality of movement it was intended to generate was supposed to be

        impulsive,

    instinctual,

               responsive.

Far from it, my movements appeared as

                  jagged,

        mechanical,

    planned,

as they felt.

The touch was new, exhilarating, and terrifying, all at once. Not because I did not trust my partner's ability to support my weight. But because my Indian, kathak-trained, solo dancing body, which had hitherto danced within a clearly demarcated space of her own, and which was coded by culturally specific regulations that govern touch, had been placed in a situation that had led to a breakdown of these very codes. There was something disempowering about experiencing the language of CI being imposed upon my brown body in that white dominant space, without making any attempt to acknowledge or even consider the differences that constituted my embodiments, that highlighted the power differentials at play in the dance studio.

But there is no monolithic brown body.

Over the decades that followed, I have come to reflect not only on the power that was being enacted upon me in that moment, but the invisibilized power I carried in my own dominant caste body, that, without a doubt, also undergirded my discomforts.

Caste is central to any interrogation of touch.

Growing up in Kolkata, in a dominant caste, heteropatriarchal, non-disabled, class-privileged Bengali family with varying relationships to faith, and with no awareness of how power operated in my family's favor, I was led to believe that caste was a discriminatory social stratification system of the past—that it had no place in our home or society, and that instead, our social categorizations were informed by class.[2] Ma tells me that my family consciously denounced our family's caste locations. I did not know my caste lineage until I started to probe while researching this project. I am told that my Baba belongs to the privileged Bengali Kayastha caste and I learn that his, and my own, surname, Mitra, is a marker of our caste-privileged lineage. Baba married my Ma despite much resistance from his family, partly because Ma's family was affiliated with the Brahmo Samaj, a reformed Hindu sect that, among many other things, claimed to have denounced the caste system. This made it impossible for my Baba's family to identify my Ma's caste location, which I am now told is a privileged mixed lineage of Kayastha and Brahmin. My own caste location is thus very clearly a *savarna* (dominant caste) one, with Brahmin lineages, and I undoubtedly grew up invisible to my own caste privileges.

The question of caste should be central to any interrogation of touch.

Built into the structure of caste supremacy are strict codifications surrounding whom (and what) one can and cannot touch, or even be in proximity with, and the violent implications of potential violations of these codes.

The social reformer, anti-caste activist, and architect of India's constitution Dr Bhimrao Ramji Ambedkar reminds us of the hereditary nature of the caste system when he writes that "the law of caste confines its membership to persons born in the caste," making the caste system "autonomous" and each caste a "closed corporation" (2016, 254). Ambedkar makes clear that this central tenet of Indian society is a discriminatory and dehumanizing system. He further argues that "the effect of caste on the ethics of the Hindus is simply deplorable," resulting in a society that operates on "caste-ridden" and "caste-bound" morality (2016, 259). It is important to note that caste supremacy also operates in distinct ways across South Asia and its diasporas, manifesting with cultural specificities across Buddhist, Christian, Muslim, and Sikh communities in India, Pakistan, Sri Lanka, and Bangladesh.

Performance studies scholar Brahma Prakash similarly argues for the foundational nature of caste in India as permeating every fabric of social interactions. He refers to caste as a "living practice" that has been "reinventing its structure, . . . to fit into the cosmopolitan society" (2019, 19). Prakash reminds us that, within the context of dance and performance, "the Indian caste system is about the politics of controlling bodies and spaces. Caste determines where one can perform and where one cannot. Performance in a way becomes enactment of power (often caste honour)" (2019, 20). This honor operates on the basis of a social hierarchy according to which the caste system classifies Indians into four *varnas*: at the top of the hierarchy are the Brahmins (the priests); next in line are the Kshatriyas (the warriors); then come the Vaishyas (the traders); and finally the Shudras (the laborers). Dalits and Adivasis fall outside of this *chaturvarna* (four *varna*) classification system, as they are considered *avarna* (without *varna*), the unclassified. Referring to Brahmins as self-proclaimed classifiers of society, Tamil writer and theater activist Srinivasa Ramanujam argues that "it is but natural that [the Brahmins] locate themselves at the apex of the social pyramid" (2020, 1) and create these hierarchized categories in order to maintain their own dominant status. This hierarchization operates in and through "the human body [which] becomes the site where the ideals and anxieties of the category are made corporeal" (2020, 2). The relationship between the Brahmins (the classifiers), the remaining three *varnas* (the classified) and the *avarna* (the unclassified) is reinforced by institutional power. And one of the most dehumanizing and defining features of this power manifests as classifying Dalit people as the "untouchables." As Ramanujam asserts, "untouchability is not the by-product of the caste system. Untouchability is the essence" (2020, 3).[3]

In her keynote address "Introduction to Caste, Intersectionality and Allyship" at University of California Riverside's Caste and Corporeality Conference through April and May 2024, Dalit feminist writer, activist, consultant, and cofounder of Dalit History Month Christina Dhanuja delineated three strands for how caste operates through social structures: firstly, she argued they are omnipresent in the *privileges* of dominant caste people through power, sociocultural capital, networks, and resources; secondly, she observed that caste is reproduced through sociocultural *practices* that manifest as culture, relationships, beliefs, and value systems; and, finally, she posited that caste-power manifests through *consequences* that result in exclusions, discriminations, and atrocities subjected onto caste-oppressed communities. Dhanuja stressed on the interconnectedness of these three strands to fully understand how caste-power shapes and is reproduced in and through South Asian and South Asian–heritage peoples (2024).

The question of caste is thus central to any project on touch.

The question of caste is thus central to my unmaking of contact.

As I reflect on my childhood, it becomes abundantly clear that many complex rituals of caste supremacy fundamentally shaped my upbringing and interactions with people, compounded further by their caste, class, faith, gender, and social mobilities, both at home and beyond. Washing our hands and feet to get rid of dirt after coming home from the outside was not only a hygienic ritual, but regularly punctuated by statements like "you never know what or whom you've touched." In the hottest of climates, where roaming around barefoot was always the desired option, we had to wear *choti* (sandals) at home, so our feet did not touch dirty floors. In contrast, however, our nannies and our domestic workers, who I suspect were from caste-oppressed communities, were expected to remain barefoot inside the home; did not join us for meals at our dinner tables; and drank and ate from cups, glasses, and plates and used toilets, that were distinct from ours. Yet, the extractive relationships between our dominant caste families and our caste-oppressed employees, often women, who were responsible for our safe and healthy upbringings and care, and whose touch healed and wiped away our tears through every scrape and cut that was our childhood, are the basis on which our families could claim to have denounced caste. Our nannies could heal our scars by applying medication, massage our heads with coconut oil, and stroke our hair till we fell asleep when unwell. But they could not eat their meals with us at the dinner table. Neither could they sit on the sofa next to us, as we watched soap operas late into the evenings.

It is also in the public sphere of 1990s Kolkata, as a young woman taking public transport to and from school, that I discovered how, in these crowded environments, people from potentially all genders, castes, faiths, and classes intersected and stood closely compressed against one another. I have disturbing memories in some of these instances of witnessing or experiencing violating, unwanted, sexual touch. On another end of the spectrum, however, I grew up watching television images of thousands of people thronging to touch the feet or hands of spiritual leaders to receive their blessings, as physical contact with them was believed to have sacred healing powers. In the aesthetic sphere of my kathak training under three different women Hindu gurus, codifications around touch persisted. In each of these tutelages, we were encouraged to touch the feet of our gurus to receive their blessings before and after each class. There were also occasional moments when my gurus would use instructional touch with their hands to correct our *mudras* or our positions.[4] I have come to look upon kathak as a predominantly solo dance form in which the dancer's personal space is clearly demarcated through extended arms, and no other body invades this space, except their omnipresent guru and their corrective touch. Even as I learned to narrate stories of love, eroticism, and intimacy, we were taught to mime these moments of relational interactions, evoked through *abhinaya*, the strictly stylized performance language of hand gestures and facial expressions. *I now wonder to what extent kathak's (and other Indian classicized dance forms') historically solo formats uphold the dehumanizing caste supremacist practice of untouchability.*

Relatedly, in this project, I consciously move away from the ubiquitous and deeply problematic label of "classical" dance, a label that was applied *to* dance forms from across South Asia through their reconstruction as Indian "classical" dances in the twentieth century, as part of India's nationalist project and in alignment with the European project of colonial modernity.[5] Thinking closely with the rightful and powerful critiques of the uncritical usage of "classical" Indian dance by anti-caste activist and hereditary dance artist Nrithya Pillai (2021), performance studies scholar Brahma Prakash (2023), and dance scholar Anurima Banerji (2023), in this book I deploy the term "classicized" throughout to signal the intellectually and materially appropriative and minoritization processes that were applied *to* the dance forms, and the hereditary artists who were their custodians, as integral to India's nation-building vision. My use of the term "classicized" problematizes the nationalist reconstruction processes that were imposed *on* the dances in the twentieth century.[6] In this, it critiques the term "classical," which has erased these processes in favor of unproblematically mythologizing the dance forms as inherently "classical" products of antiquity, placed in deemed superior hierarchy to their "folk" and indigenous equivalents.

It is surely *this* habituated codified corporeal power of the caste system in conjunction with other broader South Asian cultural norms around touch, that I shall expand on later in this book, embodied and sustained in my solo dance training, that undergirded my experience of discomfort and destabilization in that first CI class during my undergraduate years, as my caste-privilege interlocked with the racial privilege of my peers and my tutor. Therefore, as a *savarna* Indian dance scholar, working on anti-oppression in the Global North academy, while continuing to benefit from the social, cultural, and economic capital, mobility, and access I derive from my caste and class privilege in my profession, my critical interrogation of choreographic touch *has* to be an intersectional inquiry. This is necessary in order to expose the power that operates in my favor in certain dance contexts because of my dominant caste position in India and the diaspora, while simultaneously critiquing how CI wields its whiteness against me, in others.

Because there is no monolithic brown body.

Nothing evidences this more than the devastating impact of the Covid-19 pandemic, which has been exponentially worse for diasporic South Asian communities in the UK from socioeconomically marginalized (and possibly caste-oppressed) backgrounds. These communities have been more exposed to the virus while undertaking frontline menial jobs, compounded by more cramped living conditions in intergenerational homes, and structurally harmed by preexisting institutionally racist public health policies. This is also true of Black and other racially minoritized communities in the UK.

Writing a book on choreographic touch that was conceived *before* the Covid-19 pandemic, while living through its fourth year, generates very particular tensions and reflections. The last five years have changed our relationships to physical touch and social proximity with other humans irrevocably. In March 2020, when the world as we knew it grounded to a halt, as governments imposed lockdowns across the globe, people withdrew into the isolation of their own homes. In some instances, we found ourselves living with cohabitants—and in others, on our own. Depending on our circumstances, our ability to touch and be touched by other human beings was restricted by the state in significant ways. In the early days of the raging pandemic, we were told that the virus transmitted through physical contact and proximity with infected people, or by touching contaminated objects and surfaces. We were told not to touch our faces or hair after touching surfaces, as the virus would enter our system through our eyes and nose. In such state-imposed sociological restrictions on physical, human, and non-human touch, clinical attention turned to touching our own hands. Videos proliferated on social media advocating for cleanliness via choreographic rituals that brought our own hands together, meticulously and rhythmically washing them with soap and warm water, or cleaning them with hand-sanitizers. The public health discourse of touch, contamination, and transmission was turned into many creative responses—even giving guidance that the time taken to sing the first two stanzas of "Happy Birthday" is the required duration to effectively decontaminate our hands. Touch was a singular focus in the epidemiological discourse surrounding the virus—and restricting touch was an important means to containing it. Now that we know that the virus is actually airborne, and it is exhaled breath that in fact touches us in harmful ways as it migrates from one human host body to another, and most governments have withdrawn all legal precautionary measures, the discourse surrounding touch and Covid-19 has been perhaps retained only in our rigorous hand-cleaning rituals.

But a rather sinister manifestation of this discourse has emerged in caste supremacist India. Ma tells me that in a Covid-ridden world, when people have been reimagining how to greet each other as strangers, trying to avoid transmission via close physical contact like hugging, or even shaking hands in a more formal context, that India had it right all along by greeting people through the *namaskar* gesture, the folding of two hands in a prayer position and bowing one's head. I am quick to share with her the possibly casteist roots of this gesture as per philosopher Gopal Guru's speculations. Ma counters my critique by saying that she has always been told the gesture signifies "bowing down to the divinity in you" and insists I cannot deny that it does promote personal and social hygiene in a Covid-19 context. Guru suggests that the gesture was potentially designed to be as much a mechanism for ensuring hygiene by avoiding physical contact with a stranger, as it was to not have to touch the stranger without knowing their caste, to "serve the purpose of avoiding the touch of others, perhaps the repulsive other—namely, the untouchables" (2017, 213). In a panel on "Caste and Touch" in May 2024, as part of University of California Riverside's "Caste and Corporeality Conference," poet and novelist Meena Kandasamy offers greater nuance to this discourse on Covid-19 and the role that language played in policing touch and upholding caste-supremacy among South Asian people. She notes that during the pandemic, the language of "social distancing," mobilized by global scientists and healthcare professionals, led to further stigmatizing of touch in South Asian societies. As a result, she observes, it upheld caste-supremacist values that touch needs to be stigmatized and controlled in the first place, through the guise of maintaining social order, hygiene, and well-being (2024). To think that this deeply embodied gesture with its potentially caste supremacist roots is being mobilized in Covid-19 precautionary discourse, while continuing to uphold casteism, is a necessary and unsettling reckoning for me as a UK-based *savarna* Indian-heritage woman, writing a book about contact, touch, and choreography.

It makes me speculate further, as I did with philosopher Sundar Sarukkai on Skype on September 20, 2019, whether, similar to the potentially embedded casteism in the *namaskar* gesture, the habituated lack of physical contact between dancing bodies in the classicized dance forms of India, even their primary solo-ness itself, may well uphold such exclusionary politics of touch and untouchability. Although there are distinctions between how this manifests in the different classicized forms, it continues to remain pervasive across them. With this criticality in mind, I cannot help but question whether Sridevi's predominantly solo "danced-gesture" of self-fulfilled womanhood, while refreshingly anti-patriarchal and queering heteronormativity, may simultaneously carry casteist values of refraining from touch.

It is also undeniable that, in keeping with Bollywood's troubling upholding of colorism and racism through its foregrounding of light-skinned actors, Sridevi's embodiment of self-fulfilled womanhood is channeled through her own light-skinned-ness. The anti-Blackness that is inherent within caste supremacy underscores the love-dance, and indeed appears in a more obvious way through the use of blackface in the other iconic dance-number from the film, "Hawa Hawai." Here, through a series of culturally appropriative dance and dress-up sequences that reference Honolulu, Hong Kong, and non-specified Indigenous communities, Sridevi, accompanied by a chorus of men, entertains a banquet hall, singing:

> *Mai Khwabo ki shehzadi* (I set dreams free)
> *Mai hun har dil pe chhai* (I win over every heart)
> *Kehte hai mujhko Hawa Hawai* (They call me Hawa Hawai).

With a gold fitted gown and crown on her head, she is clearly set apart from her choral dancers to whom she appears as a "civilizing" presence and force. In this too, she is set apart. She is alone.

But there is no monolithic brown womanhood.

Yes. She is alone. And she is enough.

But whose humanity does she deny as a consequence?

A critique of heteropatriarchy, without a simultaneous critique of caste supremacy and white supremacy, is thus meaningless.

In an online seminar on April 26, 2022, titled "Beyond 'People of Color' Politics: Extending Ethnic Studies through Caste" hosted by San Francisco State University, Nrithya Pillai and Critical Muslim Studies scholar Shaista Patel ex/pose this very problem. They rightly challenge *savarna* scholars and artists located in white-majority Global North contexts to examine their own reductionist and monolithic self-identifications as racially minoritized and oppressed "people of color," without simultaneously acknowledging the caste, class, and other privileges and social mobilities that lend them access, sociocultural capital, and credibility to move in and through power. Pillai and Patel contend that positioning oneself as minoritized within one power structure, such as racial privilege, without simultaneously acknowledging one's position of privilege within another, such as caste supremacy, makes the "people of color" discourse a cloak, a power-move, behind which *savarna* South Asians in the Global North can hide, thus invisibilizing and remaining complicit in caste violence (2022). I take their call for the need to examine and mobilize the politics of intersectionality as South Asian scholars seriously in order to complicate and compound the analytical lenses through which we practice our scholarship. And so, as a dominant caste, racially minoritized, immigrant, class-privileged, non-disabled, cisgender, and heterosexual woman, positioned firmly in between interlocking power regimes of caste supremacy, cisgenderism, ableism, classism, whiteness, heteronormativity, and patriarchy, while negotiating power as it operates through me in some instances, and on me in others, I set forth to examine how choreographic touch in South Asian dance carries the potential to both uphold ***and*** dismantle different regimes of power, simultaneously, in my call for "unmaking contact."

In this, *Unmaking Contact* is a necessary, timely, and simultaneous unmaking of me.

References

Ambedkar, B. R. 2016 [2014]. Annihilation of Caste. London: Verso.

Banerji, Anurima. 2023. "The Epistemic Politics of Indian Classical Dance." In Performance Cultures as Epistemic Cultures, *Vol. 2*, edited by Torsten Jost et al., 191–216. New York: Routledge.

Barker, Jennifer M. 2009. The Tactile Eye: Touch and the Cinematic Experience. Berkeley: University of California Press.

Chatterjee, Sandra, and Cynthia Ling Lee. "'Out Love Was Not Enough': Queering Gender, Cultural Belonging, and Desire in Contemporary Abhinaya." In Queer Dance: Meanings and Makings, edited by Claire Croft, 45–65. New York: Oxford University Press, 2017.

Dhanuja, Christina. 2024. "*Introduction to Caste, Intersectionality, and Allyship.*" *Online Research Symposium on "Caste and Corporeality."* University of California, Riverside. May 10.
Gidla, Sujatha. 2017. Ants among Elephants: An Untouchable Family and the Making of Modern India. New York: Farrar, Straus & Giroux.
Guru, Gopal. 2017. "Archaeology of Untouchability." In The Cracked Mirror: An Indian Debate on Experience and Theory, edited by Gopal Guru and Sundar Sarukkai, 200–222. New Delhi: Oxford University Press.
Iyer, Usha. 2020. Dancing Women: Choreographing Corporeal Histories of Hindi Cinema. New York: Oxford University Press.
Kandasamy, Meena. 2024. "*Caste and Touch.*" *Online Research Symposium on "Caste and Corporeality.*" University of California, Riverside. May 10.
Khubchandani, Kareem. 2020. Ishtyle: Accenting Gay Indian Nightlife. Ann Arbor: University of Michigan Press.
Mitra, Royona. 2017. "Akram Khan on the Politics of Choreographing Touch." In Contemporary Choreography: A Critical Reader, edited by Jo Butterworth and Liesbeth Wildschut, 385–397. 2nd ed. London: Routledge.
Patel, Shaista, and Nrithya Pillai. "Beyond People of Colour Politics: Extending Ethnic Studies through Caste." *Online Research Seminar*. April 26, 2022. https://ltns.sfsu.edu/beyond-peo ple-color-politics-extending-ethnic-studies-through-caste.
Prakash, Brahma. 2019. Cultural Labour: Conceptualizing the "Folk Performance" in India. New Delhi: Oxford University Press.
Prakash, Brahma. 2023. "Opinion: To Truly Democratise Indian Art and Culture, the 'Classical' Must Be Declared Dead." Scroll.in. Accessed April 20, 2023. https://scroll.in/article/1045681/opinion-to-truly-democratise-indian-art-and-culture-the-classi cal-must-be-done-away-with.
Ramanujam, Srinivasa. 2020. Renunciation and Untouchability in India: The Notional and the Empirical in the Caste Order. Abingdon: Routledge.
Sarukkai, Sundar. 2019. *Interviewed by the author via Skype*. September 20.
Stanger, Arabella. 2021. Dancing on Violent Ground: Utopia as Dispossession in Euro-American Theater Dance. Evanston, IL: Northwestern University Press.
Subramanian, Ajantha. 2019. The Caste of Merit: Engineering Educating in India. Cambridge, MA: Harvard University Press.

Introduction

Unmaking Contact

I am seated in the concluding practical workshop to Mellon Dance Studies Seminar 2015 at Northwestern University, among a predominantly white group of participants. We have been instructed to embody the word "decolonize" in whatever way we see fit.[1] I choose to stand still, grounded, refusing to cave in the face of power, despite being questioned by some fellow white participants about how my choice of stillness could decolonize movement. I witness around me more than half the room default to the language of contact improvisation (CI) that looks like active motion, juxtaposed by my inactive choice to remain still. I encounter an interesting conundrum in this moment, as I acknowledge within myself the disjuncture between the role of stillness in early CI explorations by Steve Paxton—as captured, for instance, in his Small Dance—and the seeming move away from stillness toward perpetual motion by my fellow participants. White colleagues and some Black and racially minoritized colleagues weave in and out of weight sharing, lifting, balances, and imbalances. I am wondering: how can CI decolonize anything? Has it in fact not imposed an authoritarian language on contemporary dance, accessed by only those on the inside? Has it not in fact been an oppressive force, in its guise of liberation and democracy? As we sit in a circle to reflect on the workshop, I gently throw open these questions to the room. I share my reflection that I find it interesting that, in response to the word "decolonize," so many in the room turned to CI, and then I ask, as a provocation, "Have we in fact been colonized by CI?"[2] The room falls silent. And then, gradually, there are reflections shared on CI's exclusionary politics as experienced particularly by racially minoritized people. As the conversation moves away from the discomfort I have generated, I am left wondering just how alienating CI is to Black and racially minoritized and caste-oppressed peoples, especially in the context of decentering dance practices/studies vis-à-vis questions of power. I find myself thinking through the oppressiveness of touch within dance practices and the situations in which I am at the receiving ends of power, and those in which

Unmaking Contact. Royona Mitra with Akila, Diya Naidu, Nahid Siddiqui, and LaWhore Vagistan, Oxford University Press.
© Oxford University Press 2025. DOI: 10.1093/oso/9780197627761.003.0001

power operates in my favor, and thus, it is invisible to me. I find myself thinking about how power regimes intersect between and across cultures, knowledge-systems, and peoples within dance studios, spaces that are often upheld as epitome of liberatory politics and futures.

Unmaking Contact: Choreographing South Asian Touch interrogates "contact," understood by Global North dance discourse as a shorthand for the movement discipline of contact improvisation (CI) and its characteristic shifting points of weight-sharing between two or more bodies through physical touch, by attending to inherent power asymmetries that are foundational to this practice, yet often ignored. By placing South Asian aesthetics, bodies, discourses, philosophies, and practices on touch, at the heart of its interrogation through the lenses of caste, ecology, faith, gender, and sexuality, the book argues for an intersectional, intercultural, and inter-epistemic understanding of contact that may or may not involve touch. In doing so, the book shifts and expands understandings of "contact" in dance-making through intercultural epistemologies that examine distinct, but also overlapping, notions of touch and contact, terms that are often used interchangeably in Global North dance discourse.

In this book the term "contact" signals both a shorthand for CI *and* a shift away from it to more expansive choreographic considerations: it becomes the harbinger for dismantling power regimes (Chapter 1); it is conjured as a catalyst to examine social power relations (Chapter 2); it appears as a fulcrum of ecological relationality (Chapter 3); it arises as critical encounters full of generative and transformative potential (Chapter 4); and finally, it manifests as community (Afterwords). The book examines the interconnections between these expansive and varied manifestations of "contact" and their relationships to physical touch, specifically South Asian choreographic touch, by foregrounding South Asian aesthetics, artistic practices, philosophies and voices of four transnationally located South Asian–heritage dance-artists who become the touchstones of each of the chapters and the final Afterwords. They are India-based Akila (Chapter 1) and Diya Naidu (Chapter 2), UK-Pakistan-based Nahid Siddiqui (Chapter 3)[3], and US-based LaWhore Vagistan (Chapter 4). In each chapter, I examine a key performance by the foregrounded artist in question, and through these analyses, I theorize the culturally specific politics and power regimes that govern their respective relationships to choreographic touch, analyzing how these contribute to their respective unmaking of contact.

An integral, but not central, part of this unmaking of contact requires a critique of CI and its now ubiquitous choreographic manifestation of partnering as an aesthetic that works in infiltratory ways on South Asian dancers who train in primarily solo classicized dance forms. Indeed, it is important to recognize that the ubiquity of physical touch in many Global North dance practices beyond CI, as present in ballet, ballroom, and other social dance forms, distinguishes them from many South Asian dance forms, particularly of the classicized varieties but not exclusively so, where touching other bodies is not a prevalent practice. Thus, a particular set of tensions may arise when South Asian–heritage artists trained in South Asian classicized and other dance forms encounter CI, that the latter is not equipped to understand, let alone address. My critique of the long-standing mythologizing of CI as a democratic movement language mobilizes these intercultural considerations through the social vectors of caste, ecology, faith, gender, and sexuality to destabilize the stronghold of hitherto Global North–centric discourses on the form. This project of reorienting "contact" away from CI-driven Global North dance discourses is urgent on two counts. Firstly, while CI has been critiqued as a white-dominant practice, and its potential harmful and compulsive force on Black and racially minoritized artists has been noted by Fred Holland and Ishmael Houston-Jones (1983), Danielle Goldman (2010), Ann Cooper Albright (2017), Hannah Yohalem (2018), Rebecca Chaleff (2018), and Keith Hennessy (2019), among others, little attention, with the exception of an excellent intervention co-written by CI practitioners Guru Suraj and Adrianna Michalska (2024),[4] has so far been given to examining the implications of such a force on brown South Asian dancers within both white-majority environments, and simultaneously in elitist dominant caste environments. An interrogation of CI as socio-cultural-psychic violence, reinforced by different and competing hegemonies of caste, faith, gender, and sexuality, is therefore necessary for dance studies at large. Secondly, the project cannot stop at a critique of CI alone, as to do so would be to merely recenter the form. For it to be truly transformative, the project commits to a reframing of contact and choreographic touch itself through bringing about a fundamental shift in how we understand touch and contact in choreography, expanding our languages beyond Global North discourses on contact, through a foregrounding of South Asian philosophies and artistic practices. This is also undertaken through a simultaneous critical interrogation of the solo modality of South Asia's classicized dance forms, which follows later in this Introduction, in order to understand the ways in which this highly revered characteristic arguably upholds caste power through its negation of touch, and thus, community.

The book is therefore a simultaneous unmaking of multiple dance worlds.

On Unmaking: A Manifesto

Unmaking is a method, a politics, an emancipatory mode.
Unmaking is making, but differently.
Unmaking is not inclusion
Unmaking decenters.
Unmaking conjures new and emancipatory centers.
Unmaking is unsettling.
Unmaking facilitates through uncertainty.
Unmaking is uncertainty.
Unmaking is unsettling power.
Unmaking is messy.
Unmaking is disorder.
Unmaking is ordering but differently.
Unmaking is empowering.
   To unmake is to power, but differently.
Unmaking is making, but differently.
    To unmake is to shift the terms of making, such that,
Making is unmaking.

On Unmaking: A Method, a Politics, an Emancipatory Mode

Unmaking—as a method, a politics, a mode—is committed to the making of new and emancipatory worlds. Unmaking is processual—facilitating us through uncertainties—never pinning down destinations, ever opening up possibilities. While I arrive at this critical offering through my intimate immersions in dance worlds, I see my manifesto of unmaking—as a method, a politics, an emancipatory mode—spilling over and speaking to contexts and disciplines beyond dance studies. Unmaking foregrounds the making, the facilitation, of emancipatory worlds, led by politics of liberation across all intersecting social vectors. In this it thinks with postcolonial studies scholar Priyamvada Gopal's articulation of the project of decolonization as "a historical opportunity to remake ... lives, societies, nations, and the world itself for the better" and to "imagine the world anew, without exploitation, domination, and violence" (2023).

Unmaking generates.

Unmaking is generative.

Unmaking is critical.

Unmaking decenters.

Unmaking conjures new and emancipatory centers.

Unmaking centers uncertainties.

Methodologically, then, this book starts where my first monograph left off, by making explicit the intersectional and the inter-epistemic interrogation of power and politics that I argued is at the heart of "new interculturalism" (Mitra 2015). I want to continue to push for new interculturalism as emancipatory, ground-up, minoritized people and episteme-driven corporeality, aesthetic, and embodied politics that decenters normative white Western and Brahminical ideologies, dramaturgies, and knowledge systems—leading to the generation of new epistemes.[5] In this project, I continue to think through the stakes of new interculturalism, offering unmaking as its underpinning conceptual ethos, political mode, and practical method.

The title to this book project, *Unmaking Contact*, was born in conversation with my colleague, friend, and performance studies scholar Broderick Chow. He suggested it to signal an implicit critique of dominant discourse in cultural anthropology that often mobilizes "making contact" to describe the first point of encounter between colonial forces and indigenous groups, invariably between the Global North ethnographer and their Global South subjects of inquiry. Chow's suggestion gets to the heart of my project, and for this I am deeply grateful. But the unmaking undertaken in this project is multipronged and goes beyond a critique of (neo)colonial academic endeavors alone. The unmaking in this project dismantles several interlocking power regimes of coloniality, anthropocentrism, whiteness, heteropatriarchy, cisgenderism, faith-based hierarchies, and caste supremacy simultaneously. And as I am implicated in these power-regimes, both at the receiving end in some instances and the perpetrating end in others, as explained in my Preface, this project is also a fundamental unmaking of me.

Thinking adjacently with Kimberlé Crenshaw's foundational conceptualization of intersectionality that centers racial minoritizations of African American women and their material conditions in employment contexts, the brown South Asian dance artists in my project, who occupy different positions on the caste, faith, gender, and sexuality power spectrums, and their dance-works, are at the heart of my theorization of unmaking. I recognize Crenshaw's subject of analyses as distinct from my own. I do not wish to co-opt the concept of intersectionality from its African American contexts. I learn from Jennifer C. Nash's vital questions about the affective impact on Black women and Black feminism of how intersectionality discourse has "come to occupy the center of women's studies and to migrate across disciplinary boundaries" and remain attentive to her accompanying call for a "letting go" of the urge to retain intersectionality studies knowledge as property (2019). I am reminded by Brittany Cooper that intersectionality operates beyond individual identities, and teaches us about the interlocking, compounding, and multidimensional nature of social power regimes, depending on how social hierarchies stack up on people (2015). Unmaking our understanding of social relations and the power regimes that govern them thus requires a deep understanding of the interwoven nature of social power matrices. I thus analyze my South Asian dance artists' experiences of power and marginalizations vis-à-vis contact and choreographic touch in India, Pakistan, UK, and the United States, across social power spectrums of caste, ecology, faith, gender, and sexuality. Neither my artists nor I are exempt from this scrutiny. Our collective unmakings unfold through the pages of this book.

Unmaking is a project of (unsettling) power.

Unmaking is an emancipatory project for and by minoritized peoples, even as majoritarian views of the word dominate our simplistic understandings of it. These views consider unmaking as an imposition of power to enable the taking apart of something as we know it. I want to advocate for an understanding of unmaking that resists such destructive and imposed upon taking aparts, towards emancipation. A literal approach to the word and the action aligns with such majoritarian views and signals that to unmake is to simply take apart, to disassemble, to undo, to unravel, to dismantle, to even decimate something as we know it. At the time of writing in December 2023, we see this form of unmaking manifest in the decimation of Gaza, in the genocide of Palestinian peoples, in the scholasticidal destruction of their educational and civic infrastructures, their cultural institutions, their epistemic achievements and establishments, their homes and lands at the hands of the state of Israel, most recently since October 7, 2023, following the horrific attacks on and loss of Israeli and other nationalities' lives. But such a literal reading alone is reductive, and such a simplistic approach to unmaking, does not want to enable the emergence of new and emancipatory worlds; indeed it quells such imaginaries. It denies agency and hopes of the Palestinian peoples who continue to dream of and stuggle towards their liberatory futures, despite their over seven-decade-long history of dispossession and subjugation. Within and through and beyond the genocide of Palestinian peoples emerge hopes and resistance and dreams of an emancipatory world where Palestine is indeed free.[6] In these terms, I argue instead for an unmaking, on the terms of the minoritized, imagining its potential beyond a majoritarian mobilization of unmaking that is invariably destructive at its core. I argue for an unmaking that conjures from within the indistinguishable debris generated from these processes of decimation, new and emancipatory worlds. I argue that to unmake is to also put (back) together but differently, to (re)assemble but differently, to (re)do but differently, to (re)build but differently.

Unmaking is making but differently.

I argue against the assumption that (re)making as a process is distinct to, and follows on, from unmaking; that it necessarily and chronologically follows the process of taking things apart. I argue that unmaking—as a method, a politics, and an emancipatory mode—when embodied by minoritized peoples—witnesses and practises a collapse of temporality, and negates the assumption of such chronology and a necessary lapse of time between being taken apart and a moment of clearing in preparation for the rebuilding that is meant to follow. It is in this precise denial of, and the collapse between, such temporal and chronological assumptions of unmaking and (re)making that lurks the promise of self-determination and emancipation.

To unmake is to will on the emergence of new and emancipatory ideations, practices, politics and ways of being. Unmaking facilitates the dismantling of power in the generation of new possibilities, in and through uncertainties. To unmake is to expose and critique operating power-regimes with the intention of birthing fairer and more just worlds. To unmake requires not just questioning power structures that operate on us, but also power structures that operate in and through us. To unmake is to embrace vulnerability and demand accountability. No unmaking is complete without implicating ourselves within its very folds[7].

Unmaking is unfolding.

To unmake is to make, but differently.

Making is unmaking.

To theorize unmaking as a method, a politics, an emancipatory mode, I arrive at this "critical time of collective undoing" (Hussein 2022) by thinking with Nesreen Hussein (2022), Sandeep Bakshi (2021), Julie E Maybee (2019), Sruti Bala (2017), Dorinne Kondo (2018), Rachel Hann (2018), Tim Ingold (2013), Marta Saviliagno (2009), John Law (2004), and their respective disciplinary offerings on processes and implications of un/making across arts, humanities, and social sciences. In his attempt to destabilize social science methods' urge to strive for "certainty," sociologist John Law advocates "to unmake many of our methodological habits, including: the desire for certainty" (2004, 9), proposing instead a method that "will often be slow and uncertain, a risky and troubling process" (2004, 10). I welcome Law's call for uncertainty, conjuring unmaking as a mode and method and politics that embraces slowness, uncertainty, risk, vulnerability, disorder, destabilization; a mode and method and politics that embraces mess. These are all integral to our growth as scholars and as humans. In this, I share synergies with anthropologist Tim Ingold's meditations on the process of making as "tantamount to a process of growth" (2013). Ingold invites us to consider the process of making as "not so much an *assembly* as a *procession*, not a building *up* from discrete parts into a hierarchically organised totality, but a carrying *on*—a passage along a path in which every step grows from the one before and into the one following" (2013). I want to remain attentive to this idea of unmaking as continual, processual, collective, intergenerational, transmissive—harboring the potential to hold power accountable. Thinking through Ingold, American studies and ethnicities scholar Dorinne Kondo reminds us that, within the theater context, "making and labor, including the making of race, becomes forms of power-laden creativity." She argues that because "making is not creation ex nihilo," "making the 'world of the play' can offer opportunities to make/unmake/remake worlds inside and outside the theater" (2018). The real-life consequences of unmaking as a method, a politics, an emancipatory mode is deeply compelling to me, especially as it confronts power in its process. Kondo's emphasis on making/unmaking/remaking of race within the theater through reparative modes emphasizes the centrality of power, and its dismantling, within these processes. Also writing from within the context of theater and its practice of place-making, performance studies scholar Rachel Hann argues beyond the materiality of the place-making process, signaling toward the larger project of "political charging of place through the spatial imaginary" (2018). Hann's politically charged "spatial imaginary" find echoes in decolonial and queer studies scholar Sandeep Bakshi's postulations on the unmaking of literary canons within the university curriculum. Bakshi argues that "unmaking canons as critical pedagogy ... strives to offer an exhaustive access to pluriversal knowledge without diminishing the scope of Euro-American frames, which figure as *one* of the knowledge systems among others" (2021, 119). Driven by a similar urge to shift the dominance of Euro-American thought as central to performance studies as a field, Nesreen Hussein gifts us a way to think of birthing a decentered global performance studies, "from the border," in her commitment to speak from and "dwell in the borders ..., to engage with pluri-versal experiences, histories and epistemologies; ... challeng[ing] the illusion of universality and contribut[ing] to shifting the centrality of hegemonic forms of knowing" (2022). Dance scholar Marta Saviliagno also emphasizes the importance of the pluriversal, as she foregrounds knowledge-systems that have been and continue to be historically marginalized by Euro-US-centric frames in her theorization of "worlding" as a form of unmaking. Reminding us that "nothing is worlded without the intervention of the agential subject doing the worlding," she thinks through Gayatri Spivak to argue that "worlding amounts to inscribing what was presumed to be uninscribed" (2009, 163–164). Philosopher and disability studies scholar Julie E. Maybee foregrounds the agential subject in her call to unmake disability discourse by proposing that the "disabling [of] those who are disabled results in three socially constricted bodies"; the individual, the social, and the institutional (Zach in Maybee 2019). Maybee argues that the way to unmake disability is to "*unmake* the factors that make disability, in attitudes, social practices, workplace attitudes, and institutional policies" (Zach in Maybee 2019). All these positions individually and collectively argue for an unmaking—a reimagining of dominant epistemic, social and institutional orders that foregrounds justice and emancipation of those who have been systemically erased and silenced. Such unmaking should not be conflated with Global North academies' investments in the neoliberal project of "inclusion." And, in this, they all echo performance studies scholar Sruti Bala's critical observation that "we must not assume that inclusion is sufficient or emancipatory in itself" (2017, 339). These positions make clear that we do not need the benevolence of dominant centers to open their doors, on their terms, to include us, as they continue to dominate the center and oppress us when invited in.

Unmaking is not inclusion
   Inclusion is not emancipation.

Unmaking is making emancipatory new worlds, built by, and on the terms of, minoritized peoples.

I think here too with dance and performance studies scholar Thomas F. DeFrantz in his insightful critique of queer studies investment in "queer world-making" as a project of "rampant worldmaking" that has not necessarily delivered on its promises to create anti-oppressive worlds (2017, 175). DeFrantz offers a reorientation of such "queer world-making" through a three-act consideration of queer dance focused on being, doing, and making as a holistic combination of embodiments in the world that together unsettle the normative modes of our dominant heteronormative world.

To unmake is to unsettle.

Thinking with these multidisciplinary postulations on epistemic and social justice, and their shared commitment to interrogate and destabilise power, I offer unmaking as a method, a politics, an emancipatory mode—that takes on power. And whenever power is destabilised, challenged, and held to account, there is mess.

To unmake is to make mess.

Unmaking is a messy endeavour.

In *After Method: Mess in Social Science Research*, arguing that research methods "don't just describe social realities but also help to create them," and that in this, they are inherently political, John Law argues for the foregrounding of "vagueness and ephemerality" of social realities, over and above the foregrounding of "clarity and precision" (2004). He argues for the foregrounding of mess:

> [I]f much of reality is ephemeral and elusive, then we cannot expect single answers. If the world is complex and messy, then at least some of the time we're going to have to give up on simplicities. But one thing is sure: if we want to think about the messes of reality at all then we're going to have to teach ourselves to think, to practise, to relate, and to know in new ways. (Law 2004, 2)

While Law goes on to advocate for embodied ways of knowing as his expanded view on social science methods, approaches that dance, theater, and performance studies have long advocated for and established in our fields, it is his emphasis on the processual and generated "mess" as part of seeking new methods that I find compelling, because of its potential to acknowledge and bring disorder into social science and humanities research. Using Law's metaphoric actions and images that bring this mess into being helps me to imagine and theorize unmaking as "slippery, indistinct, elusive, complex, diffuse, messy, textured, vague, unspecific, confused, disordered, emotional, painful, pleasurable, hopeful, horrific, lost, redeemed, visionary, angelic, demonic, mundane, intuitive, sliding and unpredictable" (2004, 6).

Unmaking contact is a messy endeavour,

because it unravels several interlocking power regimes at once.

To unmake is to disorder.

Unmaking is ordering but differently.

The relationship between (dis)order and power shapes the sinews of this book project. And so much (undoing) of this power rests in the prefix "un."

Perhaps, then, unmaking is an (un)method in its call to make mess, disorder, unpower.

To unmake is to unpower.
To unmake is to empower.
To unmake is to power but differently.

Unmaking requires us to acknowledge
when we are harmed,
and also when we harm.

Perhaps, unmaking is an (un)method, a politics, an emancipatory mode, because it requires us to embrace mess and disorder to scrutinise power that oppresses us, and also power that enables us to oppress. Unmaking requires us to learn and also unlearn our relationships to power. Unmaking brings competing social realities in contact.

> *Unmaking is an (un)method, a politics, an emancipatory mode*
> *that uses contact to dismantle social order.*
>
> *Unmaking is an (un)method, a politics, an emancipatory mode*
> *that makes us make contact.*

On Encountering *Unmaking Contact*

I invite my readers to encounter, to connect with, to absorb, to reflect on, to make contact with the words on these pages in ways that unmake established terms of author-reader contracts, of knowledge-reception, such that you contribute to this project of knowledge-production. And to enable this, I want to provide a note to readers on remaining open to how you might encounter my words on the pages ahead. These thoughts arise out of the very processes that I have prioritized in its writing—processes that have attempted to unmake established norms of knowledge-production. This book hinges crucially on the long, in-depth, back-and-forth, convoluted, expansive, and critical conversations that my many artist-interlocutors have generously and graciously agreed to enter into with me. Their voices and words and thinking have informed my voice and words and thinking in inextricable ways. By foregrounding and navigating through both the connectedness and the divergences as revealed in the words and practices of my transnationally situated South Asian dance artists —both those who are the focus of the following four chapters and also others—I mobilize the theorizing of choreographic contact and touch in and through their embodied realities. I foreground their danced words in conversations with me as theory. In prioritizing the voices of these artists and their art as theory, I also wish to "make visible, open up, and advance radically distinct perspectives and positionalities that displace Western rationality as the only framework and possibility of existence, analysis and thought" (Walsh 2018, 17). In this, the book aligns with dance studies' wider understanding and advocacy for dance as knowledge-making and dancers are knowledge-makers.

This manifests in a particular way on the pages of this book, as I have consciously decided to let the words of the artists speak on their own terms, instead of paraphrasing and mediating their thinking through my scholarly voice. This is important to me so that I can remain attentive to and unmake the asymmetries of power that haunt and underpin artist-scholar collaborations. This means I have chosen, quite deliberately, to leave long quotations as they are on the page, as I have not felt it ethical to edit the artists' words, thinking and processes they have experienced to arrive at them. I urge you as readers to stay with their words as I have stayed with, and grown from, them.

A note also on the formal experimentation of words on the page, that I know you will have already encountered in the Preface and until this point in the Introduction. Inspired by conversations with performance studies scholar Kareem Khubchandani and their drag queen persona LaWhore Vagistan (subjects of Chapter 4), in this book, I have followed my instincts to loosen up as a researcher, to not take myself too seriously, and to find more creative and even fun ways to evoke my words and thoughts on the page. I have done so to seek out and experiment with affective ways to write, such that the shape and location of my words on the page, their emphasis, where they stand out, and how they stand out, have all been creative strategies with which I have wanted to make contact with, even touch, my readers through the ways in which they encounter my words on the page. I am by no means the first among dance and performance studies scholars to do so, as I explain in more detail in the Afterwords to this book, but what I can assert is that this is a first for *me*. Playing and oscillating between academic prose and more poetic modes of expression have felt liberating as these different modalities of writing interact with each other on the page, just as it has opened up the different modalities of myself—the human, the scholar, the mother, the daughter, the sister, the friend, the lover, the dancer, the writer—to interact with each other. I have tried with my writing experimentations to embody in form the different manifestations of contact I have argued for, hoping to bring my readers on an intellectual, an affective, and an emotional reading journey. In *The Cultural Politics of Emotion*, Sara Ahmed argues for how bodies and their emotional interiors are shaped by encounters and interactions that they enter into with both objects and human others. In asking questions about the "doing of emotions," Ahmed considers the "the relation between emotions and (in)justice" (2014). I have tried in my writing experimentations to extend Ahmed's ideas to also consider the relation between affect and (in)justice, asking and willing my readers to consider how these words might touch and feel, and why they touch and feel how they do, in my effort to connect with them through my words, and my attempt to unmake more established and normative terms of contact between authors and readers.

I invite you, my reader, to find your own way through this unmaking, riddled with uncertainties in the pages ahead, as you and I too make contact in our imaginaries.

On Unmaking Contact

Contact: with Touch.

Dance movement psychotherapist Katy Dymoke alerts us to the need to return to the etymology of the word "contact" (2021). The word derives from an assimilation of the Latin prefix "con" (with), and the Latin root word and participle "tangere" (to touch) or "tactus" (sense of touch). It appears to be a shortened version of the Latin "contactus" (a touching) and thus translates into "with touch." Its etymology goes some distance to explain the interchangeable use of the words "touch" and "contact" within Global North dance discourse.

Contact: with Touch.

Despite playing a key role in Global North contemporary choreographies and dance practices, touch remains relatively underexamined within dance studies but has received significant scholarly attention in other fields. Philosophy has contemplated the complex relationship between selfhood, the act of touching, and being touched (Merleau-Ponty 1962; Derrida 2005; Sarukkai 2009). Neuroscience has theorized touch as the most crucial of the senses with regard to its role in human development (Hertenstein and Weiss 2011). Psychology and somatics have championed the therapeutic value of touch-based therapies, such as massages, and somatic practices, like the Alexander Technique, for the healthy growth of prematurely born babies, and for enhancing the general well-being of people, respectively (Field 2014; Fraleigh 2015). Sociology, anthropology, and cultural studies have identified touch as the foundation of human experience, a vital medium of human communication, while also acknowledging it as a strictly regulated behavior governed by culturally specific norms (Manning 2007; Guru 2017; Sarukkai 2009; Classen 2005; Montague 1986). Geographers have noted that human geography has "quite simply and literally been out of touch," calling for a need to address this crucial gap in the social sciences (Dodge and Paterson

2016, 6). The *Anatomy of Touch* (2020), a BBC Radio 4 series presented by Claudia Hammond, recently revealed the results of "The Touch Test"—a study commissioned by Wellcome Collection in collaboration with Radio 4, and led by social neuroscientist Professor Michael Banissy from Goldsmiths University of London, that people from 112 countries participated in. Echoing some of its findings from the past, six years prior, the director of the Touch Research Institute in the United States and pediatric psychologist Tiffany Field has signaled the need for more research on the role of touch in cross-cultural environments, identifying that not enough is known about the cultural, national, racial, and gendered specificities of touch and touching (2014).

In his article "Phenomenology of Untouchability," philosopher Sundar Sarukkai examines the Indian philosophical principles of touch and contact vis-à-vis the Brahminical practice of untouchability that is foundational to India's caste system, as discussed at length in the Preface to this book. Sarukkai's project also demonstrates how this practice impacts the psyche and interactions of all in contemporary Indian society at-large. He reminds us that, in some Indian philosophical traditions, touch or *sparsha* is the most important of human senses, perceived through only one sense organ, the skin. Contact or *samyoga*, Sanskrit for linking together, on the other hand, is conceptualized as a relation, experienced by two or more sense organs. Thus, whereas *sparsha* refers to the sensation of touch, perceived through the one sense organ of skin, *samyoga* implies a relation established through two or more sense organs, of which one could be the skin. Contact therefore can, but does not necessarily have to, involve touch, and touch can, in conjunction with one more sense organ, lead to contact, or a relation (Sarukkai 2009, 40). In this sense, touch is a sensation, whereas contact is a relation, and this distinction is key for my own critique of CI in intersectional and inter-epistemic terms.

Sarukkai further explains that, while the relational capacity inherent in *samyoga* is experienced by the toucher and the touched, the sensation of touch itself is only inherent in the toucher. This distinction helps untangle the conflation of touch and contact, as is so often evident in Western discourses on touch, exemplified in cultural theorist and philosopher Erin Manning's thoughts on touch as a mechanism for "reaching toward" with its promise of generative possibilities of new relations (2007, 12). Manning proposes "that touch—every act of reaching toward—enables the creation of worlds. This production is relational" (2007, xv). In reaching toward another,

Manning argues, we "invent a relation, that will, in turn, invent [ourselves]" (2007, xv). According to Manning, "to touch is always to attempt to touch the incorporeality of a body, to touch what is not yet"; that we do not touch the person we think they are, but that we reach toward the one they will become (2007, xix). In contrast, Sarukkai's signaling of a philosophical distinction between touch as a one-way sensation, and contact as a relation-generating act, of which touch may be one part, seems key to understanding the way touch operates in Indian social interactions.

Sarukkai's mobilization of these formal Sanskrit words needs to be considered alongside the colloquial Hindi word *chhuna* or *chhuan*, which means "touch" or "to touch." Derivations of these words, *chhut* (one that can be touched or touchable, and also contagion or contamination) and *achhut* (not to be touched or "untouchable"), are embedded within everyday linguistics and corporeal practices, and signal the deeply intertwined associations between touch and contamination for Indian peoples. The potential of contamination via touch is so deeply embedded within the Indian psyche, that even the prospect of the sensorial (*sparsha*) is, in fact, thwarted via strict social codifications, in order to ensure that the relational (*samyoga*) never comes into being, or is only allowed to materialize in hierarchically controlled terms. Thus, Sarukkai's philosophical postulations, when considered alongside the colloquial position of touch in social practice, reveals that the potential for the relational (*samyoga*) is in fact socioculturally and systemically designed to be denied. *Samyoga*, in this sense, becomes a negation and a pathology.[8]

Sarukkai goes on to explain that, within Indian philosophy, the skin consists of seven layers and that the visible layer of the skin is "only the seat of the cognitive sense organ corresponding to touch" (2009, 41). This visible layer's important function is also "intrinsically related to boundaries and surfaces" (2009, 41). In order to examine the complex relationship between the boundaries of skin-to-skin contact, as embodied in the practice of untouchability, Sarukkai draws on theologist Ariel Glucklich's scholarship on principles of *dharma*, the social principles of morality in Indian philosophy, to argue for the skin as inscribed by boundaries of *dharma*. The skin therefore becomes the very mechanism through which boundaries are expected to be maintained. Sarukkai thus brings us to understanding touch as a "moral sense" before demonstrating how this manifests in the dehumanizing practice of untouchability (2009, 42). He breaks down the word "untouchable" into its constituent parts: "un-touch-able." He argues that, depending on where one places the emphasis of ability or lack thereof, two different readings of the word are produced. The first possibility is "not-touch able," in which the inability to be touched is placed on the object, such as, say, air. The second, and more troubling possibility is "touch unable," in which a subject is unable to fulfill the act of touching:

> There are important consequences for the person who does not fulfil this potential of touching. The model of touching others is that of touching oneself. Thus, in the most primal sense of the term, denying oneself the fulfilment of touch leads to denying oneself the capacity to touch oneself. . . . The person who refuses to touch an untouchable suffers from touch-un-ability. (Sarukkai 2009, 43)

In the context of the social practice of untouchability, Sarukkai argues that it is indeed Brahmins who suffer from touch-un-ability by denying themselves the ability to touch Dalits. However, he also furthers his position by adding that "the untouchability experience conditions us to be more cautious toward touching in general. So, the act of touching becomes problematical, because every act of touching becomes reflective . . . becomes a judgement" (2009, 44). This leads us to a place of distrust with making contact via touch, per se:

> The organ of touch is the skin. And if you do not like to touch something then you have to "close your skin." But closing the skin is to close the first means of contact with the world . . . simply put, the moment you close the skin you die. (2009, 44)

This closing of skin becomes apparent in the deeply embedded, culturally specific, and globally circulated gesture of the Indian greeting of the *namaskar*, the folding of two hands in a prayer position, as I have already discussed in the Preface, thinking through Meena Kandasamy's and Gopal Guru's postulations on this. And although, it can be argued, the *namaskar* gesture becomes a mechanism to avoid gender-based touch and potential for violence in patriarchal South Asian societies, ignoring its casteist dimensions would be amiss, and could therefore be considered enabling for *savarna* women, while discriminating against caste-oppressed people of all genders.

In his profound intervention, *Practising Caste: On Touching and Not Touching*, Aniket Jaaware notes that Sarukkai's and Guru's essays "seem to take touchability/untouchability as already constituted facts and/or practices" without "explor[ing] how these are constituted, in the phenomenological sense" (2019, 7). In Jaaware's book, "caste is removed from the domain of subcontinental specificity and associated with the simple divide between touching and not touching, of bringing near or keeping something or someone at a distance" (Anupama Rao in Jaaware 2019, viii) through an interrogation of the social and philosophical orders that create it, and lend it sustained credibility. Jaaware cuts to the chase when he claims that as "a matter of practice, caste is determined by birth, rather than by practice" (2019, 66), emphatically reminding us of the "tight and uncompromising fit between caste and birth, between caste and being [that] cannot be undone, or even disturbed" (2019, 67). Highlighting the obsessive interdependency between caste and touch, he astutely asks, "why there are regulations on touch when it is precisely caste that precludes the possibility of touch?" (2019, 72). He argues through this conundrum for the fragility of the Brahmin body's superiority, identifying the purifying nature of these regulations as the codes that "mark the vulnerability of the brahmanical body ... vulnerable to touch by almost everybody except the brahman himself, provided he is not in an impure state" (2019, 95). The paradox of this, he reveals, is that "the one substance that cannot ever be contaminated is ... the dalit body" as it "does not have the power to be contaminated," while "in contrast ... with increasing graduations, the non-dalit bodies have the power to be contaminated and thus must fear the contact with dalit bodies" (2019, 99).

While Sarukkai and Jawaare's scholarship speaks specifically to the practice of untouchability among Hindu Indian and Indian-heritage people in the diaspora, it is important to note that caste supremacy manifests in distinct ways across most of South Asia and in diasporas, in Buddhist, Christian, Sikh, and Muslim communities. Ethnic and critical Muslim studies scholar Shaista Patel alerts us to the manifestations and practices of casteism within Muslim communities in Pakistan. She reminds us:

> Caste dismissal in Pakistan often comes from the belief that because we are Muslim, caste does not exist in our communities and societies. Unlike Hindu scriptures, the Quran does not establish and condone a caste system.... The ritualistic, religious, familial, social, economic, political and gendered aspects of caste have their own tones in Pakistan. It is not saffron-tinted, as Hindu nationalism is, but rather it takes a green, Islamic traditional, hue. (2020)

Patel draws on Sindhi anti-caste scholar Ghulam Hussain, who notes that "Sayedism and Brahminism are infused with each other. Sayed supremacy—which Hussain labels as Sayedism—comes from the (unproven) belief that Sayeds are genealogical descendants of Prophet Muhammad and therefore have a more authentic grasp on Islam and all social and political matters" (Patel 2020). Patel also cites anti-caste scholar Haris Gazdar's observation that in Pakistan, there is a split between a public silence on caste, while within private spaces casteism and practices of untouchability proliferate. She concludes:

> There is always violence attached to caste hierarchies of which Gazdar names several examples, such as having pejorative labels to strict taboos around eating and drinking together and sharing of utensils to stealing land to beatings and rapes of men and women of lowered caste people with impunity, all to "keep them in their place." (Patel 2020)

It is therefore necessary for this project to consider the manifestations of caste supremacy across South Asians and our diasporas at large, regardless of faith affiliations, seeing as my chosen case studies represent a range of relationships with India, Pakistan, and their diasporas.

Understanding the reciprocities between social and philosophical conceptualizations and practices of touch in South Asian and South Asian diasporic cultural contexts, as described above, and their choreographic manifestations in South Asian dance practices is key to this project of *Unmaking Contact*. The specific ways in which (non/un)touch manifests in South Asian choreographic practices is thus vital to consider, as I consolidate my argument for "unmaking contact" through embodied modalities, which both speak to and cut up against the philosophical considerations already laid out in the previous section. I consider these convergences and divergences key to argue for an inter-epistemic understanding of choreographic touch. And to achieve this, alongside the words of my chosen dance-artists who are the key subjects of my chapters, Akila, Diya Naidu, Nahid Siddiqui, and LaWhore Vagistan, I foreground and interweave here the reflections of five other South Asian–heritage dance artists: Masoom Parmar[9] and Anishaa Tavag[10], whom I interviewed individually in 2020 and who worked with Diya Naidu on her choreographic project *Rorschach Touch* (2018), the subject of my analyses in Chapter 2; I also weave in the voice of British-Bangladeshi dance artist Akram Khan from an interview essay I published in 2017, and a further interview in 2022; and finally I feature the voices of US-based dance artist Hari Krishnan[11] and India-based Mandeep Raikhy[12], whom I interviewed in 2022. Over the course of this project, I posed the same questions to all these dance artists: *Do you think touch and contact mean the same thing? How has your upbringing impacted your understanding of touch and contact? Within your dance and performance training, how have you experienced touch and/or contact?* I consider their responses to the first two questions below, and return to the third question further along in this Introduction.

As I navigate their words, it becomes clear to me, and it is imperative to note, that their responses rarely overlap with one another or with the theoretical positions on touch and contact already examined in detail in this article by Sarukkai and Jaaware. Their distinct and divergent perspectives demonstrate to me the vitality of integrating their voices and lived experiences into my project of reframing choreographic touch in inter-epistemic dimensions, alongside and in conversation with the voices of the Indian critical thinkers I have already foregrounded.

For all the artists, it is clear that the concepts and experiences of touch and contact are distinct and not to be conflated. However, their views rarely coincide and start from very distinct frameworks and lived realities. Akila explains that for her "touch is *a* form of contact, but it is not the *only* form of contact... contact can go beyond touch" and that in her dance works she uses both, often observing that in it contact begins with touch (2020). Akila explains further that the logic of caste supremacy maintains that, inter-caste intimacy that arise out of touch is deemed as *the* threat to Brahminism that needs rooting out. Her anti-caste gesture to visualize full contact between spines in her choreography conjures such contact as an anti-caste promise of liberation and healing (in Akila and Chandiran; 2022). Hari Krishnan picks up Akila's thread of thinking through the relationship between touch, contact, caste politics, and its relationship to Indian visualization projects of the arts at large when he says, that for him, "front and centre of this discourse of touch and contact, with reference to Indian dance, is the displacement and replacement of values, whether its family-friendly values, or whether it is values that are about selective amnesia" with regard to the plethora of visual evidence in our visual arts histories of touch-based iconography and sculpture that is denied, erased altogether, or dangerously transformed at the hands of Brahminism and Indian nationalism (2022). Homing in on the professional and artistic context, which are of course not divorced from the broader sociocultural contexts that Akila and Krishnan evoke, Mandeep Raikhy places his articulations on the relationships between touch and contact firmly within the dance studio. As a performance-maker he uses the terms very differently. He uses contact to signal that "a generic term that possibly shrinks proximity to a point where bodies make contact," whereas touch for him conjures "intentionality, histories playing out, meaning being made and choreographic logic being constructed" (2022). He explains further that for him, the words land differently as "touch is a much more textured term and becomes a means through which we make meaning" (2022). Raikhy's reference to intentionality speaks to Anishaa Tavag's formulations on these terms in tangential ways. For Tavag, "touch is a little bit more immediate and fleeting, and contact connotes something more sustained and more shared" (2020). Tavag makes a distinction between touch and "in touch," suggesting that the latter is perhaps not so different from contact. For Nahid Siddiqui the idea of being "in touch" or making contact transpires in her endeavor as a dance artist to seek out the rhythms and pulse of her inner selfhood and its connections to the wider ecologies in which she exists. She explicates this philosophical approach to contact by observing how, despite a rotating and revolving earth, as human beings we do not lose balance as we move through our daily lives. To her, contact is a metaphysical state of being (2023). Akram Khan's thinking expands on Tavag's understanding of contact in more complex ways:

> Touch transpires as a physical action and reaction between two bodies that meet each other at two or more given points. Contact, on the other hand, goes beyond that. For example, I could make contact with someone just by looking at them, or them looking at me. Contact doesn't have to arise from touch alone... contact is more a complex form of communication between people. In that sense, touch is a simpler mode of communication to understand and react to. (Khan in Mitra 2017, 388)

In a more recent interview with me, however, Khan further nuances his understanding of contact after having worked on his directorial project *Jungle Book Revisited* (2022), an ensemble production that takes on Rudyard Kipling's novel through the lenses of colonialism, capitalism, and climate catastrophe. In this project, contact for Khan is the art of listening. He says, pointing out that an anagram of the word SILENT is LISTEN and that "it is only possible to truly listen when we stop waiting and wanting to speak," if we choose to learn the value of knowledge-production that comes from remaining silent, by listening deeply (2022). Khan's *Jungle Book Revisited* shifts attention away from human supremacy and its noise by giving voice to animals and nature. The promise of such interspecies contact between Mowgli, who learns to listen by remaining silent, and her animal companions who are given the space to use their voices, is Khan's vision of the pathway to climate justice.

Although Tavag's and Khan's understandings of these two words, touch and contact, align with Sarukkai's distinction between *sparsha* (touch) as a one-way sensation and *samyoga* (contact) as a reciprocated relation, for Diya Naidu, it is touch that is the more complex and nuanced of the two concepts, as she feels that it is "possible to touch even deeper with the eyes than the skin sometimes" (2019). It seems this is the case for Masoom Parmar, too, as he offers this beautiful meditation on the two words:

> Just to put it in one sentence, according to me, "all contact is touch, but all touch is not contact." I could touch you with my eyes, and that is also what we feel . . . you would have felt it as a woman; you know when a man is looking at you. And as an effeminate gay man, I feel it too—being touched by people's looks. So no, I don't think they are one and the same thing. Even to look at it through the prism of classical dance, especially in Bharatanatyam, we don't touch our partners. If you have to embrace somebody, you embrace the air around them. . . . So there is no physical contact, but you are touching them and this is implied. I definitely think they are two different things. I feel touch is more visceral. Thinking of travelling on the Bombay local train—you are all in close contact. But is this touch? Probably not, because your body gets so used to it. So I guess for me touch has a deeper meaning. (2020)

Parmar's reflections on the Bombay local train, and how passengers' bodies are desensitized to the close and compressed proximity to one another, making this a habituated and clinical embodiment of physical contact that is not meaningful for most concerned, aligns with Jaaware's reflections on the same instance that I discuss in the previous section. Both signal that such physical contact is clinical and mechanical and does not offer the richness of reciprocity and meaning offered by touch. However, as I have discussed in the Preface already, Parmar and Jaaware's thoughts and experiences of contact in Indian public transport scenarios remain distinct from my own memories of the same, growing up in Kolkata. My own undoubtedly gendered experiences as a woman ranged from the clinical nature of physical contact with others to attempts at deliberate relational contact, often violating and unwanted in nature, and everything in between. These differing understandings on touch and contact suggest that these considerations are deeply subjective and relational to our own cultural and social positionings, and any attempt to theorize them has to consider the landscape and complexity of this discourse as fundamentally pluralistic and divergent, placing embodied realities and understandings of these contacts at the center of these considerations. What constitutes these subjective understandings of touch and contact are embedded in our upbringings, habitus, social positions, and our lived realities, and for dance artists, reinforced in our training classrooms in both classicized and contemporary dance contexts.

Khan reflects on the familial messages he grew up with on touch and contact in his British Asian and Muslim upbringing in 1980s London:

> I grew up with the implicit understanding that touch was forbidden, especially between the opposite sexes. Although between family members it was permitted. But there was also a fine line between how your parents touch you, and up to what age this was still considered permissible. All those conditions were very finely and socially tuned. But it was very clear that touching between the two sexes was forbidden. When I say forbidden, I must emphasise that this sense of the forbidden was reinforced implicitly, without anybody ever saying so in explicit terms. I grew up in an environment where I was exposed to messages, subconscious messages, around touch. Like, for example, through Bollywood films. In that context, the touch of a hand was a huge thing. That was like sex, full on sex. (Khan in Mitra 2017, 389)

Khan's reflections take me back to my own as I recognize that touch between South Asian people of the same gender, so long as they are bounded by same caste and faith, is deemed more acceptable than touch between people of different genders. In South Asian cultures, heteronormativity operates in distinct ways to the Global North, such that, while cross-gender touching in public is stigmatized and sexually marked, people from same genders can touch and display affection freely, without social judgment. The words of these dance-artists, and my own reflections, together signal the complex and coded nature of South Asian embodiments and regulations of touch and non-touch/un-touch, and signal how deeply these practices and principles are embedded within us as social beings and, by extension, as dance artists.

Thinking through the implications of touch, untouchability, contamination, regulations, and power as both exercised by and imposed upon South Asian dancing bodies requires, then, a further unsettling of CI as a touch-reliant form that invisibles the power asymmetries that operates between them at the intersections of race and caste politics, instead of romanticizing the form as committed to politics of liberation. CI is a practice that is driven by the sensation of shifting points of touch; it is termed and framed through its aim to generate contact, and hence relations, between participating bodies. In contrast, Sarukkai's signaling of a philosophical distinction between touch as a one-way sensation, and contact as a relation-generating act, of which touch may be one part, seems key to understanding the way touch and closed-skinned-ness operates in Indian social interactions, classicized dance training, and, ultimately, choreographic processes. Understanding touch in this way might help us to consider why South Asian bodies trained in solo classicized dance forms, perhaps itself an upholding of caste politics that I shall return to later in this Introduction, and consequently participating in CI, might find the conflation of touch and contact a difficult experience to navigate at an embodied level. Although in classicized dance training, the sensation of touch is prevalent as a one-way experience, the experience of making relational contact is less so. Thus, embodying such a distinction between touch and contact, and entering the realm of CI in which they are considered one and the same, may be a fundamentally disorientating experience for many South Asian dance-artists.

On Unmaking Contact in Dance/Studies

I come to the "touch turn" in dance (and performance) studies, a relatively recent phenomenon, and perhaps following on from the "affective turn," from this very particular intercultural positioning and embodied understanding of touch, and bring to it a distinct, intersectional, intercultural, and interepistemic criticality that is currently lacking in this emerging discourse. As I navigate my way through the dominant whiteness and Euro-centricism of this discourse, I pause and breathe deeply, inspired by dance scholar Prarthana Purkayastha's haptic orientation and framing of the agential hauntings of dancing women artists in nineteenth-century Bengal visual culture archives, the subjects of her forthcoming monograph *The Archives and Afterlives of Nautch Dancers in India* (forthcoming 2025). Purkayastha conceptualizes the encounter between these archival women dancers and their audiences as "holding dance." She conjures these women as being "held" by their audiences, both literally in the palms of their hands, and also metaphorically in their imaginaries. For Purkayastha, "the hold in dance is capacious, often if not always still, yet alive with tension" (forthcoming 2025). And while she continues to consider the asymmetries of power in the "beholdenness" she conjures between these dancers and her audiences, for me, the haptic dimension of her conceptualization lends me the breath with which to consider the possibilities that open up between the unmaking of contact and how it might "hold" dance through South Asian epistemologies and aesthetics. I embrace this capaciousness knowing that I am about to wade through the whiteness and Euro-centricism of this discourse, before I can emerge on the other side.

Writing on touch in contemporary dance, with a dominantly US-Eurocentric focus, dance and theater studies scholar Gerko Egert argues that "dance intensifies touch" (2020, 3) because "contemporary dance ... takes up the manifold touches of everyday life, modulates them, intensifies them, and dramatizes them" (2020, 3). Invested in theorizing touch in dance as relationality in movement and its affective dimension, Egert argues that "[t]ouches are movements, they are events and relations, they are sensations and they are affective, but above all, they are corporeal. A touch without a body ... is impossible" (2020, 52). This corporeality of touch underscores more recent scholarly attention on touch and contact within dance studies. In the introduction to her edited anthology *Thinking through Partnering and Contact Improvisation,* dance scholar and choreographer Malaika Sarco-Thomas invites us to consider what constitutes "to be-in-touch" through partnering in dance, arguing that it embodies intellectual processes of "thinking touch" and "understanding connection" (2020, 1). Sarco-Thomas complicates the relationality between thinking and touching as distinct and inter-related processes:

> The invitation "to think touch: is tricky for several reasons. Focusing on tactile activity can be a great antidote to an overactive brain, yet the reverse can also be true: certain kinds of thought can bring us away from sensation. Can thinking itself be touched? ... Can touch be thought?" (2020, 1)

While questions around the relationships between embodiments, selfhoods, intellect, and cognition in choreographic or danced touch are central to these recent scholarly projects, they rarely foreground questions of power and even more rarely focus beyond the US-Eurocentric contexts. These are, however, taken up in refreshing ways in the call for contributions for a special issue on "Touch and Training" (2023), by the journal *Theatre, Dance and Performance Training*, led by an editorial team across national and cultural contexts, and bridging the Global North and South divide: Ha Young Hwang (Republic of Korea), Tara McAllister-Viel (UK), Liz Mills (South Africa), and Sara Reed (UK). They write:

> The special issue will: (re)consider the role of touch in training in which race, gender, dis/ability, and health have a significant place in shifting understandings of why/when/where and who can/should touch; examine the power relationships during touch between teacher/student; performer/ audience; between performers in rehearsal rooms; critically examine the ways in which touch is (re)framed and negotiated through policy-making and revolutionary protest in drama schools, rehearsal rooms and training studios; address questions such as "How do these movements influence and cross-fertilize each other?" (2022)

They invited contributions that reconsidered, among other positions, "touch as violence" alongside "touch as revolution" (2022). The publication of this special issue coincided with a publication of another special issue "On Touch" (2023) in *Performance Research: A Journal of the Performing Arts*, coedited by Asher Warren and Martin Welton. Together these special issues dedicated to the subject of touch extend our fields' understandings of the multiple ways in which hapticity manifests in performance, providing a helpful, even if predominantly Global North–focused, overview of this emerging discourse. Borne of a lament of the touch deprivation that necessarily accompanied the Covid-19 pandemic lockdown, the contributions in "On Touch" attest that "the loss of contact with others, and with the stuff and fabric of lives beyond locked-down confines, has been the source of pain, hunger and injustice," as they simultaneously demonstrate that "touch also endures, in pain, in pleasure, in play and in memory" (Warren and Welton 2023, 5). Speaking to the irrevocably changed sociocultural consciousness that emerges out of social-justice seeking temporality that frames "recent global happenings, specifically #MeToo, #blacklivesmatter, and the Covid-19 pandemic" (Hwang et al. 2023, 81), "Training and Touch" as a collection of essays asks:

> What is taking place when touch happens within a network of power positions, layers of institutional practices, systems and infrastructure? Who touches, how does/should one touch, why and when can/should touch occur? How did/do these happenings influence and cross-fertilize each other? How have recent human conditions provided us with a fundamental (re)thinking about touch in its epistemological and experiential terms? (Hwang et al. 2023, 81)

My book remains in dialogue with these urgent critical interventions and invitations to critically interrogate touch within dance and performance, placing at its heart questions of power, violence, revolution, and justice, and contributes to this emerging criticality in fundamentally intercultural, intersectional, and inter-epistemic ways. Where it remains unique is in its foregrounding of caste politics in its interrogations of touch and contact in performance, arguing that any research that examines touch without engaging with the vector of caste is incomplete. This critical stance complicates scholarship that has tended to advocate the use of CI and touch in dance and movement therapy as healing, generative, and liberatory forces, without fully considering how power and compounded social positionalities impact CI dancers and participants (Novack 1990; Houston 2009; Dymoke 2014). This is a necessary intervention to the body of work on CI and touch-driven choreography, in order to challenge 1960s/1970s Global North dance/studies' attitudes that have equated touching bodies with counterculture liberation; and remains in critical dialogue with Guru Suraj and Adrianna Michalska's critical intervention (2024).

In her groundbreaking ethnographic study of "contact improvisation as [American] culture" (Novack 1990, 4), anthropologist, dancer, and educator Cynthia J. Novack traced the emergence of CI in the United States and argued that "we perform movement, invent it, interpret it, and reinterpret it, on conscious and unconscious levels" and through this "we participate in and reinforce culture, and we also create it" (Novack 1990, 8). We have already learned with Dorinne Kondo that such creative, inventive, making actions are "power-laden" acts, in and through which power asymmetries can be upheld or challenged. Novack attributes the "invention," and in that sense the steering of, CI to Steve Paxton in 1972 (1990, 10), while also exposing some fundamental contradictions within the movement's guiding principles and the narratives that have been written about it:

How does someone exert leadership within a movement which denies it? How do people take action when the prevailing ideology is to let whatever happens, happen? How is egalitarianism maintained within an individualistic community? (1990, 12).

Following through at some levels with questions on egalitarianism and CI, Novack notes that while "in America, one body touching another body is highly charged with meaning and appropriate only in certain contexts, ... contact improvisation presents a unique situation within dance" as an anomaly (1990, 160). She claims though that "in contact improvisation, the functional use of touch predominates" (1990, 163), and explains further that her ethnographic conversations with dancers from all spectrum of experience in CI suggest that many "related touching to a freedom from the restriction of gender roles and from accompanying expectations about what kind of movement suits men and women, and what parts of the body can and cannot be touched" (1990, 168). While Novack notes that in those early years of 1970s CI practice, most participants were "young, college-educated, white, middle-class Americans" (1990, 10), the egalitarian principles of CI do not move beyond gender, and to some extent sexuality. But questions of egalitarianism vis-à-vis CI and choreographic touch cannot stop at gender, and need to develop in intersectional dimensions, taking into consideration other social power regimes.

In a historically (and predominantly) ableist practice, Katy Dymoke's work with Touchdown Dance based in the UK has brought necessary complexity to the discourse on CI and power. Through listening in to the experience of touch dispossession experienced by visually impaired and deaf people, Dymoke "became aware of the absence of touch in society and the negative impact of touch deprivation on health and well-being" (2021, 4). By interrogating how CI can become an empowering force for disabled and visually impaired people, Dymoke's leadership at Touchdown Dance has demonstrated that CI "has turned out to be a kind of Braille for the body, instinctively available to those who can see and those who cannot, alike— shared language learned through the body" (Paxton and Kilcoyne quoted in Dymoke 2021, 5). Dymoke's scholarship has thus attempted to advocate for the beneficial role of touch within health and social care, arguing that "CI liberates us from many social and cultural constraints, allowing a rethink based on a subjective internalized perception of self in the world" (2021, 10). CI as a liberatory force for disabled and visually impaired people also rests on its ability to work with and through non-linearity with regard to shape and also by influencing the movement of someone else's body weight across a horizontal plane, in opposition to the vertical uprightness of ballet and other Euro-US dance forms of the twentieth century. But internalized perceptions of our selves do not exist distinct from interlocking regimes of power that operate in and through us.

Intersectional interrogations of such power regimes as upheld by CI are thus, still, few and far between. And I can see why. For a practice that was premised on modeling egalitarian society, and could be argued as modeling white liberal formulations of democracy, championed by a group of people who were predominantly invisible to their own power and privileges, CI remains clouded in floaty ideals of democracy and freedom. This is foregrounded in its movement language invested in notions of abstraction underpinned by technique, invisibilizing the politics of the lived realities of the people that perform them. The link between abstraction and (colonial and racialized) power is explored by US choreographer Miguel Gutierrez, the son of Colombian immigrants, in his article "Does Abstraction Belong to White People?" Gutierrez poses a necessary and rhetorical question before going on to answer it: "who has the right not to explain themselves? The people who don't have to. The ones whose subjectivities have been naturalized" (2018). Dance scholar Arabella Stanger complicates the question (and its possible responses) further by compellingly arguing that the ideals of abstraction and democracy as promised in "utopian choreographic projects" of US-European modern dance are, in fact, built on "violent ground" (2021, 3). She challenges "the corporeal forms of harmony and freedom promised in Euro-American theater dance," arguing that they "conceal material conditions of imperial, colonial, and racial subjection" (2021, 3).

Thinking collectively through these critiques, it is not difficult to locate the multiple formal dimensions at which CI manifests as an exclusionary movement practice. CI as a practice and CI practitioners are cloaked in deeply troubling narratives of universalism invested in and stemming from an even more troubling notion of "neutral" scientific inquiry. Its commitment to experimentation and a deemed, exploratory, and open-endedness is contrary to the ways in which the participants all arrive at the same point through identical vocabulary, energies, and dynamics through training in a shared and formulaic vocabulary. While these principles and practices underpin CI's claims to its liberatory form and spirit, the absence of a specific vocabulary can, ironically, become an exclusionary experience for many who are not from within the CI world.[13] There is then also something exclusionary in the "improvisation" part of this practice. Witnessing CI in practice has made me aware of how physical touch appears to travel seamlessly between different points of bodily contact, regardless of the potential of social and bodily harm that might be generated by such intimacy. A key component of this appearance of seamlessness rests in this notion of "improvisation"—the inherent idea that our responsiveness has to be instinctual and not intellectual, spontaneous and not premeditated. I strongly contend, based on my own experience, that being instructed and able to improvise spontaneously within CI signals its deeply privilege-wielding white and other socially dominant foundations. And I can also see this translates into caste supremacist contexts within contemporary Indian dance experiments. In reality, therefore, not everyone can improvise freely without the fear of how power might enact on and harm our bodies in and through our CI partner's relational social positionings. The hardest part of CI for me has always been to stop myself from preplanning my next response—in order to try to control and preempt how and where I am comfortable being touched back. Simply put, it is the improvisational dimension of CI that really reveals the asymmetries of power that are foundational to the form (i.e., as participants, we are never sure where and how we will be touched).

These complex relationships between US-European ideals of abstraction, democracy, technique, form, claims of universalism, and racialized power are at the foundations of my published interview with Paxton, where we engage in a conversation about CI's histories and contemporary implications. Paxton reflects on how CI began as somatic explorations into how inter-bodily communications transpire through shared points of physical touch (Mitra 2018, 9). He notes that "if you feel like you are being supported, say, under your rib, you can then use that as a fulcrum to test out the possibilities of movement that would not be possible if that point of contact or touch was removed. So suddenly, your whole body-surface becomes a possible connection to the earth.... Your partner is connected to the floor, you are connected to the floor, and you are mutually supporting and using the supports to discover and provide new movement possibilities" (Paxton in Mitra 2018, 9). Physical touch is thus central to and the driving force of CI, through which contact of many kinds are initiated and maintained.

Keen to consider the intersectional ways in which CI carries the potential to harm its participants through upholding power asymmetries in its founding principles and continuing practice, in our interview I questioned Paxton about the form's predominant whiteness:

RM: You mention that contact has been less successful in integrating Black and brown people into its practice, and that it does remain a predominantly white movement practice. Would you have an answer as to why this is the case? (Mitra 2018, 13)

His response is significant:

SP: I've been thinking about this question for a very long time and yet I am not sure that I do have an answer. There have been a few of course. As the recent Black Lives Matter movement signals to us, what we once considered was institutionalized racism as practiced by the police is in fact systemic in our society, our culture. So, it might well be that rubbing skins with your oppressors is not an appealing prospect within contact. It seems to be a bit of a canary-in-a-coal-mine situation, this. It warns us that something might be up, and has been, for the whole time that contact has been around. (Paxton in Mitra 2018, 13)

Paxton's reflections signal his whiteness as he articulates the realization that the democratic principles, which he and his generation of CI practitioners felt were foundational to the practice, do not in fact hold true vis-à-vis race and racially minoritized bodies participating in CI.

In many ways, Paxton's words consolidate ongoing lines of inquiry into the whiteness of CI as unpacked by Fred Holland and Ishmael Houston-Jones (1983), Danielle Goldman (2010; 2021), Ann Cooper Albright (2017), Hannah Yohalem (2018), Rebecca Chaleff (2018), and Keith Hennessy (2019), among others, all noting and problematizing the white and racist foundations and ongoing practice of CI to various degrees, and Hennessy most recently acknowledging its culturally appropriative foundations in erased borrowings from Black embodiments of walking, Japanese Aikido and Zen Buddhism, Chinese Taoism, and Africanist music and dance approaches to the idea of the "jam" sessions (2019). In *"Wrong" Contact Manifesto* (1983), exposing the exclusionary and codified performance conventions and tactics of CI, Fred Holland and Ishmael Houston-Jones note that "Contact Improvisation remained in 1983 and remains still a dance form done largely by people who are liberal arts educated and are not Black" (2022). Their protest transpired in the following proclamations and also aesthetic and movement choices in their duet that countered CI's normative and exclusionary codes:

> We are Black.
> We will wear street clothes.
> We will wear heavy boots.
> We will play a loud, abrasive sound score.
> We will have non-performative conversations.
> We will fuck with flow.
> We will stay out of physical contact as much as possible.
> (Holland and Houston-Jones 1983)

Holland and Houston-Jones's "C.I. duet that [broke] every rule of C.I. orthodoxy" (Houston-Jones in DeFrantz 2017) was a crucial commentary on the engrained CI's exclusionary politics into the formal, visual, and movement dimensions of the practice. I am struck particularly by the statement to "stay out of physical contact as much as possible." It reinforces that the imposition to share physical touch that is woven into the very fabric of the practice is a deterrent for Black and racially minoritized participants due to the power asymmetries that always already shape the space they, we, move in. Writing on touch and Black subjectivity in the African American context, Rizvana Bradley notes that "touch . . . evokes the vicious, desperate attempts of the white, the settler, to feign the ontic verity, stability, and immutability of an irreducibly racial subject-object (non) relation" (2020). Bradley proposes that this creates "subjects whose conditions of existence sustain the fantasy of being-untouched" (2020). I find Bradley's postulations on touch as violent and harmful to Black subjectivity, crucial here to delineate from white ways of thinking about touch, particularly in CI, as healing and generative. They further alert us to the need to be attentive to the ways in which whiteness exerts and maintains power in CI through touch.

I observe, in the conclusion to this published interview, that Paxton's honest and generous reflections necessitate an urgent consideration of the relationships between CI and broader politics of power:

Where this interview offers a valuable new perspective on this discourse is Paxton's observation that the form's whiteness points to a "canary-in-a-coal-mine situation," . . . Paxton reflects on this in two ways: first, by acknowledging that claiming democracy between bodies that are historically in hierarchical relationships with each other with regards to continuing unequal power structures, may well make contact improvisation a form difficult for black and brown bodies to feel welcomed into . . .; second, Paxton suggests further that perhaps racial and cultural divides in our societies are too deeply engrained in a way that contact improvisation's democratic principles are not equipped to acknowledge or address. (2018, 16)

Paxton's reckoning with the foundational whiteness of CI, signaled in his speculation that "something might be up, and has been, for the whole time that contact has been around," has led me to my own. Listening to him consider the potential of harm that can be inflicted by CI on racially minoritized bodies achieved in me two simultaneous realizations: the first, a much needed validation of my first-ever experience of CI, when I was at the receiving end of whiteness's violence in the dance studio, which I have described in the Preface; and the second, an admission that, in some instances of participating in CI, I must surely wield power against fellow participants in the room who are located in different social positions to my own.

Although my line of questions for Paxton came from my position as a brown, immigrant, Indian woman at the receiving end of CI's racialized power matrices in the UK, Paxton's response has alerted me to consider further how the intersections of power work within a CI session in, say, India or in the diaspora between brown-only South Asian bodies, in which caste alongside race becomes the lines through which power is exercised, invisibilized, and experienced. My interview with Paxton has been a wake-up call for myself, as a dance scholar, to think beyond power and oppression in ways that fundamentally intersect, most importantly in myself. Locating Paxton's words in the caste-apartheid context of South Asia and its diasporas, I must necessarily consider the implications of "rubbing skins with your oppressors is not an appealing prospect within contact" (Paxton in Mitra 2018, 13). And to understand physical contact and touch within the Indian caste supremacist context, which is built on the very premise of whom one can (and cannot) touch, critique of CI has to be intersectional through the interconnectedness of race, caste, and gender politics. I return here therefore to a second set of interwoven reflections from Krishnan, Raikhy, Naidu, and Khan as they reveal their encounters with touch and CI within contemporary dance contexts responding to my second question: *Within your dance and performance training, how have you experienced touch and/or contact?*

Krishnan shares that his first encounter with touch in performance training was within theater as a child, long before he began studying Indian dance, which made him "much more cognizant of the varied possibilities of how touch can be performed through relationships beyond the solo dancing figure" (2022). This encounter within the theater training context, in a looser environment free from stylization, heightened his awareness to a different sense of "emotional linkage via contact" that touch in theater enables. His subsequent training in Indian dance and then in contemporary dance in the United States, and the ways in which contact and touch transpired very differently in these environments, he says, are fundamentally entwined with his emerging queer identity (2022).

Raikhy's experience of contact during his CI training in the UK makes him reflect on its virtuosic and mechanical particularities, which places a specific "kind of attention on contact pertaining to questions of efficiency, questions of organicity, to ensure safety in flow and weightbearing in CI training" (2022). When he went on to work with British-Asian choreographer Shobana Jeyasingh, he encountered the virtuosity of contact and touch anew, driven not by efficiency and relationality of bodies of his CI training, but rather by a visuality that made physical demands to solve aesthetic puzzles such as "could you lift this body above your shoulder level? Or could you invert this body?" (2022).

For Naidu and Khan, gender and race intersect in the studio space to shape their understanding of touch and contact. Naidu recalls that teachers and modes of pedagogy "in these spaces are more tactile in the way they transfer information or give feedback and there is a general sense of liberated, non-gendered and able-bodied safety one experiences" (2019). However, she also reflects on the seemingly gendered nature of these interactions within the classroom, and how these impacts their behaviors and beings beyond it:

> I do remember teachers having to really talk through and hand-hold some students into being comfortable with touch with the opposite sex. An experience I remember very clearly is how our bodies changed during those first

months of contact improvisation classes. We were all walking around with this sense of openness, freedom and awareness, reveling in the momentary freedom from gender. And then, when class finished, we would go outside onto the street in large groups as dance students do. Day after day, I would watch as the girls, me included, systematically and sadly closed our bodies again. The walk home would prove very unpleasant if we continued to have that sway and exuberance, indeed that inviting quality. The boys on the other hand, barely seemed to notice they had left the studio. This is something I still feel poignantly till today and it influences much of my research and work. (2019)

The theme of discomfort, although not necessarily gendered in this instance but instead racialized, is echoed in Khan's memory of his first contact improvisation class at De Montfort University in Leicester, UK, where he enrolled in the undergraduate dance program:

It was terrifying. But to be honest, even before I encountered my discomfort with touch in the studio, there was a whole other issue I had to confront. Before touch ... before touching somebody else, I had to get to grips with the idea of touching myself, but in a non-sacred context. Because in Islam, we are constantly touching ourselves; we wash our face five times a day to cleanse our bodies. But this emphasis on self-touch is that it is once again framed as sacred, between oneself and God. In addition to confronting these complex emotions around touch and touching, I had to confront the issues I had with the medium of such touch itself—my own body, and how I perceived it from within. In a contemporary dance environment, where most women and men were absolutely fine with revealing their bodies in very open ways, I concealed myself more and more. And I did this quite literally by putting more and more layers of clothes onto me. So I would wear a t-shirt, on top of another t-shirt, on top of another t-shirt, and then a cardigan, and a hat, and trousers and a hoodie. And to be honest, I've never been able to shake off this vulnerability of revealing myself, fully. This sense of self-concealment continues to shape my work. This is why I cannot perform naked, because of the fear of revealing my body. During my movement training this feeling was heightened because most of the bodies of my peers around me fitted the mold of what a Western dancing body is expected to look like. But my body did not fit this image at all. So, for me it was frightening ... terrifying. And then, on top of that, there was touch. (Khan in Mitra 2017, 391)

When I asked if his tutors at university ever made space to discuss the different cultural codes bodies of color bring into the studio space in negotiating contact, he said:

> No, not once. But I want to clarify that this does not necessarily mean that the teachers were not aware of the issues. My teachers might well have been aware and felt that they were helping me deal with my awkwardness by guiding me through it? But nobody questioned . . . nobody directly asked me "are you feeling uncomfortable?" But the thing is, the body doesn't lie, so of course they saw I was uncomfortable in my body. (Khan in Mitra 2017, 391)

Naidu's observations about the tendency of white teachers of CI workshops within Indian settings is equally troubling:

> I think the sensitivity of a teacher to the exact individuals in the room is of paramount importance. I have seen many European teachers talk rather patronizingly to Indian students, assuming they never touch the opposite sex, and now they will be liberated from their social conditioning via this class. . . . I think what annoys me most is when the teacher, usually from a first world country, assumes that this is somehow a superior way to be, interact, touch or think about other bodies and to then witness very naive, unsuspecting and awestruck young dancers lap up that discourse because they are so smitten with the skill. There is barely any real time spent on talking about how or why this way of moving with other bodies in space came about and what it meant socially or culturally at the time. (2019)

Both Khan and Naidu, implicitly and explicitly, signal the condition of Sarukkai's concept of "closing the skin" through their distinct South Asian upbringings, when reflecting on their training in CI. For Khan, the potentiality in making contact, as per Sarukkai's understandings of *samyoga*—that is, to enter into a relation with another body—is where the place of discomfort opens up, as his skin, his moral sense, mobilizes boundary maintenance. For Naidu, the potentiality in making contact with other bodies within a studio environment comes somehow supported and sanctioned by accepting the norms of Western pedagogies. These knowledge systems momentarily disorient, destabilize, and undermine her own innate ways of knowing that are inscribed into her skin, but she is able to navigate them within the studio. However, as she leaves the studio walls and walks onto the streets, her skin or her body closes up again to keep moral boundaries in place, and to protect herself from the potential of unwanted or even violent touch. Despite their very distinct South Asian upbringings and lived realities in India and the UK respectively, Naidu and Khan seem to be bound by an embodied moral sense. Their experiences with the whiteness of CI are further complicated and nuanced by their own respective embodiment of gendered brownness. Whereas it is true that Khan would have encountered the whiteness of CI more explicitly during his dance training in the UK as the only racially minoritised person in the class, Naidu's experience of the form's whiteness is perhaps more implicit in a class of other Indian students, being taught and led by a white CI teacher. For both of them, what is undeniable is the experience of destabilization in having to navigate the whiteness of the form in their respective brown skins.

I notice that, although power asymmetries related to race and gender are spoken about with ease, questions of caste politics are not explicitly and sustainedly present in my conversations with the four artists. The closest we come is Parmar's reflections on the hierarchies in classicized dance because of the love expressed in narratives between human and divine characters (2020). Tavag mentions that, although she is not fully certain, she wonders whether urban and elite CI spaces in India may well operate in exclusionary ways because of India's inherent and internalized practice of discrimination via colorism, excluding participants with darker skin from the practice (2020). Colorism and casteism are closely related discriminatory realities and practices in India and the Indian diaspora. The absence of a more substantial discussion of caste politics from my conversations with many of the artists signals a caste-blind phenomenon akin to the colorblind rhetoric of whiteness. To move to a place of caste justice, or race justice, or both, vis-à-vis choreographic touch requires a deep reckoning with how power operates in these practices, and a recognition of how power asymmetries are perpetuated and kept in precisely through such invisibilization of power. It requires a reckoning with our role as artists and scholars in these invisibilizations. My conversations with these artists thus open up generative and necessary spaces for such reckonings. And they take me back to a scrutiny of the ways in which caste supremacy is potentially upheld in invisibilized ways in the classicized dance forms practiced across South Asia and its diasporas, in their solo presentation mode.

On Unmaking Contact in South Asian Dance/Studies

Foundational to the practice and presentation of the classicized dance forms from India, and sustained beyond its borders, is their highly revered predominant solo presentational mode. Even when these classicized forms are presented as ensemble productions, the spatial dynamics and lack of choreographic touch between the dancers replicate the deemed self-sufficiency of the solo dancer in the visual design.

She is alone and she is enough.

During the nationalist reconstruction of the classicized dances, the centrality of the solo dancer on the proscenium stage became paramount. This solo form in classicized dances emerged, in part, out of dialogue with contemporary US-European modern dance initiatives that initiated a collapse between the role of the "dancer" and the "choreographer," or indeed through the rise of the category of the "choreographer" itself, as dance commentator Sally Gardener notes (2007). This is how perhaps Rukmini Devi Arundale and Birju Maharaj, for instance, became deemed as solo architects of bharatanatyam and kathak respectively, carrying out appropriative erasures of caste-oppressed communities of hereditary dancers and Muslim dancers respectively who were the custodians of these dances, Brahminizing these forms in the name of "classicization."[14] The alignment of colonial modernity and Brahminism finds a particular manifestation in the classicized dance forms, and thus tuning into the workings of caste politics on the solo architectural form of these dances seems crucial. As is leaning into the importance of community in artistic efforts that undo these erasures.

Anti-caste activist and hereditary dance-artist Nrithya Pillai has argued that "[b]haratanatyam is permeated by a deeply affective and somatic form of Brahminism" (2022). I speculate whether the solo modality of these classicized dance forms that were reconstructed during India's nationalist project, and upheld as ideal and norm, is an integral part of this "somatic form of Brahminism"—in dialogue with US-European modern dancers and their embodiment of the individual as genius. Describing the ways in which her caste-oppressed body poses a challenge to "Brahminic Bharatanatyam" (2022), Pillai writes:

In my own performances, I deploy my Bharatanatyam to imagine new regimes of mobility and equity for women like me. A large part of this has to do with the retrieval—through largely oral sources—of dance repertoire of historical import that was created by and for my direct ancestors. I perform such pieces not only as a counterpoint to the acts of upper-caste appropriation and stewardship, but also to acknowledge the deep levels of mediation through which I myself have received the very practice of Bharatanatyam, across the deep vectors of reform discourse, aesthetic refashioning, and moral and cultural nationalisms. Built upon the thematic of courtly love, as opposed to nationalist neo-Hindu devotional modes, my reclaiming of my community's repertoire, asserts old familial genealogies into the dystopic spaces of capitalism where today's corporate-funded "classical" dance thrives for the upper castes. I perform dance compositions that were created or revivified for the new elites by hereditary dance masters (*nattuvanars*) in my family, except that now, I perform these through my Bahujan body. (Pillai 2022)

By claiming the solo format and taking up space in and through it, Pillai's choreographic challenge to the dance form that was designed to exclude hereditary dancers like herself during the nationalist reconstruction of bharatnatyam aims to center Bahujan women artists, oral histories, genealogies, and sources from within her own ancestral community. Pillai holds to account both Brahminism and men from her own community in their patriarchal complicity, in her critiques of these appropriative erasures. Her solo performances are a reclamation of her own erased ancestries, their labor and art. Pillai's danced interventions are crucial as she foregrounds (her own) community through them, in contrast to the solo bharatnatyam danced by *savarna* elites, whose aesthetic foregrounds individual genius.

Approaching questions of cultural appropriation and caste justice from a diametrically differing position to Pillai by focusing more on the role of patriarchy in the erasure of her ancestors, the Kalavantulu women, and their art, Kuchipudi dancer Yashoda Thakore too turns our attention to community and begins her "research by conversing with Kalavantulu women—women whom I thought had disappeared." She reminds us:

The role of the Kalavantulu women in Kuchipudi did not end there. It was the presence and the performance of the Kalavantulu practitioners that contributed to Kuchipudi's classical status. This is a poignant and often overlooked reminder of the contribution of these women to the history of Kuchipudi. (2022)

Thakore's emphasis on the pluralized "women," the ancestry of hereditary artists from whom she hails, signals the importance of community to these dances and their erasures by *savarna* elites in favor of the solo dancer as the individual genius.

I want to recognise that the impetus and stakes of reclaiming their dance forms through the solo format are different for hereditary dancers, as they seek justice for their communities. I thus wish to critically interrogate the dominant Brahminical solo format within the classicized forms itself, particularly when danced by *savarna* artists, vis-à-vis its rejection of touch by form and, potentially, community by architectural design. I am thinking through here the relationship between the negation of touch of others due to the architectural design of the solo format, and its potential negation of community, and considering if they are mutually exclusive. Can we affirm community formations without touch? Yes, most certainly so. Does the avoidance of touch necessarily lead to a diminishment of community? Very likely not, because we know that contact, without physical touch, can also lead to community. But what is at stake here are the ways in which caste supremacy is upheld by the avoidance of touch in the solo format, which constraints the possibility of cross-caste choreographic community formations. So, while community is not denied per se due to an absence of touch of others in the solo format, its cross-caste formations are most certainly constrained, even denied, as a result of it.

Nearly two decades ago in my first academic publication, reflecting on the relationship between space, contact, touch, and kathak (the classicized form I trained in), I wrote:

> The spinal column of the Kathak dancer is upright and the use of the extended arms marks out a very clear personal space which is never invaded. This demarcation of physical space, this deliberate denial of physical contact reflects the post-colonial conditioning of India.... As a result no physical contact or any form of intimacy is ever expressed with another dancer. (Mitra 2005, 4–5)

While I write about my experience of embodying kathak in this passage, this demarcation of personal space is just as applicable to the other classicized dance forms of India. And, twenty years on, I find myself considering not only how such an individualistic aesthetic informs the architectural form of the dances, but more important, how this aesthetic is designed to impact the interiority and sociocultural formation of the identities of the dancers themselves. During his kathak training in the UK, Akram Khan observes that "the caste system itself didn't quite reveal itself" in the solo form, even as it was present in themes and content that were explored in his multiethnic and multiracial classroom. But as he reflects further on the ways in which the solo format *might* uphold caste supremacy during our conversation, Khan observes, "I think it is built in sub-consciously. I think it's there, for sure it's built in. Absolutely! In the solo form—you are sacred—you are not of the people" (2022). Reflecting on the relationship between the solo form of bharatanatyam and caste supremacy, Mandeep Raikhy too observes "there is no other truth to this" (2022). He notes the casteist foundations in the reconstruction project of the art form and shares with certainty that the negation of "touch had everything to do with it" because "a caste framework for its reinvention, would mean that touch is central to it" (2022). Echoing similar sentiments, Hari Krishnan explicates and complicates Raikhy's and Khan's observations further by arguing that the architectural "distancing between gesture and torso is very clearly demarcated" in the solo dancer (2022). And that such demarcation was embedded into the nationalist revival of bharatanatyam where "intimate moments of human contact are physically actualized through a deliberately dangerous stylization of gesture, torso, and physicality," which results in a "distancing that becomes an absolute counterproductive enterprise in these really intense moments of contact representation" in the dance repertoires, which are only allowed to play out at the interdisciplinary levels of lyrics, poetry, music and narrativizations, but not in the visualization and corporealization of the dance (2022). Krishnan calls for the need to repair this disjuncture in the art form, which he believes is the result of Brahminic architecture of the solo form, and leads to the upholding of caste supremacy (2022).

With these perspectives in mind, it becomes important to consider the many advocates of the solo form in Indian classicized dances. Dance scholar and choreographer Ananya Chatterjea attributes to the solo format of these classicized dance forms the ultimate goal for the student-artist, which is "to render herself devoid of *aham* (egotism) and to become a selfless devotee of the dance" (1996, 74). Chatterjea's observation of the goal to move beyond the ego, in order to serve the dance, however, seems to enter into tension with the recent emphasis that has been placed by other dance scholars and writers on the vitality of the individual dance-artist's growth and sustenance through the solo format. Is it possible to transcend the ego if the architectural design of the dance, the solo, is individualism?

The late dance historian Kapila Vatsyayan claimed that the solo presentation of the classicized dance forms is integral to its identity:

> The Indian classical dance form is largely an Ekal Nritya (a solo dance form). It is in sync with our philosophy that we come alone, and die alone.... By not investing in the creation of solo dancers, the very foundation of the tradition of Indian classical dance is rattled. Whatever the challenges, this central character of the solo dance needs to nurtured, protected and promoted. (quoted in Jafa 2019)

Kathak dancer and cultural activist Navina Jafa writes that the solo format is under threat and reinforces Vasyayan's argument that "the anchoring feature of most Indian classicized dances is the solo dancer" (2019). Jafa argues that the "solo has to survive to conserve the Indian classical dance" (2019) and that it must withstand the "the pressure of succumbing to popular forces of group performances" (2019). Dance-scholar Padma Subrahmanyam also echoes the need to salvage the solo form to preserve the rigor of Indian classicized dance:

> Dance like Hindu practice is individualistic and not collective devotion. It is a one to one journey of realisation. In the Natya Shastra, solo is one form among the ten categories of drama. The emphasis in the Indian dance is on nurturing individual creativity and not factory productions, or cloning as evident in the process of group productions. (quoted in Jafa 2019)

Subrahmanyam's words suggest that, in her opinion, the nurturing of the individual solo artist, which must be upheld at all costs, is at odds with ensemble performance training and making, which she compares to factory cloning processes. She claims, therefore, that the presence of multiple dancers, sharing the same space within a common choreographic vision, devalues the potential that lies in an individual dance-artist and also their dance; that somehow bodies sharing space leads to a contamination of the dance itself; and that the potential of collective knowledge-making is a threat to the individual star culture of the classicized Indian dance world. I am intrigued by this downright rejection of dance as community. However, as dance scholar Janet O'Shea helpfully points out to me, there is need to exercise further nuance in the implications of Subrahmanyam's words, not only on its upholding of the solo artist, but also on its critique of ensemble innovations with the bharatanatyam world:

> Subrahmanyam rejects collectivity and favors individuality, but she also rejects the uniformity of a particular style of bharata natyam ensemble production, in which dancers are expected to match each other's movement exactly. Neither the solo star nor the ensemble model is collectivist in nature. Rather the ensemble production replaces one form of hierarchy with another. (O'Shea 2023)

This reading of the ensemble format of South Asian classicized dance forms as also anti-collectivism helpfully complicates what constitutes dance as community. Moreover, both Vatsyayan and Subrahmanyam locate this solo pathway of classicized dance forms in "our philosophy," based in "Hindu practice" of individual "and not collective devotion." This formulation of Hinduism as a practice of individual devotion, devoid of contact/relationality with other human beings, that is, devoid of community in devotional mode, is noteworthy here, especially how this manifest in the upholding of the solo dance form. I pause here to consider a potential link between such advocacy of the solo dance format as intrinsically Hindu, its underpinning ideology of Hindutva, a politicized form of Hinduism, and neoliberalism, and their interlinked advocacies of individual decision-making and choices, on the basis that social and "human welfare is dependent on the freedom to choose, and the market facilitates and allows individual choices to run the economy" (Siddiqui 2017, 152). Dance scholar Anurima Banerji has alerted us to the potential connectedness and "presence of dancers in movements allied with the ruling regime" in India (2022, 1), giving us reason to consider the potential ways in which dance and dance discourse in contemporary India may be informed by the political and ideological persuasions of the "ruling regime."

Such considerations signal the Brahminical body-politic that intersects with and is upheld by the classicization project of the dance forms, captured in the exclusive solo dancer, and her embodied politics of individualism. By implication, then, those "folk" (dances of the people that are not considered worthy of being deemed as classicized) and Adivasi (indigenous) dance practices from across India that foreground collectivity in their touch-driven movement languages, and their community-building aesthetic (Assamese bihu, Santhali dance from West Bengal, lavani from Maharashtra, among others), are relegated to the realm of the non-devotional, the non-Hindu, the non-Brahminical, the collectivist, the Other. These dance forms are permitted to be consumed by the urban dominant caste and class elites from a distance, that is strictly codified and maintained by the Brahminical world-order. And when this distance is permitted to collapse even momentarily as part of this codified design, the cross-caste and class touch and community that emerges from such instances is experienced and processed as superfluous, and not to be dwelled on (Sengupta 2024a). In a conference paper titled "Un/comfortable Encounters: Tourist Experience of Adivasi Performance", doctoral researcher Tirna Sengupta at the University of Leeds, UK examines the tensions exhibited in and embodied by urban Bengali tourists when visiting rural Bengal as they witness and are invited to participate in Adivasi dance performances that are curated for their pleasure and consumption. Sengupta deftly analyses the asymmetries of power that frame such interactive spectacles, observing both the chasm maintained between tourists and Adivasi dancers during the course of the performance, *and* the momentary disruption of the Brahminical world-order in the physical contact between the two groups in the last routine presented by Adivasi dance troupes (Sengupta 2024a). In personal communications with me Sengupta offers further critical observations about these interactions:

> The physical distance between the tourists and the Adivasi dancers, Adivasi safari drivers who usher the tourists into the space where the dance happens and the Adivasi staff of the tourist lodges who serve tea remains intact during the performance. The last routine presented by the troupes invite participation from the tourists where some tourists (by choice) come in contact with Adivasi bodies. I express my suspicion in the thesis that these moments of choreographed contact with marginalised bodies do not necessarily constitute a sustained challenge to the tourists' Brahminical world view in their return to daily lives. Literature on tourism activities suggest that people do things during their travel that they would not otherwise do in their daily lives. Besides, the overall curation of the programme is such that stereotypes about the Adivasis are reinstated rather than challenged. The performance does not provide space for uncomfortable reckoning with caste or class. I interviewed tourists who participated in the dance and came in contact with the Adivasi dancers, and they denied the practice of caste in urban Bengal altogether, making further conversations about the

significance and meaning of their experience with respect to caste and class-based segregation of bodies irrelevant or impossible. (Sengupta 2024b)

Thinking with Sengupta's observations lends weight to my own suspicions about how caste politics shapes, and are upheld and invisibilized by the solo format of the classicized dance forms, vis-à-vis the threat posed by the collectivism of "folk" and Adivasi dance practices and their touch-driven aesthetics. As Sengupta explains, while the Brahminical world-order is disrupted, even momentarily, in this interaction between the Adivasi dancers and the Bengali elite tourists, their collectivism is deliberately undermined and overlooked in favour of denying opportunities for caste-class reckonings on the part of the tourists. As they return to their urban lives, their experiences are deliberately left behind without further reflections. I acknowledge here of course that not all Indian folk dances are collective in their form, and indeed some are also Brahminical in origin. But it is still worth noting that none of the eight classicized dance forms of India is by design advocated as a collectivist art form, signaling that the rigor and excellence deemed requisite to become a carrier of national culture in order to be conferred "classical" status can only be attained by solo dancers. This segregation of the individual from the community, how they manifest in the actual architectural forms of the variegated landscapes of dance across India, and what this means for which dance (and dancers) are allowed to represent the collective nation-state (and which are not), deserve critical attention.

Brahma Prakash argues that "a monoculture, a Brahminical ideology defin[es] Indian cultural and aesthetic discourse at large" (2022). He reminds us that "the focus of Indian aesthetic and cultural discourse has remained so narrow and so exclusive that in this diverse country, it can be termed as a discourse of one community. It is the discourse of the upper caste *kula* (the family and lineage). In cultural discourses, *kulas* are cool" (2022). Compellingly contending that archives, the institutionalized repository of texts and artifacts on which cultural aesthetic discourse is premised, and the classicized dance forms of India were reconstructed "are a SCAM!" (2021), Prakash argues that "what we see in the archive is an uncritical celebration of Brahminism and its cultural manifestations" (2021). One such manifestation, I contend, is the revered solo format of the classicized dance forms, embodied predominantly by *savarna* elite dancers. I wish to examine it through two simultaneous negations: that of touch and that of community.

To unmake contact in South Asian dance/studies

    is to consider and critique

                          the sociocultural implications
of making contact between bodies

    who have been choreographed

to never share space,

        to negate *touch*.

To unmake contact in South Asian dance/studies

    is to consider and critique

           the sociocultural implications

    of making contact between bodies

           who have been choreographed

  to negate *community*.

Having trained in kathak, a dance form designed to negate touch (of self and other) and community, Khan, Naidu, and I were undoubtedly going to be jolted during our initial encounters with CI, a form that is founded on touch and community-building. It seems important, then, to ruminate further on my speculation with Sarukkai in 2019 about the relationship between caste politics and the solo modality of these classicized dance forms. I consider here the impact of this solo design in classicized dance forms and to what extent it embodies Indian sociocultural codes of touch and untouchability, principles foundational to Brahminism, as those of us trained in these solo forms encounter practices such as CI. And to segue into this discussion, for one final time, I interweave further interview excerpts between Naidu, Parmar, Tavag, and Khan, still in response to my third question to each of them: *Within your dance and performance training, how have you experienced touch and/or contact?*

For all four of the dance artists, within the context of the classicized dance training world, touch was experienced as a corrective gesture. Tavag recalls that, during her childhood bharatanatyam classes, she was "afraid of being hit by the little stick" and remembers "seeing some students being hit on the knuckles with it" (2020). Her memory of this stick, the *tattakali*, was that "it kept time and also kept us in check" (2020). Parmar, too, remembers the disciplinarian *tattakali*, but his memory provides an insight into its gendered use in his bharatanatyam classroom in a small town in Gujarat with a female teacher. He says that, while his teacher would correct the postures or gestures of the female students in the class by touching them with her hands, "she would walk up to me but the touch would be with the *tattakali*," regardless of what part of his body was being corrected (2020). He reflects that, growing up in a liberal and physically demonstrative home, this experience in the classroom was eye-opening and disorienting, but it taught him that not everyone experienced or understood physical contact in the same way as himself. Naidu, too, does not "remember any form of touching in the bharatanatyam or kathak classes except maybe to correct a posture or gesture by shifting or aligning it a little differently" (2019).

In addition to experiencing touch as a corrective experience in his kathak training, Khan says he "experienced touch while learning to dance narrative components of Hindu myths of, say, Krishna and Radha" (Khan in Mitra 2017, 390) and was made to understand that in this context touch was permissible as it was framed as sacred. Parmar astutely questions the inherent hierarchization and potential exclusion of bodies within classicized dance spaces through precisely this pervasive idea of the sacred:

> What I have always thought, and maybe I am wrong, but this is my interpretation, that dance always talks of the lover—but one of them is divine, and the other is human. So even if it's the divine embracing the human or the other way round—there is a hierarchy? Right? And embedded in this hierarchy there is touchability and untouchability. The supposed divinity of the form—that lends itself to keeping such hierarchy in place. (2020)

Parmar's reflections are vital here, as Brahminical supremacy is woven into the fabric of the Natyashastra, the foundational text for Indian classicized dance forms, as argued by Anurima Banerji (2021). Its inherently violent casteist, gendered, and classist histories of erasures and appropriations are also foundational to the formational histories and practices of Indian classicized dance forms, for instance, bharatanatyam, as explicated by Nrithya Pillai (2021).

From the interview excerpts I cite above, Khan, Masoom, Tavag, and Naidu signal the three interactive components at the heart of this solo design within their dance training: bodies (the dancers and the *gurus*), space (the training studio), and objects (human and non-human interactions used within training). They all speak of their corporeal relationships to their *gurus* and the nature of instructional physical contact between them. In this, some experience direct physical touch from their *gurus*, while others experience it via the *tattakali*. They all imply, through their memory of the rejection of touch with other bodies, the strict demarcation of space maintained between the dancers themselves, and also between the dancers and their gurus. The *tattakali* becomes the mechanism through which not only are disciplinarian instructions imparted but spatial order is maintained. Touch is only evoked as an imagined desire between the human dancer and their projected love for the divine. Such an individualistic aesthetic is designed to focus on an internalized interiority of the dancer, and prevents dancers from "reaching towards" (Manning 2007, 12) others. Thinking through Sarrukai's critique of Brahminism's denial of the touching of others as inducing "touch-un-ability" toward their own selves leads me to consider that the solo format of classicized forms may well uphold both the ideology of untouchability, and the resulting "touch-un-ability" as experienced by the dancers. Such "touch-un-ability," for instance, is exhibited in the choreographic language of the solo dancer as she mimes putting on jewelry, while getting dressed for her beloved's arrival, a popular motif in classicized dance recitals. While her fingers trace an imaginary necklace around her neck, clip imaginary earrings onto her ears, and place an imaginary *tikli* along her middle parting, the only lightest of touch that transpires in these choreographic arrangements is between her thumb and forefinger. Not even the tip of the triangle created as her forefinger and thumb touch comes into physical contact with the dancer's actual neck, ears, or hair-parting. An empty space is maintained between the edge of the triangular tip and the body-part she is conjuring in her dressing-up ritual. Even as her imaginary beloved arrives, their presence is symbolized by her arms holding their invisible waist in an embrace as her neck tilts into the embrace resting on an imaginary shoulder, but her two hands never touch to complete the circle around their waist. In other motifs, as she picks up the imaginary water container and places it on her head to carry home, there is an empty space between the base of the palm of her hands and her head. In the signature *salaam* gesture, where the kathak dancer slowly raises a loose and open, upturned palm gesture toward their forehead, as they bow their eyes and neck gently to meet the hand, an empty space is held between the forehead and the hand. Unable to physically touch others, and also unable to touch oneself, the dancer embodies the Brahminical design of the solo choreographic language, devoid of tactility and community, even with one's own body.

> *She is alone.*
> *And (we have been made to believe that) she is enough.*
> *She is the nation, the community, the whole.*

Political theorist Benedict Anderson's foundational conceptualization of the nation as "an imagined political community—imagined as both inherently limited and sovereign" seems important to consider here, seeing as the classicized dance forms were so integral in the Brahminical elitist imagination of the Indian nation, even before it existed (Renan quoted in Anderson 2016 [1986]. Anderson argues for the imagined nature of this community as most of the members of a nation will never know, meet, or hear of each other, even as they are brought together under the guise of a political "image of their communion" (Anderson 2016 [1986]). The *savarna* elite solo dancer, in and through her dance, represented this imagined communion of masses without ever knowing the vast majority of peoples they were symbolically representing. It begs the question: how can an individual, choreographically designed to negate community, represent an imagined community? Anderson signals the power asymmetries that are foundational to these imagined communities when he claims that "regardless of the actual inequality and exploitation that may prevail in each, the nation is always conceived as a deep, horizontal comradeship" (Anderson 2016 [1986]) vis-à-vis other nations. This horizontal comradeship sees to the erasure of inequalities in the ruling *savarna* elite's narrativization of Indian nationalism, through which oppressive power structures are both invisibilized *and* kept in place by the slogan "unity in diversity." We see this play out in the way that classicized dances represent high culture, while "folk" and indigenous dances are hierarchized as lesser, even as they, together, represent the diversity of India.

Dance scholar Urmimala Sarkar-Munsi reminds us:

> For a long while, the elite in India did not acknowledge the presence of dance as part of their culture and existence; then came a stage when dance became *the* emblem of rich and glorious history and tradition. . . . Folk and tribal dances were part of the culture of the unrepresented few, good for showcasing the variety and the "ethnicness" of the Indian people, . . . but never deemed good enough to be representative of "high" Indian culture. (2011, 124)

This segregation between the individual classicized solo dancer representing the nation as high culture, while collective and communal danced expressions of "folk", tribal, and indigenous peoples were/are cast aside as worthy of mere spectacle on regional, national and international platforms as displays of Indian "ethnicness" (Sarkar-Munsi, 2011, 124) is insightful of the fraught relationship between the individual and the community in the Brahminical vision of the Indian nation and its dialogue with capitalist modernity. It would seem that corporeal collectivism that stands for "social values" (Joseph 2007) poses a threat to Brahminism's (and Hindutva's) colonial, capitalist, and neoliberal impulse to turn inward, emphasizing individualism and its advocacy for "economic value" (Joseph 2007) for the state. This is perhaps why Vatsyayan, Jafa, and Subrahmanyam all argue that the solo dancer, deemed to be under threat in twenty-first-century India, must prevail (Jafa 2019).

The individual solo dancer, heralded as the symbol of excellence and rigor, the "classical," thus prevails through a rejection of community, and a negation of sharing of space and touch. This mythologizing of collectivism as contaminated, messy, and unordered, is exactly what is deemed a threat to the highly codified touch-un-abled world of South Asian classicized dances practices. Dance scholar Andre Lepecki's call here seems fitting as he provocatively asks: "in an era of supposedly free individualization, how does one perform and enact other modalities for collective life" (2016, 14). In the context of South Asian dance, this might involve unmaking the power upheld by the solo dancer while moving towards community and contact.

*Unmaking contact in South Asian dance/studies
thus requires
a reckoning
with its caste supremacist roots
that are foundational
to its formal,
architectural,
and
intellectual
design.*

This project's critical scrutiny of CI as an exclusionary practice is not only worth reinforcing through the consideration of caste politics, but this very scrutiny of CI has also opened up the possibility and the necessity of a similar scrutiny of the solo format of South Asian classicized dance forms, through the same lens. It may seem like a juxtaposition at first to critique CI in its insistence on touch without due consideration to caste politics, while also critiquing the classicized dance forms in upholding caste supremacy via negation of touch. But what it hopefully reveals is the need to become attentive to the ways in which power regimes inform, and are upheld, within these dance languages' formal and architectural codes that are taken for granted. It is with this double-edged criticality that I have approached each of my carefully chosen transnationally South Asian dance artist-interlocutors.

On Unmaking Contact with My South Asian Artist-Interlocutors

I have chosen Akila, Diya Naidu, Nahid Siddiqui, and LaWhore Vagistan as the South Asian dance artists I wish to foreground in this project with great care, as I value the transnational and intergenerational dialogue they have enabled in my thinking, from varying social positionalities along the power spectrums of caste, faith, gender, and sexuality, and from varied career locations. My mobilization of the geopolitical category of "South Asia/n" as an umbrella in which to locate these artists is also deliberate in its capaciousness to accommodate a range of lived realities, theoretical offerings, trans/national identities, professional connections, and diasporic heritages that link to South Asia in myriad ways. While two of my case-study artists, Akila and Naidu, live and make work in India about contemporary Indian life, Naidu has also presented her work in Europe, and Akila's commentary on inter-caste intimacies is just as relevant to South Asian communities in the diaspora. My remaining two case-study artists, Siddiqui and LaWhore, test the porous and political boundaries between homeland and diaspora in thrilling ways. Siddiqui's location between Pakistan and the UK impacts the British dance landscape in significant ways, while LaWhore's drag-art in India, the UK, the United States, but perhaps most importantly on social media, enables an identification of South Asia that is malleable and spacious. For these reasons, despite all its potential pitfalls, "South Asian" is capacious enough to signal the scope of these four artists' interventions within their respective local, national, and global dance landscapes, particularly with regard to their unmaking of contact through alternative embodiments of choreographic touch. Some of my chosen artists also share distinct relationships with classicized dance forms from different regions in India that are practiced across South Asia and its diasporas. Akila and Naidu have trained in bharatanatyam (the form attributed to the state of Tamil Nadu with influences from Andhra Pradesh). Siddiqui and Naidu have trained in kathak (the form attributed to the unspecified and expansive area considered north India). In order to examine how my chosen artists unmake contact in their respective choreographic journeys, the book will consider how the aesthetics of and training in these classicized dance forms, including their solo format, impact their understandings of contact and touch.

Moving away from the focus of my first monograph on Akram Khan, a cisgender man, I wish to focus this study first and foremost on women and gender-minoritized dance artists. I have also taken a deliberate step toward considering dance as the most capacious container, beyond the theater-dance contexts in which I have located my body of dance scholarship to date. In doing so, I have tried to respond to Indian performance studies scholar Brahma Prakash's call for the need to democratize the discourse around South Asian dance:

> Decentring dance would involve a democratisation of movement itself so that a new practice can be conceived—to bring it to the simplest form, as it is articulated in the Oraon belief that "ekna dim tokna, baa'na dim parna," that walking is dancing and talking is singing. (Prakash 2023)

Accordingly, my chosen case studies' performance locations/formats are varied and range from outdoor locations in Indian university campuses (Akila), to performance and art galleries (Naidu), to the English countryside (Siddiqui), and finally to social media and the internet (LaWhore). What is common as methodology toward the close dance analyses that underpin each of my chapters is, unlike my previous scholarship where I based my encounters with my case studies in live performance, constrained by Covid-19 lockdowns, in this book project, I have encountered all my case study performances in digital formats as recordings of live performances (Akila and Naidu), dance-films (Siddiqui), and social media reels (LaWhore).

In each chapter I propose a particular mode by which the artist in question unmakes contact through its reframing and contextualisation within

South Asian and South Asian diasporic contexts, with or without touch. In Chapter 1, titled "Contact as Caste Justice: *Theenda Theenda* (2018) by Akila and the Touch of Death," I argue that Akila conjures contact as caste-justice in her dance as education and activism piece *Theenda Theenda* (2018), arguing for inter-caste intimacies and touch as the promise of liberation from caste supremacy and violence. The chapter examines this performance-duet and social commentary on the deeply entrenched attitudes of caste dominance that motivates horrific hate-crimes referred to in common parlance as "honor killings" within the southern Indian state of Tamil Nadu. Tamil for "as we touch," *Theenda Theenda* is a choreographic debut of dance-artist and anti-caste activist Akila, performed by artistic collaborators, dancers, and body-based movement practitioners Akila and Chandiran in the outdoor grounds of a college campus in Tamil Nadu, India. Thinking through Dr. B. R. Ambedkar's powerful articulation that the caste system hierarchizes "castes arranged according to an ascending scale of reverence and a descending scale of contempt" (quoted in Chakravarti 2018, 7), the chapter examines what transpires materially and socioculturally when such a violent system, built on the premise of impermissibility of contact between an "ascending scale of reverence" and a "descending scale of contempt," is challenged by inter-caste intimacies through touch. Such intimacies call Brahminism's founding principle of caste purity (and hence self-asserted superiority) into question, as dominant caste and caste-oppressed people engender social and physical relations, and thus simultaneously unmake the very social contracts upon which caste supremacy's notions of purity rest. I examine the unmaking of such impermissibility of inter-caste contact through a close analysis of *Theenda Theenda* a full-length choreographic debut by Chennai-based dancer-choreographer-singer Akila.

In the second chapter, titled "Contact as Reframing Sociality: *Rorschach Touch* (2018) by Diya Naidu and 'Normalizing Touch,'" I propose that Naidu evokes contact as sociality in her dance as social experiment project *Rorschach Touch* (2018), arguing for the need to "normalize touch" in an Indian sociocultural context that, in fact, stigmatizes it on the lines of faith, gender, and sexuality. Bangalore-based dance-artist Diya Naidu's choreographic debut and ensemble social experiment is examined through Naidu's desire to "normalize touch" in the hope of conjuring contact as the promise of new and liberatory socialities, while acknowledging the complex Indian sociological codes that govern touch and touching. The chapter undertakes a choreo-analysis of selected sections of *Rorschach Touch* (2018) through an intercultural theoretical nexus that brings together two conceptual frameworks: philosopher Sundar Sarukkai's premise of touch as a moral sense that drives the socialization of Indian peoples as "closed-skinned," and Asian American dance scholar SanSan Kwan's critical intervention that "love is an essential condition of interculturalism" and that, relatedly, "we must love one another in order to connect... and, at the same time accept one another's ultimate inaccessibility" (2021, 14–15). Through this intercultural entwining of Sarukkai and Kwan's critical positions, the chapter examines Naidu's choreography to ascertain the extent to which *Rorschach Touch* is successful at moving beyond our closed-skinned-ness through foregrounding love, not just of the "hopelessly romantic" (Kwan 2021) kind, but love as a choreographic method that binds humanity and desire for human connection. It is this critical love with which Naidu places the responsibility of unpacking socialized stigmas around touch and touching on her audience members, in how they read, respond to, and interact with the touch-based-intimacies that they witness in the piece. By placing on her audience members a charge of an awakening through confronting their own prejudices, desires, and discomforts, Naidu's *Rorschach Touch* offers us glimpses of "normalizing touch." In this, it builds alternative imaginaries and socialities through an unmaking, albeit partial, of Indian closed-skinned-ness.

In Chapter 3, titled "Contact as Ecological Relationality: *Mirror Within* (2022) by Nahid Siddiqui and Shakila Maan and Touch without Tactility," I contend that Nahid Siddiqui summons contact as ecological relationality in her dance-film *Mirror Within* (2022). Made in collaboration with British-Asian filmmaker Shakila Maan, and arguing for a kathak that moves beyond human supremacy in order to coexist in relationality with her natural environment and ecological companions, Siddiqui's choreography embodies the vitality and life-giving force of such contact without tactility as a mode of deep immersion channeled through the Sufi principle of *wahdah* (unity). British-Pakistani kathak maestro Nahid Siddiqui's embodied provocation to the kathak world "when you harmonize with nature, then you are doing kathak" (in Maan 1995) becomes the fulcrum of my analysis of *Mirror Within*. I examine Siddiqui's unique embodiment of kathak in this dance-film as an ecological meditation, resting on a complex and beautiful relationality between the interiority of her womanhood, the exteriority of the environment in which she dances, and its connections to living beings at large. Siddiqui's words signal a fundamental relationality, a contact, between nature, and ecosystems, and kathak and unsettles kathak's focus on human supremacy, inviting us to necessarily consider humanity's ecological relationality in and to the world. Aligned with Sufism's foundational practice of caring for, protecting, and living with the environment (Qudosi 2010), Siddiqui's own desire "to connect to the sky and the earth at the same time, feeling the core of my existence at the centre of the Universe as my navel" (Siddiqui in Sadler's Wells 2022), comes alive in this the dance-film, which I examine at the intersections of feminism, ecology, and Sufism, arguing that Siddiqui's anti-patriarchal choreography emerges at the junctures between her own selfhood and its relational synergies with her ecological surroundings.

The fourth chapter, titled "Contact as *Adda*: Critical Encounters in *#KaateNahinKatte* Instareel (2020) by LaWhore Vagistan and Digital Touching," moves between critical essay narratives and a conversation between US-based LaWhore Vagistan, the drag queen alter ego of performance studies scholar Kareem Khubchandani, Khubchandani, and myself. Framed and theorized as an *adda*, a Bengali speech genre that is an open-ended, dialogic, critical and intellectual encounter between participants, this conversation exposes the historic hierarchies between conventional interviews as method between artists and researchers, in its seamless shift of power between LaWhore and me. In this we generate together three kinds of contact making: firstly, we together choreograph contact between our artist-scholar positionalities; secondly, and more specifically pertaining to LaWhore's drag art itself, we consider contact as the building of community that she choreographs on social media for people of all genders and sexualities, between queer and non-queer peoples; and finally, between the formal essay modes and the more informal *adda* modes that this chapter explores. Anchored in a close analysis of LaWhore's *#KaateNahinKatte* Instareel, created during the pandemic lockdowns and bringing to life Sridevi and Anil Kapoor's love-dance from the Bollywood blockbuster *Mr India* where this book began, the chapter examines through its critical essay narratives and the *adda* how communities are touched, and are made and sustained through the power of the digital and social media.

Finally, in search of an alternative ending to the book that makes a case against conclusions, I offer my "Afterwords: Against Conclusions," where I evoke contact as community through a fabricated WhatsApp thread between my four artist-interlocutors, imagining what a virtual conversation between them might look like if they had actually made contact on their own terms. This book is the result of a series of long, inter-connected, entwined, and open conversations that have opened conversations. This book is the result of connecting thinking and actions and feelings of, and between, artists and people who do not know each other. And yet they have contributed collectively to its knowledge-making. This book is borne of collectivity. To mark this vital process of coalitional world-building in my final gesture on the page, I enter into this fictive relationship with my four transnationally situated artist-interlocutors Akila, Diya Naidu, Nahid Siddiqui, and LaWhore Vagistan, and end this book with this short and fictional WhatsApp conversation between them, imagining their unmaking of contact on their own terms.

References

Ahmed, Sara. 2014. The Cultural Politics of Emotion. Edinburgh: Edinburgh University Press.
Akila. 2020. *Interviewed by the author via Zoom*. December 6.
Akila and Chandiran. 2022. *Interviewed by the author via Zoom*. July 13.
Albright, Ann Cooper. 2017. "The Politics of Perception." In The Oxford Handbook of Dance and Politics, edited by Rebekah J. Kowal, Gerald Siegmund, and Randy Martin, 223–243. New York: Oxford University Press.
Anderson, Benedict. 2016 [1986]. Imagined Communities: Reflections on the Origin and Spread of Nationalism. London: Verso Books.
Bakshi, Sandeep. 2021. "Towards the Unmaking of Canons: Decolonising the Study of Literature." In Doing Equity and Diversity for Success in Higher Education, edited by D. S. P. Thomas and J. Arday, 117–126. Basingstoke: Palgrave Macmillan.
Bala, Sruti. 2017. "Decolonising Theatre and Performance Studies: Tales from the Classroom." Tijdschrift voor Genderstudies 20 (3): 333–345.
Banerji, Anurima. 2021. "The Laws of Movement: The Natyashastra as Archive for Indian Classical Dance." Contemporary Theatre Review 31 (1–2): 132–152.
Banerji, Anurima. 2022. "The Award-Wapsi Controversy in India and the Politics of Dance." South Asian History and Culture 14 (2): 263–284.
Bradley, Rizvana. 2020. "The Vicissitudes of Touch: Annotations on the Haptic." Boundary 2: An Online Journal. November 21. https://www.boundary2.org/2020/11/rizvana-bradley-the-vicissitudes-of-touch-annotations-on-the-haptic/.
Chakravarti, Uma. 2018. Gendering Caste: Through a Feminist Lens. New Delhi: Sage Publications India Pvt Ltd.
Chakravorty, Pallabi. 2008. Bells of Change: Kathak Dance, Women and Modernity in India. Kolkata: Seagull Books.
Chalef, Rebecca. 2018. "Activating Whiteness: Racializing the Ordinary in US American Postmodern Dance." Dance Research Journal 50 (3): 71–84.
Chatterjea, Ananya. 1996. "Training in Indian Classical Dance: A Case Study." Asian Theatre Journal 13(1): 68–91.
Classen, Constance, ed. 2005. The Book of Touch. Oxford: Berg.
DeFrantz, Thomas F. 2017. "Queer Dance in Three Acts." In Queer Dance: Meanings and Makings, edited by Clare Croft, 169–180. New York: Oxford University Press.
Derrida, Jacques. 2005. On Touching—Jean-Luc Nancy. Stanford, CA: Stanford University Press.
Dymoke, Katy. 2014. "Contact Improvisation, the Non-Eroticised Touch in an 'Art-Sport.'" Journal of Dance and Somatic Practices 6 (2): 205–218.
Dymoke, Katy. 2021. The Impact of Touch in Dance Movement Therapy. Bristol: Intellect.

Egert, Gerko. 2020. "Moving Relation": Touch in Contemporary Dance. Abingdon: Routledge.
Field, Tiffany. 2014. Touch. Cambridge, MA: MIT Press.
Fraleigh, Sondra, ed. 2015. Moving Consciously: Somatic Transformations through Dance, Yoga, and Touch. Urbana: University of Illinois Press.
Gilson, Ruth Wilson. 2017. "Abolition Geography and the Problem of Innocence". *Futures of Black Radicalism*. Ed Gaye Theresa Johnson, and Alex Lubin. London: Verso.
Goldman, Danielle. 2010. I Want to Be Ready: Improvised Dance as a Practice of Freedom. Ann Arbor: University of Michigan Press.
Goldman, Danielle. 2021. "A Radically Unfinished Dance: Contact Improvisation in a Time of Social Distance." TDR: The Drama Review 65 (1): 62–78.
Gopal, Priyamvada. 2023. "Is Decolonization 'Genocide'? Let's See." Accessed December 19, 2023. https://zen-catgirl.medium.com/is-decolonization-genocide-lets-see-de91184cb8af.
Guru, Gopal. 2017. "Archaeology of Untouchability." In The Cracked Mirror: An Indian Debate on Experience and Theory, edited by Gopal Guru and Sundar Sarukkai, 200–222. New Delhi: Oxford University Press.
Gutierrez, Miguel. 2018. "Does Abstraction Belong to White People?" Bomb Magazine. Accessed January 15, 2022. https://bombmagazine.org/articles/miguel-gutierrez-1/.
Hammond, Claudia. 2020. "The Anatomy of Touch." BBC Radio 4. Accessed January 1, 2022. https://www.bbc.co.uk/programmes/m000n484.
Hann, Rachel. Beyond Scenography. Abingdon: Routledge.
Hennessy, Keith. 2019. "Questioning Contact Improvisation." Dancers' Group. October 1. Accessed November 1, 2019. https://dancersgroup.org/2019/10/questioning-contact-improvisation/.
Hertenstein, Matthew J., and Sandra J. Weiss, eds. 2011. The Handbook of Touch: Neuroscience, Behavioral, and Health Perspectives. New York: Springer.
Holland, Fred, and Ishmael Houston-Jones. 1983. "The 'Wrong' Contact Manifesto 1983." In Contact at 10th and 2nd. Accessed April 1, 2019. https://vimeo.com/114657723.
Houston, Sara. 2009. "The Touch Taboo and the Art of Contact: An Exploration of Contact Improvisation for Prisoners." Research in Dance Education 10 (2): 97–113.
Hussein, Nesreen. 2022. "Editorial—Decolonisation and Performance Studies: Questions from the Border." Global Performance Studies. Special Double Issue: "Decolonisation and Performance Studies" 5 (1–2).
Hwang, Ha Young, Tara McAllister, Liz Mills, and Sara Reed. 2022. "CfP: TDPT Special Issue: 'Touch and Training.'" TDPT Blog. Accessed March 1, 2023. https://theatredanceperformancetraining.org/2022/02/cfp-tdpt-special-issue-touch-and-training/.
Hwang, Ha Young, Tara McAllister, Liz Mills, and Sara Reed. 2023. "Editorial: Training and Touch." Theatre, Dance and Performance Training Journal 14 (2): 81–85.
Ingold, Tim. 2013. Making: Anthropology, Archeology, Art and Architecture. Abingdon: Routledge.
Jaaware, Aniket. 2019. Practicing Caste: On Touching and Not Touching. New York: Fordham University Press.
Jaffa, Navina. 2019. "Why the Solo Classical Dancer Needs to be Saved." The Wire. Accessed February 15, 2022. https://thewire.in/the-arts/indian-classical-dance-soloist.
Joseph, Sarah. 2007. "Neoliberal Reforms and Democracy in India." Economic and Political Weekly 42 (31): 3213–3218.
Khan, Akram. 2022. *Interviewed by the author via Zoom*. June 6.
Knowles, Ric. 2010. Theatre and Interculturalism. Basingstoke: Palgrave Macmillan.
Kondo, Dorinne. 2018. World-Making: Race, Performance, and the Work of Creativity. Durham, NC: Duke University Press.
Krishnan, Hari. 2019. Celluloid Classicism: Early Tamil Cinema and the Making of Modern Bharatanatyam. Middletown, CT: Wesleyan University Press.
Krishnan, Hari.2022. *Interviewed by the author via Zoom*. June 7.
Kwan, SanSan. 2021. Love Dances: Loss and Mourning in Intercultural Collaboration. New York: Oxford University Press.

Law, John. 2004. Mess in Social Science Research. London: Routledge.
Lei, Daphne P., and Charlotte McIvor, eds. 2020. The Methuen Drama Handbook of Performance and Interculturalism. New York: Bloomsbury/Methuen.
Lepecki, Andre. 2016. Singularities: Dance in the Age of Performance. Abingdon: Routledge.
Maan, Shakila. 1995. A Thousand Borrowed Eyes. Maan Made Films.
Maan, Shakila. 2023. *Interviewed by the author in person.* May 18.
Manning, Erin. 2007. Politics of Touch: Sense, Movement, Sovereignty. Minneapolis: University of Minnesota Press.
Maybee, Julie E. 2019. Making and Unmaking Disability: The Three-Body Approach. Lanham, MD: Rowman & Littlefield.
McIvor, Charlotte. 2016. Migration and Performance in Contemporary Ireland: Towards a New Interculturalism. Basingstoke: Palgrave Macmillan.
McIvor, Charlotte, and Jason King, eds. 2019. Interculturalism and Performance Now: New Directions? Basingstoke: Palgrave Macmillan.
Merleau-Ponty, Maurice. 1962. Phenomenology of Perception. London: Routledge.
Mitra, Royona. 2005. "Cerebrality: Re-writing Corporeality of a Female Indian Dancer." In Tanz im Kopf *(Dance & Cognition)*, edited by Johannes Birringer and Josephine Fenger, 15: 1–17. Accessed December 15, 2023. http://www.digitalcultures.org/Library/Mitra.pdf.
Mitra, Royona. 2015. Akram Khan: Dancing New Interculturalism. Basingstoke: Palgrave Macmillan.
Mitra, Royona. 2017. "Akram Khan on the Politics of Choreographing Touch." In Contemporary Choreography: A Critical Reader, edited by Jo Butterworth and Liesbeth Wildschut, 385–397. 2nd ed. London: Routledge.
Mitra, Royona. 2018. "Talking Politics of Contact Improvisation with Steve Paxton." Dance Research Journal 50 (3): 6–18.
Nakase, Justine. 2019. "'Recognize My Face': Phil Lynott, Scalar Interculturalism, and the Nested Figure." In Interculturalism and Performance Now: New Directions?, edited by Charlotte McIvor and Jason King, 257–280. Basingstoke: Palgrave Macmillan.
Naidu, Diya. 2019. *Interviewed by the author via email.* February 26.
Nash, Jennifer C. 2019. Black Feminism Reimagined: After Intersectionality. Durham, NC: Duke University Press.
Novack, Cynthia J. 1990. Sharing the Dance: Contact Improvisation and American Culture. Madison: University of Wisconsin
O'Shea, Janet. 2023. *Personal correspondence with the author.* October 18.
Parmar, Masoom. 2020. *Interviewed by the author via Zoom.* September 9.
Patel, Shaista. 2020. "It is Time to Talk about Caste in Pakistan and Pakistani Diaspora." Accessed February 2, 2022. https://www.aljazeera.com/opinions/2020/12/15/it-is-time-to-talk-about-caste-in-pakistan-and-pakistani-diaspora.
Pillai, Nrithya. 2021. "The Politics of Naming the South Indian Dancer." In Conversations across the Field of Dance Studies: Decolonizing Dance Discourses, edited by Anurima Banerji and Royona Mitra, 40: 13–15. Oak Creek, WI: Dance Studies Association.
Pillai, Nrithya. 2022. "Re-Casteing the Narrative of Bharatanatyam." Economic and Political Weekly 57 (9): 2–12.
Prakash, Brahma. 2021. "Archives Are a SCAM!" Interventions in Contemporary Theatre Review. Accessed December 20, 2022. https://www.contemporarytheatrereview.org/2021/archives-are-a-scam/.
Prakash, Brahma. 2022. "Dialogue with a Dancer." India Seminar Magazine 753. Accessed June 1, 2022. https://india-seminar.com/2022/753/753_BRAHMA_PRAKASH.htm.
Prakash, Brahma. 2023. "Opinion: To Truly Democratise Indian Art and Culture, the 'Classical' Must Be Declared Dead." Scroll.in. Accessed April 20, 2023. https://scroll.in/article/1045681/opinion-to-truly-democratise-indian-art-and-culture-the-classical-must-be-done-away-with.

Purkayastha, Prarthana. Forthcoming 2025. The Archives and Afterlives of Nautch Dancers in India. Cambridge: Cambridge University Press.
Qudosi, Shireen. 2010. "Sufi Muslims Are Islam's Eco Guardians." The Eco Muslim. Accessed June 1, 2023. https://www.theecomuslim.co.uk/2010/11/sufi-muslims-are-islams-eco-guardians.html.
Raikhy, Mandeep. 2022. *Interviewed by the author via Zoom.* June 23.
Sadler's Wells. 2022. *Mirror Within*: Sadler's Wells Digital Stage. Directed and Edited by Shakila Taranum Maan. Choreographed and Danced by Nahid Siddiqui. Accessed February 1, 2023. https://www.sadlerswells.com/digital-stage/longevity-in-dance-elixir-on-digital-stage/commissioned-by-sadlers-wells/mirror-within-nahid-siddiqui/.
Sarco-Thomas, Malaika, ed. 2020. Thinking Touch in Partnering and Contact Improvisation: Philosophy, Pedagogy, Practice. Cambridge: Cambridge Scholars Press.
Sarkar Munsi, Urmimala. 2011. "Imag(in)ing the Nation: Uday Shankar's *Kalpana*." In Traversing Tradition: Celebrating Dance in India, edited by Urmimala Sarkar Munsi and Stephanie Burridge, 124–150. London: Routledge.
Sarukkai, Sundar. 2009. "Phenomenology of Untouchability." Economic & Political Weekly 44 (37): 39–48.
Sarukkai, Sundar. 2019. *Interviewed by the author via Skype.* September 20.
Saviliagno, Marta Elena. 2009. "Worlding Dance and Dancing Out There in the World." In Worlding Dance, edited by Susan Foster, 163–190. Basingstoke: Palgrave Macmillan.
Sengupta, Tirna. 2024a. "Un/comfortable Encounters: Tourist Experience of Adivasi Performance." Conference Paper at Theatre and Performance Research Association Annual Conference. 4-6 September 2024. Unpublished.
Sengupta, Tirna. 2024b. Personal communications via email with the author. October 12.
Siddiqui, Kalim. 2017. "Hindutva, Neoliberalism and the Reinventing of India." Journal of Economic and Social Thought 4 (2): 142–186.
Soneji, Davesh. 2012. *Unfinished Gestures: Devadāsīs, Memory, and Modernity in South India* I. Chicago: University of Chicago Press.
Suraj, Guru, and Adrianna Michalska. 2024. "Making Contact: Practicing and Creating Spaces of Contact Improvisation in India." In Resistance and Support: Contact @ 50, edited by Ann Cooper Albright, 276-290. New York: Oxford University Press.
Tavag, Anishaa. 2020. *Interviewed by the author via Zoom.* September 18.
Thakore, Yashoda. 2022. "Dancing Caste, Rethinking Heredity: A Kuchipudi Artist Reflects on Her Multiple Lineages." Scroll.in. Accessed May 15, 2022. https://scroll.in/article/1021494/dancing-caste-rethinking-heredity-a-kuchipudi-artist-reflects-on-her-multiple-lineages.
Thobani, Sitara. 2017. Indian Classical Dance and the Making of Postcolonial Identities: Dancing on Empire's Stage. Abingdon: Routledge.
Walker, Margaret. 2014. India's Kathak Dance in Historical Perspective. Farnham: Ashgate.
Walsh, Catherine. 2018. "The Decolonial For: Resurgences, Shifts, and Movements." In On Decoloniality: Concepts, Analytics, Praxis, edited by Walter D. Mignolo and Catherine E. Walsh, 15–32. Durham, NC: Duke University Press.
Warren, Asher, and Martin Welton. 2023. "On Touch." *Performance Research: A* Journal of the Performing Arts 27 (2): 1–6.
Yohalem, Hannah. 2018. "Displacing Vision: Contact Improvisation, Anarchy, and Empathy." Dance Research Journal 50 (2): 45–61.

1
Contact as Caste Justice

Theenda Theenda (2018) by Akila and the Touch of Death

She slowly raises her right hand above his head, and even more slowly brings it down to rest her palm on his right shoulder, clasping and resting her fingers gently over his shoulder bone. He flinches at her touch, and raises his shoulders in response, making them both turn together to face backstage-left corner. Their gazes together directed at the floor, their left feet ahead of their right, her right arm resting along his back and holding his right shoulder with so much gentleness and care.

Contact.
Touch.
Contact.

They momentarily part ways, and then run back to each other. This time, they make contact with each one's right hand clasping the other's right forearm. They lean back, giving into and supporting each other's weight fully. Their eyes lock. They playfully pivot a while at their point of counterbalance, before falling out into the space to find their own selves again. They continue to find each other again, and again, and again. Hand to wrist, countering each other's weights and eyes forever locked. He raises his left leg as he lowers his body weight to the floor. She counters his weight as she remains standing, her knees unlocked, supporting him. She helps him up, letting him work his way through choreographic and social precarity. He folds her into his outstretched right arm, shifting his contact from her wrist across her back and onto her right shoulder. She slides her left arm across his back to rest around his waist, as he allows his right arm to rest around hers. She moves around him until she is behind him, supporting his entire upper body and allowing his spine to rest across *the length of her spine, as he gradually lowers himself to sit on her left thighs. She leans in to caress his right shoulder with her right hand and cradles his head gently in the crook of her neck.*

The mutuality of their touch hinges between curiosity, exploration, support, solidarity, friendship, resistance, care, love, sensuality, and intimacy. It carries the burden of its impermissibility, the resistance to such impermissibility, and the hope that such resistance engenders and enables.

Contact
Akila and Chandiran
Chandiran and Akila.
Contact
Entwined in new beginnings.

The complex relationships between Indian sensibilities and codifications of touch (*sparsha*) and contact (*samyoga*) as discussed in the Introduction, the Brahminical pillars of caste purity, and its misplaced concept of (dis)honor that is threatened by inter-caste contact lie at the heart of this first chapter. Thinking through Dr B. R. Ambedkar's powerful articulation that the caste system hierarchizes "castes arranged according to an ascending scale of reverence and a descending scale of contempt" (quoted in Chakravarty 2018, 7), this chapter examines what transpires materially and socioculturally when such a violent system, built on the premise of impermissibility of contact between an "ascending scale of reverence" and a "descending a scale of contempt," is challenged by inter-caste intimacies through touch and/or even relational proximity. Such intimacies call Brahminism's founding principle of caste purity (and hence deemed superiority) into question, as caste-oppressed and dominant-caste people engender social and physical relations, and thus simultaneously unmake the very social contracts upon which caste supremacy's notions of purity rest. I examine the unmaking of such impermissibility of inter-caste contact through a close analysis of *Theenda Theenda* (2018), a full-length choreographic debut by Chennai-based dancer-choreographer-singer Akila. Tamil for "as we touch," *Theenda Theenda* is a performance-duet and social commentary on the deeply entrenched attitudes of caste dominance that motivates horrific hate crimes referred to in common parlance as "honor killings" within the southern Indian state of Tamil Nadu. The duet is performed by the artistic collaborators, dancers, and body-based movement practitioners Akila and Chandiran.

Through the analysis of this duet, I also conceptualize the *savarna* spine, a violent and everyday manifestation of caste power that is embodied in the skeletal-musculature presentation of an upright spine.[1] I examine the *savarna* spine as activating physiological, neurological, sociological, and phenomenological power in order to subjugate and control anyone it comes in contact with, or indeed who dare cross its path. I argue that if caste supremacy is physiologically and sociologically upheld via the practice of endogamy and segregation of peoples, its everyday dominance manifests in the Indian social order via a highly intricate choreography, performed through the *savarna* spine.

I stumbled upon *Theenda Theenda* by serendipity in spring 2020, when I was researching transnationally located South Asian dance artists whose choreographic endeavors were unmaking contact and decentering discourse on choreographic touch. I remember Googling "contemporary dance + caste + touch + India." And the very first result that Google yielded for me was a performance review for *Theenda Theenda* titled "The Touch of Love, the Touch of Death and a New Dance in Tamil Nadu" by the dancer and illustrator Madhushree. Intrigued by the review and accompanying photos from the performance, I made contact with Akila via Indianostrum, an organization that was hosting the duet and described it on their Facebook page as a "narrative on the attitude of caste dominance and oppression, and its consequences, struggle, resistance and countering with equality, in the body" (Indianostrum 2018). Days later I received a warm response from Akila, followed by our first Zoom conversation in December 2020. In the summer of 2022, Akila and I reconvened on Zoom, and this time we were accompanied by Chandiran.

Choosing to write about *Theenda Theenda* and its focus on inter-caste intimacies and related critique of hate crimes of "honor killings" is not a decision I have taken lightly. My lived experience of growing up in Kolkata as a Bengali is far removed from the performance's evocations of inter-caste relationships and its repercussions in Tamil Nadu in particular, and through it, its critiques of caste violence. Despite the pan-Indian manifestation of caste supremacy, I am not privy to regional specificities that nuance its discriminatory codes and violent practices. Moreover, as a *savarna* woman who has never experienced inter-caste intimacies and the punitive actions they trigger in India's caste society, I have never been at the receiving end of either caste oppression or the related violence of Brahminical patriarchy. Indeed, through my upbringing as a young *savarna* woman, I never had to think about caste oppression and its intersections with gender-based violence in any meaningful way. It is therefore neither my place nor my intention to speak *for* those who are caste-oppressed, or even those who experience the violence of caste supremacy because of being deemed as caste traitors, due to willfully embracing inter-caste intimacies. To write about *Theenda Theenda* as part of this book, for me, has thus needed clear parameters of engagement that do not reinforce caste dominance. To write about *Theenda Theenda* has meant to examine the ways in which the piece simultaneously critiques caste supremacy that delivers violence and death sentences to many who embrace inter-caste touch and relational contact, *and* to recognize the performance's promise of healing and liberation in its signaling of radical emancipatory futures offered in precisely such touch, through a conscious undermining of, and challenge to, caste supremacy.

Theenda Theenda
is thus a harbinger of death
while it simultaneously heralds
the promise of (new) and emancipatory life and worlds.
As it dances such promise of justice into being,
Theenda Theenda
speaks to
and stirs
my relatively recent
anti-caste consciousness
and commitments to dance studies.

In methodological terms, this means that in this chapter I analyze the depictions and embodiments of Brahminism, its dominance and violence, and how they physically manifest in *Theenda Theenda*, instead of writing about the performance's representations of caste oppression. Of course, at times these embodiments are entangled, mutually codependent, and hard to delineate as distinct. But my criticality in this chapter is primarily focused on locating and critiquing caste supremacy as it manifests in the choreography, with particular attention to gestures that threaten Brahminism through the mobilization of inter-caste contact that transpire between Akila and Chandiran. I achieve this through conceptualizing the idea and practice of "choreopower of Brahminism," that is, power that is choreographed, learned, held, and unleashed as everyday movement as we *savarna* people move through the world through the upright *savarna* spine, whose architecture negates contact. In this critique of the choreographic dimensions of Brahminism, my words, Akila's choreography, and Chandiran and Akila's danced intimacies are aligned in our collective and individual anti-caste endeavors.

Akila: Dancing Activism

Akila is "hesitant to identify her attitude towards her work as activism" (Madhushree 2018). However, her political commitments toward anti-oppression and caste annihilation are inseparable from her dance-making, and she says as much to me when she states:

> I never had the dilemma in locating myself between artist and activist and I don't see any hierarchy between the same. I'm clearly locating myself as an artist who sees through the social hierarchies through the art. (Akila 2022)

Akila's keen awareness of the complex relationship between art and social hierarchies comes from being "raised as an artist" during her childhood in a political environment deriving from her "father's association with Tamizh national communist party," which equipped her with a "basic understanding of issues around class, caste, gender and environment in society" (Akila 2022). Such a political and artistic upbringing inspired her to pursue master's and MPhil degrees in music at Madras University, where she completed a project on "Thappattam, a folk dance form of Tamil Nadu, a community form" that belongs to one of the major Dalit communities—Paraiyar (Akila 2022). During her project, Akila visited many villages to meet with Thappattam artists, in order to understand their art practices. And it was during this time that she came to witness and understand the predicaments of these caste-oppressed peoples:

> I understood the social position of the lower caste more deeply through their art and the artists. The social hierarchies between the Brahminical classical art world and the folk-art world became more evident for me. (Akila 2022)

Akila was also immersed in the Brahminical classicized world. She shares that, while she trained in the classicized form of Bharatnatyam (and Kuchipudi) from a young age, she always struggled to make sense of, and reconcile between, the religious fervor of these forms that appeared to her to be disconnected from the real world and her own social realities. The late Indian choreographer Chandralekha also echoed Akila's sentiments, unable to reconcile these disturbing disconnects in the Indian dance world:

> One of the crucial experiences that shaped my response and attitude to dance was during my very first public dance recital (*arangetram*) in 1952. It was a charity programme in aid of the Rayalseema Drought Relief Fund. I was dancing "Mathura Nagarilo," depicting the river Yamuna, the waterplay of the sakhis, the sensuality, the luxuriance, and abundance of water. Suddenly, I froze, with the realization that I was portraying all this profusion of water in the context of a drought.... Art and life seemed to be in conflict. The paradox was stunning. (Chandralekha 2003, 50)

Moving into contemporary dance, for Akila, consequently meant carrying with her an innate "resistance to the content of religiosity and patriarchy in line with the questions that were also asked by many first generation of contemporary dancers" (Akila in Akila and Chandiran 2022). However, even as she shifted into contemporary dance training and spent a significant part of her dance career working with the choreographer Padmini Chettur, initially she struggled to understand how the abstraction of the dance-works she was performing with Chettur's company could speak to everyday social struggles in India. This echoes in many ways the critiques levied at CI vis-à-vis its advocacy of abstraction as an apolitical force, as discussed in the Introduction. She wrestled with the elitism of these "art-world bubbles" (Akila 2022) that continue to fail to engage politically with the world around them:

> While I worked with Padmini, I went through the whole enquiry on the body and movement in relationship to space and time. But there was always one vacuum present for me—the connection between the body and society. Because of the vast differences between realities of the art world and the social world. (Akila 2022)

Akila's artistic journey has since continued independently, committed to seeking "the inextricability of dance from agitation" (Mills 2021, 2), through finding "a new form, a new language, to express new content" (Akila in Akila and Chandiran 2022):

> This new content in dance for me always occurs in the vacuum between the art world and society. Some may argue that there is no distinction—and that artists too are located within the same society along with everyone else. But I would argue that artists in society tend to operate within bubbles that can be removed from reality. From that vacuum, my interest is to reflect on what is happening around me. And the caste system is one very strong dimension of society that affects me. So, I am driven by a very basic question, "what can artist do about this?" As a body-based danced practitioner, my response to a caste society begins from the body. (Akila in Akila and Chandiran 2022)

Akila notes that her points of departure from Chettur's aesthetic and bodily inquiries are as follows: firstly, she is interested in critically engaging questions of caste oppression and the hate crimes of "honor killings" at a corporeal dimension—locating them at the intersections of bodies, movement, space, and time; secondly, and following on, she is invested in exploring movement language that explores "attitudes in the bodies of oppressor and the oppressed, emotion in the bodies, struggle and resistance in the bodies, and responses in the bodies to invisible, external controlling forces" (Akila 2022); and finally, through a deconstructed relationship between movement and music structure, moving away from "strict metronomical time structures" that bind classicized dance forms, and toward a soundscape that is responsive to the moods, attitudes, emotions, and responses of people in relation to the caste society they live in (Akila 2022). She makes very clear to me that her anti-caste commitments for making *Theenda Theenda* were sown in her during her politically charged upbringing, enhanced further by her educational experiences of working closely with the Thappattam artists from the Paraiyar community, and a reckoning with how to mobilize her art toward social change from her own position of privileges (Akila 2022).

Akila is dedicated to engaging with, speaking to, and critiquing "contemporary social ideologies and realities within the contemporary dance space, not as a propaganda but as a statement/opposition" (Akila in Madhushree 2018). In this resistive mode, Akila asserts that she is particularly committed to making dance-works that are meant to be performed outside of elite high-art spaces, reaching out instead to young people in educational institutions, college campuses, and community spaces with the intention of educating, initiating conversations and aspiring toward mobilizing social change (Akila 2020). I align with Madhushree's sentiments when she notes that, despite Akila's discomfort with the label of activism, "works like Akila's could be a welcoming and well-required beginning of a collaboration with social activism against honour killing and the anti-caste movement in Tamil Nadu in general" (2018).

We know from dance scholar Sherry Badger Shapiro that dance plays an important role in activism through its latent power to "envision, move and create change" (2016, 3). If, as Akila believes, dance-works can become a vehicle through which we exercise criticality about the human condition (Shapiro 2016, 4), they can also "expose questions of social injustice, inequality, asymmetrical power, and the lack of human rights or dignity" in any given sociocultural milieu (Shapiro 2016, 10). Thinking of the potentiality of dance-works in this way allows us to consider the possibility that not only do we as artists create dance, "but dance also creates us" (Shapiro 2016, 12). And to extend this line of thinking further, if dance has the capacity to create or make us, might it also harbor the capacity to unmake us as peoples? Might it hold space and time to expose the asymmetries of power that we take for granted, and the prejudices that constitute the very interiorities of our personhoods? Might its unmaking of us be fundamentally linked to our making? Akila's dance-activism takes on these very questions. Through her work we see the promise of invoking such socially just worlds, through an attempted unmaking of its caste supremacist foundations as we live and breathe them in our caste society, signaled and choreographed through the power of inter-caste intimacies. Her choreography thus makes it possible to visibilize both what is, and "equally importantly, to imagine what is not yet" (Shapiro 2016, 21). Aligned with choreomusicologist Chelsea Oden's thinking on dance as political activism, Akila wills her audiences of *Theenda Theenda* to "listen more deeply ... to hear bodies in sounds ... to hear stories in bodies ... to hear hate in violence and empathy in love" (Oden 2021, 105).

An intrinsic component of *Theenda Theenda*'s choreographic vision is to encourage such active listening in her audiences through creating a "post-performance conversation on the form and content of the piece," without affecting their thinking in any particular way (Akila 2022). Akila contemplates that this second choreographic component is perhaps where the real potential for social change lies, as she reaches out to "younger generation in educational institutions, college campuses, community spaces"—generating a discussion about the performance they have witnessed, and coaxing them to respond to the movement language, the content, and the responses that these elicit in them. Akila is crystal clear in her intentional call to these young people:

> These younger generations will very soon, after their education or during their education, be making a choice of life partners or already made choices. And if there is a choice of inter-caste relations, they will be encountering the very problem of caste. Agenda here is not to propagate or romanticize inter-caste marriage, but to confront the problem of caste oppression and honour-killings. Finally, questioning themselves to locate themselves within the problem. (Akila 2022)

I am intrigued by Akila's clear articulations that *Theenda Theenda*'s main premise is not so much to advocate for inter-caste intimacies, but to confront the problem of caste oppression itself. I wonder if it is possible to disentangle between the two quite so starkly, considering Ambedkar's sustained critique of Brahminical patriarchy and endogamy, which he believed was the mechanism that "functioned to regulate the sexuality, social mobility, and economic resources of women—especially *surplus* (i.e., unmarried or 'unmarriageable') women—and thus safeguard brahman male power and sexual privilege by preventing those women from seeking intercaste marriages and transgressing the boundaries of the caste hierarchy" (Paik 2022). For me, *Theenda Theenda* raises awareness of both the horrors of caste violence and "honor killings", while simultaneously offering the promise of liberation from a caste society through inter-caste intimacies, whether Akila intends this or not. I hear its double-edged call loud and clear in the piece's choreographic vision, aesthetic, and politics.

Chandiran: Dancing between Therapeutic Touch and Social Touch

In *Theenda Theenda*, Akila's urge toward mobilizing dance for social change comes coupled with Chandiran's experience and knowledge of the power of social and individual healing as a movement therapist, based in what he refers to as "traditional body therapies like yoga and kalarippayattu" (Chandiran in Akila and Chandiran 2022). Chandiran explains that in his practice as a therapist he works with disabled and non-disabled bodies, and this gives him insight into how marginalizations work along the social axis of ableism. As he moves between his therapy practice and his dance practice, he has come to notice a significant difference between how touch operates in these two worlds. He explains that as a therapist he very often is required to apply direct pressure onto clients' bodies through his hands to release muscular tensions in different body parts. In this mode of touch, which he describes as "healing and clinical" (Chandiran in Akila and Chandiran 2022), he feels the energy flowing from his active self to his passive recipient clients, whereas he feels that "touch in the dance world is completely different," where passive and active energies flow back and forth through "give and take" (Chandiran in Akila and Chandiran 2022). His insights on the role and manifestation of touch within the contemporary dance world in India at large, and *Theenda Theenda* in particular, are important as someone who navigates his social positioning between his rural upbringing in a village in Tamil Nadu and his present urban life in Chennai.

Chandiran was born in a remote rural village in Tamil Nadu. He explains that, growing up in these geographical and social circumstances, he did not experience discrimination because his ancestors had worked hard to ensure their future generations were protected from harm within their own village locations, among their own communities. His desire to move to the city to learn movement practices, however, brought him into contact with the deeply hierarchical realities of Tamil Nadu's caste society. In Chennai, within popular dance class environments, Chandiran came to realize that urban caste supremacy operates in surreptitious ways, based on language (operating against those who do not speak English), anti-Blackness and colorism, and manifests as discriminatory and segregationist behaviors over sharing of food and social and dining spaces. The dehumanizing Brahminical principles of (im)purity and untouchability thus proliferate into everyday social interactions within the urban cityscape, and is undergirded by spatial and social segregation and the upholding of a lack of English-education and darker complexion as a signifier of one's caste oppressed location. To support himself and his family financially while training as a dancer, Chandiran turned to the therapeutic body practices of yoga and kalarippayattu, where he was able to immerse himself in the healing language of touch. Chandiran's complex relationship to touch thus informs his performance in *Theenda Theenda*, both in its form and in its subject matter, in intricate and important ways.

Touch, Inter-Caste Intimacies, and Caste Violence

When we Zoom in December 2020, Akila shares with me that the first version of *Theenda Theenda* was made with four dancers and was an attempt to respond to and narrate the story of a particular "honor killing" that shook Tamil Nadu in 2013. "Honor killing," a much-disputed label in itself, is used to refer to a category of hate crimes across India and South Asia where the actions of individuals are deemed by their community to have engendered familial dishonor and disrepute. Writing about transgression of caste society laws through inter-caste intimacies, Sunalini K. K. et al. provide a helpful overview of the practice of "honor killing" as a particular kind of hate-crime:

> Honour Killing is deemed to be a crime that jeopardizes the unity and harmony of the community. Violence against men/women in the name of safeguarding families' honour has become a serious problem in India, across regions and communities.... Honour killing is not gender specific. Whoever violates social and moral codes of conduct is subjected to ruthless killing with the family's honour placed first. Any kind of premarital, extramarital, or postmarital sexual relationship may lead to honour killings. This practice is prevalent in tribal and rural areas, but it is also spreading rapidly to urban and metropolitan areas such as Delhi. Men frequently use honour killing as a pretext to subjugate women in patriarchal hegemony. (2022, 3929–3930)

Further context about "honor killings" in the state of Tamil Nadu itself reveals that its state government is in denial about the high prevalence of these hate crimes:

> Tamil Nadu—a progressive state with above-average literacy rate and sex-ratio, bearing witness to one of the richest histories of caste movements in India—alone has seen 187 cases of brutal murders (with women as 80% of the victims) in the name of "caste honour" in past 6 years.... Though Tamil Nadu has rarely seen honour killings based on religion unlike the rest of the country, inter-caste honour killing have been rampant as yet another manifestation of the general air of severe caste conflict. (Madhushree 2018)

Akila further nuances my understanding of the complex power dynamics that undergird these hate crimes, caste violence, and caste oppression, explaining that "honour-killings are more frequent in inter-caste relationships between most backward classes and Dalits," and that "caste oppression also happens between dominant Dalit and very oppressed Dalit communities" (Akila 2022). Consequently, she clarifies that *Theenda Theenda* aims its critiques at "all levels of caste hierarchies" (Akila 2022).

The rampant and prolific nature of these hate crimes in Tamil Nadu means these tragic and violent stories emerge and are forgotten endlessly. But for Akila, this particular one stayed with her:

> 5 years ago, on the 4th of July, 19 years old Dalit youth named Ilavarasan's body was found by a railway track in Dharmapuri in Tamil Nadu—reported as a suicide, but with all the evidences of being a homicide. He was married to Divya, who belonged to the Vanniyar caste, for eight months, during which they were repeatedly threatened by Divya's family. Finally, Ilavarasan was arrested by police based on false cases and Divya was abducted by her own family, house-arrested and made to present false statements to the media. The incident—less "spectacular" than some other cases of honour killing in Tamil Nadu—eventually disappeared from most of our minds as one of the many real-life horror stories that the society amply gifted us with. Yet, some of us remembered it well enough. (Madhushree 2018)

And Akila is one of these people who could not forget it. The particular story ignited in her, the artist, a sense of responsibility into mobilizing their art toward social change. She asked herself, "what am I going to do as an artist, and also what can an artist do?" (2020). She recognized of course that she had to find a means of response that acknowledged that she was "not a part of any of the communities [she would be] representing" and that she "didn't have any direct experience of oppression" (Akila 2020). Yet she felt it was precisely from her position of privilege that she needed to speak out, joining the dots between her lifelong and political education of her childhood, her close encounter with Dalit communities through Thappattam artists, and her quest for speaking truth to power through her art. Akila explains that in her first attempt to bring *Theenda Theenda* to life, she found a way to dance her personal response to Divya and Ilavarasan's tragic story by choreographing a piece with four dancers. Following this first version, she retrospectively recognized that a literal narration of Divya and Ilavarasan's violent and violated circumstances was in fact not appropriate. Akila remembers that through a conversation with, and guidance from, her writer-journalist friend, Mr. Gnani, she was encouraged to divest from literal representations of the story. Instead she was encouraged to find danced ways to capture, more generically, caste violence and discrimination that is aimed at people in inter-caste relationships by working with only two dancers (2022). Working with the conceptual structure offered by Mr. Gnani, Akila found ways to transform the original piece toward "a more general statement of protest—less narrative, less emotional, more bent on a general note of dissent as well as of disillusionment with the patriarchy that weakens the anti-caste movement" (Madhushree 2018).

This is how Akila and Chandiran, who had both worked in the original version, came together in the duet that became *Theenda Theenda*, the subject of this chapter.

This is also how they met.

This is how they touched.

This is how they made contact.

*This is how they unmade
(social codes and unwritten contracts around the impermissibility of
inter-caste)
contact.*

This is how they unmade theendamai (Tamil for untouchability).

This is how they made Theenda Theenda (as we touch).

*This is how their touch became the genesis of new life, new hope and new
futures.*

Theorizing the relationship between the role of education and inter-caste marriages, Tridip Ray et al. remind us that "caste endogamy [is] the pillar of caste system," that "violations of caste endogamy are often punished by social ostracism," that "inter caste marriages can directly weaken the foundations of caste system" (2020, 620), and that this is why such marriages remain as low as 5.82 percent of marriages in India in 2011, with little upward trajectory in forty years (2020, 620). Thinking through Tanika Sarkar, V. Geeta, and Uma Chakravarti, gender and caste violence scholar Sowjanya Tamalapakula nuances this observation further by bringing gender into the equation:

> Endogamy is a very significant feature of the caste system. However, the freedom given to upper-caste men with regard to polygamy and access to lower-caste women is apparent throughout history. According to the Hindu scriptures, a Brahmin/uppercaste man is allowed casual sexual access to lower-caste women, but giving the status of wife to Dalit/lower-caste women is offensive, due to the purity/pollution associated with caste position. On the other hand, the Brahmin/upper-caste woman is confined to caste-endogamous marriage and constrained by the ideology of wifely devotion (*pativrata dharma*). Caste purity is ensured through stringent control of an upper-caste woman's sexuality, so no lower-caste man may plant his seed (sperm) in her.... The stringent control over the sexuality of upper-caste women determines the hegemonic position of upper-caste women within the ideology of sexual purity/pollution. (Tamalapakula 2019, 316–317)

Tamalapakula argues that patriarchy prevails in the way caste and gender politics play out vis-à-vis inter-caste relationships. She notes that Dalit (and non-Dalit men) "do not become polluted by any sexual activity," and that in fact some Dalit men may consider "inter-caste marriage to an upper-caste woman an honor to Dalit masculinity" (2019, 324). However, she also points out that while "the practice of inter-caste marriage of Dalit men" can be read as their resistance against "the traditional ideology that Dalit men have no access to upper-caste women" (2019, 324), it "doesn't mean that the Dalit man can become an upper-caste man by marrying an upper-caste woman" (2019, 324). They therefore cannot escape their caste-oppressed location in society, even as they gain patriarchal power. Conversely, by embracing inter-caste sexual unions, Tamalapakula notes that it may be argued that "upper-caste women suffer a severe loss of honor from cohabitation outside their caste" (2019, 331–332). Tamalapakula observes that through entering into inter-caste relationships, Dalit masculinity is reinforced through patriarchy, while *savarna* womanhood may have the potential to escape patriarchy's grasps even as she is deemed impure on caste lines. However, she also notes that Dalit women experience the double-binding discriminations of caste and gender at once which deems them unworthy of being categorized as both human and woman simultaneously, and thus struggle with inter-caste marriages as a site of resistance for their socially oppressed positions (2019). Tamalapakula reminds us that:

> The perception in the Dalit movement of the status of Dalit women in inter-caste marriage has strong patriarchal undertones. While the inter-caste marriage of Dalit men is considered an annihilation of caste, Dalit women's sexual choice is perceived as a betrayal and "against the interest of the community." Thus, the inter-caste marriage of Dalits is constructed within the ideology of Brahminical patriarchy, which advocates freedom of sexuality for men, but not sexual choice for women. (Tamalapakula 2019, 335)

We thus have to consider the "sex-gender-caste complex," as formulated by historian and gender studies scholar Shailaja Paik, as the intersecting social power matrices within which the lives, dignities, and sexualities of Dalit people of all genders play out. Paik nuances this complexity by pointing out that "while dominant caste, and in general caste Hindu women are deemed socially respectable, Dalit women are exploited, denied respectability, and rendered sexually available," thus making "caste violence . . . central to constituting Dalit women's subjectivity" (2022). Paik notes further that "many dominant-caste (and Dalit) men are oblivious to the deep systemic workings of the sexual-caste economy, the sex-gender-caste complex, that generate[s] both difficulties and possibilities for Dalit women" (2022).

It is within these complex and interlocking grids of power regimes of caste, gender, and codes of heterosexuality that *Theenda Theenda* locates its politics, knowing full well that the fulcrum of inter-caste intimacies that crumbles the foundations of the caste system is touch. The willful act of touching "the untouchable" leads to a breakdown of caste society, and leads to a simultaneous genesis of a relationship, and a social order, that cannot be categorized by Brahminical codes of purity and hierarchizations. It leads to caste annihilation.

Akila is clear in her thinking about the centrality of touch, choreographically, conceptually, and ideologically within *Theenda Theenda*:

> When it comes to *Theenda Theenda*, touch is a very key word. It is everything. It is because of the potential of two hands from two different communities touching that the problem arises. It is all about that touch. When these bodies unite, everything goes wrong. (2020)

Akila echoes Tamalapakula's argument that "caste supremacy is challenged and broken through inter-caste relationships" (Akila 2020) and, in this, the inter-caste physical contact that leads to intimacies that are embodied in *Theenda Theenda*, becomes the pivotal point between a death sentence and the promise of new life, of liberation. As discussed in the Introduction, the basis of caste supremacy rests on the fundamental belief that touching a Dalit, a person deemed "untouchable," especially a touch that can lead to the potential of a sexual union between inter-caste people, results in the dilution and contamination of caste purity. Paik asserts that this is why upholding caste supremacy is so closely linked to the control of female sexuality in particular:

> the control of sex and female sexuality leads to the reproduction of caste.... The mechanisms of caste created and maintained hierarchy, untouchability, and inequality and strengthened boundaries, reinforcing the benefits of the sex-gender-caste complex for touchables and the basis for the exploitation of Dalits. (2022)

It is to counter such potential impurifications that the hate crimes of "honor killings" are practiced as punitive acts, meant to function as deterrents to others seeking similar intimacies. Akila explains that usually families of women from "upper caste backgrounds do not want them to have children from relationships with lower caste men because they do not want that [contaminated] caste lineage for the next generation" (2020). This is when "honor killings" are most prevalent, as patriarchy and caste supremacy come together in a violent double-bind, often resulting in gruesome murders of these *savarna* women who dare to enter relationships with people from caste-oppressed backgrounds. Akila notes that while the reverse circumstances are also not uncommon, the extent of discrimination aimed at *savarna* men for entering into inter-caste relationships is nowhere near as violent. This is explained by gender studies scholar Uma Chakravarti's observation that caste-privileged women are constructed as the gateways and custodians of caste hierarchies through their ability to procreate and keep caste-lines pure and alive, and as such their sexualities are controlled by the forces of Brahminical patriarchy (2018).

Dancing Touch, Choreographing Caste Justice

In *Theenda Theenda*, Akila is keen to expose and critique caste violence as embodied in controlling, arrogant, and oppressive attitudes and actions of dominant-caste people and their self-appointed superiority, and her intention comes alive in her solo that begins the performance.

The film settles on an open-air courtyard with two trees, both leaning to the stage left, one at the front and the other at the back of the performance space. The ground is covered in soil. Dressed in a sleeveless pale-yellow kurta and churidar, Akila enters the space, running across from backstage right and stops center stage as she looks to her right and stops abruptly. In her two hands she clasps two ends of a green towel that is wrapped with tension around her upright shoulders. Her spine is erect as she takes up space, matching the confidence in her gaze that she directs straight at her audience. A droning soundtrack begins immediately, rhythmic, and monotonous. She flicks the towel behind her shoulders to reassert the tension back into the fabric. She turns her back to the audience and continues to flick the towel, shaking it out on her right-hand side, with her right hand. She then flicks it over her left shoulder like a scarf, letting it hand loose and low like the pallu of a sari.

As she slowly pulls the towel off her left shoulder, the precision in her gesture and the slowness with which she carries it out,
    accentuates her straight spine,
        her upright neck
            and her head held high.

Even as she has her back to the audience,
    we know that her gaze is directed at the horizon and above.
        Never to the ground.

The sound of tweeting birds intermingle with the droning soundscape, emphasizing the apposition between the rigidity of Akila's bodily movements to the rhythmic score, and the natural environment in which it resides. Akila walks around, up and down, in horizontal pathways through the space. She uses the towel in various ways to drape across her shoulders and her elbows. She interposes these statuesque positions with standing still, arms clasped behind her back as though in the army. She wraps the towel briefly around her head, like a turban. She releases the towel to rest and hang across the back of her shoulders as she starts to bring her limbs into gestural moves that become an extension of the towel's rigidity, presence, arrogance.

She kicks high,
beats the left side of her chest with her right hand,
fists her hands as her arms are held away from her,
taking up more and more space as she surveys it.

She owns the land.
She is a landowner.
She owns the people on the land too.

She extends her left arm and index finger
as though pointing at someone in the distance—
exposing them,
apportioning blame,
bringing them shame.

She continues to repeat the gesture of pointing fingers, now to the other side, all the while handling the towel as an extension of the power she wields and (up)holds in the space, flicking, shaking, twisting the fabric between her hands. Without the use of text or dialogue to underscore this visual and gestural world Akila occupies, she and her towel embody power. The droning soundscape starts to build in percussive rhythms into a frenzy. The repetitive nature of Akila's movements reinforces her all pervasive presence and authority.

Akila explains to me her very deliberate choreographic choices of her upright spine and the choreographic prop of the towel:

> When I am playing this dominant caste woman, the spine is always erect and vertical. It never collapses. It has its own freedom of movement. The spine has the power to choose what to touch and what not to touch. And this choice is made in the spine, and the spine determines the space I occupy and how I occupy it. The towel is an extension of the caste dominance attitude as embodied in the spine. The spine is thus the internal metaphor of power and the towel is its external manifestation. (Akila in Akila and Chandiran 2022)

Akila shares that in her opening solo, her "spine is always erect, never collapses" and, in this, she references the late Indian choreographer Chandralekha's piece *Shri* (1991), who used the metaphor of the erect spine as a resistive, anti-patriarchy feminist call to liberation, the "greatest metaphor for freedom," and "an act of resistance [to] not bow to the oppression of patriarchy" (Doshi 2012). Over both our conversations, Akila and I talk about the points of convergences and departures between her deployment of the vertical spine and Chandralekha's. She makes clear that working with Chandralekha's choreographic principle of the "spine as the dignity of the body" bears the potential to have different choreographic manifestations whether it is "countering against patriarchy, oppressing others, criticizing caste arrogance, or distributing the power and dignity of the spine equally; using the strength of the spine to impose power or to distribute power" (Akila 2022). I listen to Akila's words as I try to process my prior reading of Chandralekha's feminist deployment of the anti-patriarchy spine. I read it now with more nuance, as a potentially *savarna* feminist gesture, re-encountering it through Akila's deployment of the spine as a redistribution of social power to all marginalized peoples, women and the caste-oppressed. Thus, for me, while in Chandralekha's choreography the upright spine becomes a metaphor for resistance against patriarchy, in Akila's choreography the upright spine becomes a critique of caste dominance.

I am compelled to consider more closely the violent implications of caste power that is embodied in this skeletal-musculature presentation of the upright spine. As Akila's posture in this opening solo demonstrates, the upright spine enables a way of walking through the world, a way of taking up space, a way of punitively acting on the infiltration of someone else into our space, and a way of impacting one's environment where nothing matters more than this individual's place at the center of the(ir) world. Indeed, if their spine is the axis through which they orientate themselves in and to the world, the upright spine *is* the world. And it directly impacts their piercing gaze at the horizon, annihilating anything or anyone that is deemed unworthy of being looked at. The physiological, neurological, sociological, and phenomenological power that is activated via such a spine has the ability to control anything it chooses to come in contact with. Everything is entirely at this upright spine's mercy. Such is the power of the *savarna* spine, and such is the potential of violence that lays dormant in it, ready to unleash onto anyone in its path who is deemed unworthy of their encounter.

I would propose, then, that if caste supremacy is physically and sociologically upheld via the practice of endogamy, its dominance manifests in the Indian social order via a highly intricate choreography, performed through the *savarna* spine. Following performance studies scholar Brahma Prakash's call to become attentive to the complex interplay between the "biopolitics of the neoliberal state and the choreopolitics of the lower caste labouring bodies" (2018, 185), I want to name and critique this phenomenon as "the choreopower of Brahminism," where, thinking through Gerko Egert, choreopower "denotes the execution of power on and by movement" (2022, 99)—captured in this instance in the choreographic everyday manifestation of Brahminism. This choreopower is learned, stylized, repeated, and perfected, Judith Butler style, to be performed and unleashed through the *savarna* spine to assert supremacy in retaliation to the potential of any liberatory "mode of organization in which the body becomes the site where power has to be reinforced, enacted and resisted" (Prakash 2018, 185). Through this conceptualization of the "choreopower of Brahminism," I wish to extend Vivek V. Narayan's study of caste as performance, in which he argues for the regulatory and governable dimensions of caste choreography in the embodiment of caste-oppressed peoples (2021, 273), by focusing instead on the choreography of caste and its violent power as embodied in and through *savarna* spines.

As *Theenda Theenda* extends into Chandiran's solo, we witness Akila's continued critique of the choreopower of Brahminism as her choreography of "caste attitudes through the spine" (Akila in Akila and Chandiran 2022) manifests in the metaphor of his collapsed spine, demonstrating that there are power regimes other than patriarchy that dehumanize Indians.

Akila's focus turns to stage left, as her gestures build in aggression and arrogance, like it is now aimed at someone in particular. Into the frame walks Chandiran dressed in dark gray trousers and a lighter gray fitted sleeveless t-shirt. His presence in the space is full of uncertainty, as he reveals his reticence to traverse it. His gaze, unlike Akila's, is focused staunchly on the ground. With great hesitation he wraps a red towel around his waist. Akila watches him enter the space, and slowly exits backstage right, from where she had entered. Chandiran takes a long time to tie his towel around his waist, pensive and precise. A slow accompanying percussion accompanies his movements—distinct from the drone that accompanied Akila's.

Akila speaks to the relationship between percussion instruments that permeate the landscape in *Theenda Theenda* and caste politics:

> From my research experience and working experience with folk forms, artists and instruments, the inseparable connection between the percussion instruments and the caste were apparent to me. Skin of the percussion is very much tied to the lower caste of the society. Each folk instrument is very caste specific and used in social/religious rituals within the caste. Parai or Thappu is the only instrument which becomes the identity of current Dalit politics beyond its socio-ritual role and has become overused as an art form of Thappaattam itself. (Akila 2022)

She explains further that in *Theenda Theenda,* the "religious and ritual roles of the caste specific percussion instruments are deliberately changed" (Akila 2022):

> For example, Urumi is the instrument which manifested the caste arrogance from its constant rupture. It is the instrument for Devarattam, the community dance form of Kambalathu Nayakar. The instrument Makudam, which is played only in the Kaniyan community's (a scheduled tribe community)

rituals, shouted out caste equality at the end of the piece. Because of the relationship between each instrument and its associated caste, the choice and the usage of the percussion instruments in the music is very crucial to this piece. (Akila 2022)

Chandiran lowers his head slowly until his gaze is directed at the ground. Keeping his gaze at the ground, he turns his neck toward his right, as though to look behind him, over his shoulder, to see if anyone is watching him, surveying his presence. With one swift jerk to his spine he flicks his upper body back before curving his spine forward toward the ground, arms hanging loose in front before him.

He slowly unfurls his spine, but his gaze never averts from the ground.

He flicks the towel off his waist, and buries his face in it, as if to protect himself. He keeps looking over his shoulder, tracing surveying gazes on his presence. He repeats the throwing back of his upper body backward before collapsing his spine over his legs in front of him, clasping onto his towel to hide in. He walks backward, curled up, gaze lowered, squeezing into as little space as he can possible take up on the land he doesn't own. He shifts left and right on his feet, unsure of his footing or his place on this land. His body flinches in response to the sound of trains and horns—hard to know if this is intended to be a part of the soundscape or a coincidental intermingling of art and life.

Akila reveals to me on reading this chapter that the trains and horns are indeed coincidental, but to *Theenda Theenda* this unplanned soundscape of "the train horns is a very crucial coincidence, as the Dalit youth Ilavarasan's body was found by a railway track" (Akila 2022).

Chandiran slowly stoops low onto the ground, and then collapses onto his left into rolls on the ground. He repeats his movement sequence across the ground, wrapping himself up in dirt, dust, and soil as he traverses the space.

His relationship to dirt and soil and dust is really distinct to Akila's in her opening solo, where although bare feet, her spine does not make contact with such impurities. Prakash poignantly reminds us of the biopolitics of dirt within Indian caste society:

Dirt is not only understood in the context of its materiality but also in the context of its subjectivity. It has two meanings. In the former case, dirt is dirt because of its materiality and whoever engages with those materials is impure. In the latter case, dirt in terms of subjectivity is associated with the Dalit community and therefore, in spite of the nature of the work they do . . ., they generate impurity. (2018, 192)

The towel is always clutched into a ball and held close to his belly, over his legs. Or he curls it into a ball and holds it under his left armpit. Or he ties it around his waist.

> Unlike Akila's,
> Chandiran's towel takes the reduced shapes he does,
> due to the way he handles it.
> But these shapes are diametrically opposite;
> Akila's towel is tense, terse, works in straight lines
> and is held with strict visibility and tension.
> Chandiran's towel works in curvatures,
> furling and unfurling,
> twisting and turning into oblivion.

Akila and Chandiran's towels perform the choreopower of Brahminism, of dominance and oppression respectively, becoming metaphoric extensions of their respective spines.

His movements build to a frenzy, forward rolling, backward rolling across the ground. His spine bends, flexes, contours, twists, curves, furls, unfurls in rapid succession in response to the building percussion and the invisible forces that contain him in the space, shaping his movements. It's a permanent push and pull between his body, and the ground that both consumes him, flattens him, brings him down and gives him the energy to push back up and rise again. To keep going. His spine is a battleground of these forces.

Chandiran articulates his own experience of using the spinal metaphor for caste dominance and the material impact that it has on oppressed communities:

> In the piece I play a lower caste person and my body language reflects this through the way I use my spine, the way my eyes try to track who is watching me.... My spine is always collapsed, I never stand erect and I never stand in a vertical capacity. I am unsure to walk freely in the space, and my body language always asks "can I move this way?," "can I look this way?" My towel is an extension of my collapsed spine, always wound up, always taking up less space. And choreographically it is always around my hips. I want to explore freedom and liberation, but I am not allowed. I am not allowed to look at the space, or to look into the upper caste person's eyes. I am not even allowed eye contact. (Chandiran in Akila and Chandiran 2022)

CONTACT AS CASTE JUSTICE 89

Akila explains the inherent caste politics choreographed in and through towel with regard to where it is positioned on the two bodies. She also explains that she chose the colors of their costumes and towels with much care, such that Akila's yellow costume and green towel, and Chandiran's gray costume and red towel, did not signify any specific caste locations. She wanted to evoke through their respective spinal and towel choreographic expressions the two distinct roles of the oppressor and the oppressed, and how they impact each other materially and corporeally as they share space, and eventually make contact (Akila 2022). She also explains that in rural Tamil Nadu the dominant-caste landlord always wears the towel over their shoulder, but people from "lower caste are never allowed to wear their towel on the shoulder in front of the upper caste. Instead, having a towel around the hips is a symbol of subjugation and servitude" (Akila in Akila and Chandiran 2022). Later on in the piece, the towels become the oppressive force through which Akila and Chandiran's agency is stripped off them, making them unable to "see, hear, speak or do what they want to" (Akila 2022). Endowing a physical object with human attitudinal qualities makes for powerful theatricality in a piece dependent solely on the relationship between visual and the aural, devoid of text. Madhushree describes the strategic politics of nonverbal silence, aside from the accompaniment of various rural percussions from Tamil Nadu and Kerala: urumi, thudumbu, thappu, tavil, edakka, kanjira, udukkai, and makudam (2018), as deployed by Akila in the duet:

> The non-verbal nature of this work has a complex politics of its own. On one hand, as Akila and Chandiran point out in their dance, body-language has an important role to play in the context of caste oppression, which has a curiously silent nature. The lower caste people, in not being allowed to look into the eyes of the upper caste, lay their shadows on the road where the upper caste walks, desire the upper caste as partners, drink water from the same source as the upper caste does, cover their bodies as the upper caste does, touch anything or anyone that the upper caste "owns" and in many such restrictions are constantly under a silent supervision within and without, lest their lower caste body resembles the upper caste body in movement or appearance. The surveillance is so overpowering that an option of a dialogue does not even arise. That is why, when in Teenda Teenda the dancers—constantly revolving in a circular path in diametrically opposite positions, symbolizing the circle of perpetuality of the horrific practice

of honour killing—begin to acknowledge each other's existence in space through eye-contact, it creates a subtle but magically emotive moment.... In Akila's choice of silence lies the silencing of the most violently oppressed Dalit castes such as Pallar, Sakkiliyar, Vannaan, Thoatti, Arundadiyar and others, who are caught helplessly in the socio-political turmoil, facing the brunt of caste violence, losing on all opportunities. (2018)

But Chandiran is quick to remind me that the aesthetic of "non-verbal performance is not something new to traditional art forms of the region" (Chandiran in Akila and Chandiran 2022). Rather, this familiar tactic becomes a mechanism through which the duet communicates with its audiences who find comfort in the nonverbal form to access uncomfortable dancings of truths to power. The sound of silence brims with transgressive noisiness as Akila and Chandiran's solos give way into a duet of touch.

Chandiran's frenzied dance is brought to an abrupt end, as he sees Akila re-enter the space from backstage-right. He turns to face away from her, as he ties his towel hesitantly around his waist once again. What begins is a fast-paced duet between the two of them:

> Akila takes up space,
> traverses across the ground,
> gaze directed at the horizon,
> wielding her towel to claim space and assert power.
>
> Chandiran reverts to the ground,
> rolling,
> tumbling,
> diving in and out of it,
> gaze averted to the ground,
> allowing the limpness of his towel to shape his body movements into
>   contortions.

They repeat each of their solos, this time fast-paced, and alongside each other. And for the first time their respective spines appear in choreographic tandem—making their distinctive embodiments come alive with clarity and precision vis-à-vis being in each other's presence. Their towels too embody different attitudes, as choreographic extensions of their respective spines. Performing alongside, Akila flicks her towel in the air and then over her shoulder as

Chandiran's spine feels and internalizes the terror-ridden impact of the flick, and falls to the ground, flattened by its power. She controls his movements through her towel. What once stood for self-contained choreographic solos now can be read in their relationalities to each other. We see before us a duet that, relationally, conjure the oppressive embodiment of Brahminism: Akila exerts power over Chandiran, as the power asymmetry plays out through their distinctive uses of their spines and by extension, their towels. They do not make eye contact.

Akila's performance of the choreopower of Brahminism in and through her spine is no longer about merely enforcing and maintaining her own place in the environment, but much more about responding to the potential of threat to her own deemed purity and superiority that comes attached to Chandiran's infiltration of her space.

Over time, as they circle and move through the performance space, very gradually and almost not possible to trace when this transition starts, Chandiran's towel starts to imbibe the attitudes of Akila's towel. For the first time it ends up wrapped around his neck and shoulder—and as this happens, Chandiran's spine slowly becomes more upright, losing its tendency to collapse in on itself.

This stage in the duet starts to dismantle and unravel the foundations of the choreopower of Brahminism.

The first choreographic mirroring of contact that happens between them is striking. Both stand center stage: Akila located backstage with her back to the audience and her right arm extended out, palm facing up. And Chandiran located frontstage, facing and meeting the gaze of the audience for the first time, his right arm extended out, palm, facing up. Their spines upright. They traverse the space, but this time Chandiran's movement language seems changed as he takes up more space, directing his gaze at and above the horizon. There are tiny shifts between his old body language and his newfound embodiment. They are in sync insofar as they want to find a new way of moving with and for each other, but they still haven't fully acknowledged each other's presence, let alone shared eye contact. And then, they do.

Akila starts to move her left hand across her chest and lets her hand rest on her right upper arm. She reaches out to extend the touch into the space, toward him.

The second choreographic mirroring of contact transpires as each of them stand next to each other, separated by the tree. Akila is located center-stage-left and faces backstage, her right arm extended out, palm facing down, as though resting on someone's shoulder. Chandiran is stood center-stage-right and faces the audience, his right arm extended out, palm facing down, as though resting on someone's shoulder. Ever so slowly, they turn center stage and look at each other. It is such a powerful moment that conjures imagined physical contact and intimacy between them. Akila continues to repeat the gesture of touching her upper arm with her other hand across her chest. They build up to the moment when they face each other, on the diagonal, eyes locked.

Akila extends her right arm out toward Chandiran. He unfurls the towel off his neck and flicks it over his left shoulder, just as she did at the start of her solo, and slowly, and precisely leans toward her extended arm, lunging on his right leg.

But, still, they do not touch.

They play endlessly, engaged in a ritual of getting closer and closer to each other and then moving away just as they are about to touch, Akila's hand to Chandiran's shoulder, in different permutation combinations.

This time Akila scrunches up her towel and extends toward Chandiran.

He leans into her extended arm and allows the towel to touch his shoulder.

They circle out of each other and let go of their respective towels. Devoid of the constraints the towels brought onto their embodiments, they walk toward each other, eyes locked, still. They face the audience diagonally toward the downstage-left corner. Chandiran stands with his hands in his pockets, Akila behind him.

She slowly raises her right hand above his head, and even more slowly brings it down to rest her palm on his right shoulder. Clasping her fingers gently over his shoulder bone. He flinches and raises his shoulders, making them turn together to face backstage-left corner, their gazes together directed at the floor, their left feet ahead of their right, her right arm resting along his back and holding his right shoulder with so much gentleness and care.

Contact.
Touch.
Contact.

Akila describes in careful detail the choreographic trajectory of touch and contact in the duet interactions of *Theenda Theenda*:

> In *Theenda Theenda*, the initial inter-caste contact happens through eye contact. And it is the nature of their eye contact that reflects the caste and power differentials between them. Exposing the way you look at someone

who is lower caste as an upper caste person is key to a critique of caste society in the choreography. But once the distance diminishes between the male and female bodies and they are in physical contact, that contact makes another statement. That moves into a commentary about the touch of love. Initially the touch begins with seeking out friendship and then moves into a more romantic exploration. During the periods of hesitation of the hands touching, the towels get in the way and indicate the caste difference between them, that governs their inability to touch. Only once the towels are discarded, does actual contact between the bodies happen. The clasping of the wrists as opposed to hands is to indicate a symbol of developing trust between the two. A kind of trust-touch. This trust builds dignity and equality between the people. The last intimate and most intimate contact is the placement of her palm on his chest. (Akila in Akila and Chandiran 2022)

They separate out and then run back to each other. This time they make contact, each one's right hand clasping the other's right elbow, and lean back, giving into and supporting each other's weight. Eyes locked. They pivot a while at their point of counter-balance before falling out again into the space to find their own selves again. They find each other again, hand to wrist, countering each other's weights and eyes forever locked. He raises his left leg as he lowers his body weight to the floor. She supports his weight and helps him up, letting him work his way through choreographic precarity. He folds her into his outstretched right arm, shifting his contact from her wrist across her back and onto her right shoulder. She slides her left arm across his back to rest around his waist, as he allows his right arm to rest around hers. She moves around him until she is behind him, supporting his entire upper body and allowing him to rest across the length of her body as he sits on her left thighs. She leans in to caress his right shoulder with her right hand, and cradles his head gently on the crook of his neck.

Akila traces the shifting patterns in their spines as the piece moves on, explaining that as they make contact "the differences in the spine somehow start to shift and diminish, and gradually becomes one, because of contact between the spines" (Akila in Akila and Chandiran 2022), which are now both upright. She is very clear that if "the spine carries the dignity of the human" then she choreographs this dignity equitably, sharing it across both spines, both humans. And it is in this intention of choreographing human dignity equitably that Akila's conceptualization and anti-caste gesture of contact as caste justice is born.

Akila pivots across Chandiran's upper body until she rolls over to his front, her back leaning onto his chest as he leans his spine backward to take her weight. Their spines support each other, their arms loose, her head tucked into the space between his chin and his chest. Two people, locked in mutual support. They start to walk stage-left, their right feet taking a step forward in sync as they upper bodies remain connected. And then their right feet. And their left feet again. They move in sync with each other's spines, listening through them, moving through them, talking through them. They face each other as Chandiran's wrist rests gently against Akila's forehead. She leans in, giving him her full weight, and for the first time she averts her gaze to the ground.

Their dance of mutuality and symmetry continues to build, shifting between the everyday gesture of a caress, and the abstract movements of weight bearing, of taking responsibility for each other's safety and well-being. Of building mutual trust. One could read the abstraction in their movement sequences as clinical, technical choices, that test the relationship between mass, weight, and gravity.

> *But their movements are so much more because of what they stand for.*
> *Because of the impermissibility of contact they willfully ignore*
> *and push-back against.*
>   *Because of all they risk.*

Their full spine-on-spine contact becomes a powerful anti-caste gesture. But in a caste society within which they are dancing their protest, "when two inter-caste bodies make such intimate contact, this is where violence starts" (Akila in Akila and Chandiran 2022). Akila explains that it is shortly after this moment of full spine-on-spine contact between them that "the problem arises" (Akila in Akila and Chandiran 2022). That while the two bodies will continue to try to make further intimate contact, they "will always be kept apart by some violent external force that will tear them apart" (Akila in Akila and Chandiran 2022).

Chandiran and Akila face away from each other while reaching backward to hold each other's wrists, as they lean away from each other. As though being forced to walk in opposite directions by invisible forces, but being hinged together by their intentional choice to hold on to each other's wrists. Chandiran starts to walk forward, toward stage-right, bringing Akila on his journey, despite the pull he feels from her in the opposite direction. And then in one swift motion, he pulls her in so they can rest in contact.

> *Back-to-back.*
> *Spine to spine.*

They each share the other's spine across their back as they lean forward, carrying the other with them. Forever in touch—and if, for a split second their contact breaks, they reach out to each other by extending their open palm hand, inviting contact again. Akila wraps Chandiran in a hug from behind him, resting her head on his shoulders, her eyes closed. Her right arm comes round to his chest as she stretches out her fingers and places them intentionally and carefully and lovingly on the left side of his chest. They hold the embrace, breathing together, standing together. Listening to and feeling each other's heartbeats (Image 1.1).

They support the most fragile parts of each other's bodies: their heads, their necks (Image 1.2).

Image 1.1 Akila and Chandiran in *Theenda Theenda*
by photographer Sridhar Balasubramaniyam

Image 1.2 Akila and Chandiran in *Theenda Theenda* by photographer Sridhar Balasubramaniyam

> *There is care. There is risk.*
> *There is even more care in mitigating against the risks.*
> *There is love.*
> *There is intimacy.*

Chandiran raises his right arm and stretches out the fingers. He slowly brings his hand down to meet Akila's hand on his chest. But just as he is about to touch her hand, the sound of a percussive blow pushes them apart. She runs backward away from him. He stands frozen on his spot, on tiptoes, his shoulders raised to his ears, his arms unsure and fists curled up. He slowly releases the tension in his body and returns his heels to the ground. The percussion sounds again, he repeats his gesture of tension as she runs to him and places her left arm on his shoulder, a counter gesture of calm, urging him to release and return to the ground. On the third percussive blow, her shoulders tense up too as she goes onto tiptoes. They begin a repetitive tension and release section, cutting across the space, sometimes triggered by the percussion, and sometimes not, having internalized the sequence into their bodies. They return to their respective towels and pick them up. The struggle begins with each of them trying to manipulate the towels in ways opposite to their intrinsic and original attitudes. Akila tries to scrunch up her green towel as it forces itself open into straight and upright lines. Chandiran tries to straighten his red towel across his shoulders, as it insists on curling round his waist. Both of them are silenced by their towels as they tighten over each of their mouths. The towels tie them down, rooting their legs and limbs from free movement, forcing them to conform. Each of them spreads their towel wide and places it over their faces, invisibilizing themselves, holding the towel on the top of their heads in a fist. Their heads are forced up and down, left and right, by a force controlling their hands. The towels become the mechanism through which they are controlled and moved around the space. Into these disturbing imagery creeps in the silencing gesture of their own left hands clasped over their mouths. This builds into a frenzy until the towels come off. They tie their towels around their right hands, unable to part with them. Their contact duet continues, but with the towels on their hands, the energy in their duet is about opposition and conflict. They are torn apart even as they try to return to each other. Exhausted by their efforts, they give into the ground, disheveled, disillusioned, demoralized. When they finally find the energy and purpose to move, they return to their own solo worlds, carrying the traces of the contact they had made inside them. They try to reach out to each other, and every time they touch each other, they explode apart. Against all odds, they keep on trying to make contact with their hands. Against all odds they are kept apart. The social violence of caste apartheid is reflected in the physical violence reaped in their bodies. They end up lying next to each other, one's feet next to the other's arms, facing the sky, arms above their heads, legs sprawled. Hyper-ventilating.

Over what seems like the longest time, Akila's feet makes the gentle and surreptitious contact with Chandiran's hands. And the cycle starts again. They seem unable to move forward as a unit, held back by invisible ties that they have wound around their right wrists in the forms of their respective towels, that weight them down. Stuck in an endless back and forth of making and breaking contact, Akila and Chandiran enter the final stages of their meditative longing for each other.

Their bodies are tired, their clothes covered in sweat and soil, their bare arms glistening in the dusk light. A stagehand enters at the backstage-right corner with an earthen pot burning, what Akila clarifies is, mosquito repellant to keep the audiences safe at dusk. To me this is reminiscent of the Bengali dusk ritual of burning dhuno, frankincense, slowly fumigating the air with the smoke as it infiltrates and purifies their space of encounter.

Their space of contact.

The juxtaposition between the slow and intentional movement gestures of holding hands through mutually locked eye-contact, with what to me evokes the everyday Brahminized ritual of purifying their space of inter-caste encounter with dhuno is a subtle and sinister reminder of the deemed threat their attempted contact and desired union holds for the caste supremacist society at large. As the smoke continues to bellow into the space, Akila and Chandiran's duet gets more and more intense, exhausting, and frenzied. They move between upright and collapsed spines, between drawing each other into their spines and spiraling each other out into the space. The percussion builds in tempo and pace as Akila and Chandiran sit frontstage left, facing each other, holding each other's hands. Locking their gaze at each other, they start to unravel each other's towels. They twirl the towels in their hands, moving swiftly and smoothly, such that after a point it is no longer clear which towel belongs to whom. They go through a series of quick movements in succession, repeatedly swapping towels, placing the red one on Akila's shoulders and the green one on Chandiran's. They swap them back and forth, taking on the statuesque arrogance of Akila from the beginning of the performance. They hand both towels to each other, and one in each hand, they shake them out, twirl them through the space, and hit the ground with them. As the percussion builds to a crescendo, they use the towels as extensions of their arms, countering each other's weights, leaning in and out, supporting each other's existence until they wrap themselves up tight in each other's towels, tangled through their limbs, impossible to tell the difference between them. The towels are a part of them and they are a part of each other. They want to reject the towels, push them through and bury them under the soil. They dance around the two entangled towels lying in a heap between them, pushing down against the resistance they feel emanating from them. The performance ends on this relentless ritual of violence and resistance, resistance and violence, and resistance against violence, as Madhushree notes:

> It ends on a simultaneously hopeful and grim note: the dance speaks of dissent and a prospective interlocking of caste identities as a means to that, but at the same time, the lights go dim over a repetitive ritual of movements symbolizing the endless saga of honour killing. (2018)

Akila's danced discourse on inter-caste intimacies embodies her intentions "to address the very core issue of caste dominance, and one of its main consequences of honour-killing which is ongoing, relentless, and everywhere" (Akila in Akila and Chandiran 2022), due to the threat that inter-caste intimacies pose to Brahminism's social order. By bringing Brahminism's fragility to the fore in such bold and candid terms, Akila and Chandiran's duet starts a long overdue and urgent conversation on India's caste society through dance, foregrounding the role of social and choreographic touch in the dismantling of caste supremacy. In this, the duet also instigates a conversation about dance in India itself as a field of the creative arts whose histories and presents are long tangled up with caste dominance, appropriations, and violence. In this, Akila's reflections on the world of both classicized and contemporary Indian dance as a place that is disconnected from contemporary social realities manifests as a double-thronged critique of both Indian caste society and Indian dance-works simultaneously, demonstrating the violence of the former and the apolitical politics of the latter. But most important, in *Theenda Theenda*, Akila and Chandiran's inter-caste intimacies evoke critiques of Brahminism through their compelling depiction of the redistribution of power that lies latent in, and is inherent to, Brahminism's metaphoric and material spine, through their mobilizations of inter-caste spine-to-spine contact, heralding emancipatory futures for all spines and their willful intimacies.

Reflections: On *Savarna* Spines and Dismantling the Choreopower of Brahminism

In the preface to my first book *Akram Khan: Dancing New Interculturalism*, reflecting on the role of the spine in negotiating tensions between different movement methods that my body was moving through during my intercultural performance training, I wrote:

> I began to notice that in shifting between one language and another, my spine was suffering from negotiating the different demands of my performance training. The creative tensions that surfaced in moving smoothly between different embodiments of my body's central axis, different relationships to verticality and horizontality, and most importantly different explorations of the relationship between gravity and my body weight, were gradually manifesting as physiological tensions at the base of my spine. Even though I was advised to discontinue working with multiple

corporeal languages, an intellectual reading of my physiological condition instigated interesting questions about the role of the spine in such intercultural negotiations. (Mitra 2015, xiii–xiv)

Thinking through *Theenda Theenda* with Akila and Chandiran and their pivotal choreographic mobilizations of the spine in the equitable redistribution of power and dignity in their duet through inter-caste spine-to-spine contact has made me return to my earlier reflections on "the role of the spine in such intercultural negotiations." They now seem not only incomplete, but also inadequate, devoid of considerations of the competing power regimes of race, caste, and gender that constituted the ways in which my spine, and by extension my personhood, felt compromised, maybe even threatened, when having to negotiate the demands of horizontality of my contemporary dance training. I realize now that the verticality of my spine and the way it allowed to carry myself, take up space, and potentially deny the same for others, during my upbringing in India-the verticality that I felt was being challenged by the horizontality of my floor-bound contemporary dance training was in fact not *just* an embodiment of my kathak training, as I claimed in my first book's preface. Instead, I have now come to understand as I watch Akila's vertical and erect spine exert her caste dominance in *Theenda Theenda* that my vertical spine was also a marker and embodiment of my own *savarna* personhood, my performance of the choreopower of Brahminism. Thus, the "intercultural tensions" my spine was experiencing between my long-held and unquestioned verticality of my spine and its affiliated social superiority, and the newly imposed horizontality that was being expected of it, was not just about the encounter between white Western performance aesthetics and my Indian kathak training, but also about the innate sense of (loss of) power I experienced when my vertical *savarna* spine was threatened to cede space within a context where the codes of social hierarchies were different to the ones where I grew up in a position of dominance. What I experienced in those "intercultural tensions" was contact with another social order, which constituted an unmaking of my personhood.

The unmaking of contact in *Theenda Theenda* thus signals more than its very important critique of Brahminism's founding principles of caste purity through the practice of untouchability through its evocation of inter-caste touch and intimacies. It also, and importantly, systematically and choreographically exposes the manifestation of Brahminism, the choreopower of the spine, in the embodiments of *savarna* personhoods within the body, more specifically through the spine as a metaphor of caste power. It signals how caste is choreographed into our bodies, and learned, sustained, and performed through repetitive embodiments of dominance (and subservience) through our spines. It provides glimpses of social repercussions, both violence and emancipation, when such encoded and hierarchized choreographies are dismantled through inter-caste spine-to-spine contact that equitably redistributes empowerment between Akila and Chandiran. It demonstrates the threat such choreographic reorientations of the spine poses to Brahminism's social order in its evocation of inter-caste intimacies and its promise of emancipatory worlds.

References

Akila. 2020. *Interviewed by the author via Zoom.* December 6.
Akila. 2022. *Personal communication via email with the author.* September 28.
Akila and Chandiran. 2022. *Interviewed by the author via Zoom.* July 13.
Chakravarti, Uma. 2018 [2003]. Gendering Caste: Through a Feminist Lens. Rev. ed. New Delhi: Sage Publications India.
Chakravorty, Pallabi. 2008. Bells of Change: Kathak Dance, Women and Modernity in India. Kolkata: Seagull Books.
Chandralekha. 2003. "Reflections on New Directions in Indian Dance." In New Directions in Indian Dance, edited by Sunil Kothari, 50–58. Mumbai: Marg Publications.
Doshi, Tishani. 2012. "Chandralekha: Rainbow on the Roadside." KindleMag. Accessed August 23, 2023. http://kindlemag.in/chandralekha-rainbow-on-the-roadside/.
Egert, Gerko. 2022. 'Operational Choreography: Dance and Logistical Capitalism'. Performance Philosophy. Vol 7. No 1. 97–113.
Indianostrum Theatre. 2018. Facebook post. December 20. Accessed October 20, 2020. https://www.facebook.com/photo?fbid=1957641784334418.
Kanu, Haja Marie. 2019. "'Have You Noticed White People Never Move out of Your Way?': The Politics of the Pavement." Gal-Dem. Accessed November 9, 2023. https://gal-dem.com/have-you-noticed-white-people-never-move-out-of-your-way-the-politics-of-the-pavement/.
Madhushree. 2018. "The Touch of Love, the Touch of Death and a New Dance in Tamil Nadu." GroundXero Facts as Resistance. Accessed July 1, 2022. https://www.groundxero.in/2018/07/07/the-touch-of-love/.
Mills, Dana. Dance and Activism: A Century of Radical Dance across the World. London: Bloomsbury.
Narayan, Vivek V. 2021. "Caste as Performance: Ayyankali and the Caste Scripts of Colonial Kerala." Theatre Survey 62: 272–294.
Oden, Chelsea. 2021. "Dance as Political Activism: Two Popular Choreomusical Responses to the Orlando Shooting." Pop—Power—Positions. Vibes. Accessed July 2, 2022. http://vibes-theseries.org/oden-dance/.
Paik, Shailaja. 2022. The Vulgarity of Caste: Dalits, Sexuality, and Humanity in Modern India. Stanford, CA: Stanford University Press.
Prakash, Brahma. 2018. "'Dangerous' Choreopolitics of Labouring Bodies: Biopolitics and Choreopolitics in Conflict in the Act of Jana Natya Mandali in India." In Shifting Corporealities in Contemporary Performance: Danger, Im/mobility and Politics, edited by Marina Grzinic and Aneta Stojnic, 183–201. Basingstoke: Palgrave Macmillan.
Ray, Tridip, Arka Roy Chauchuri, and Komal Sahai. 2020. "Whose Education Matters? An Analysis of Inter-Caste Marriages in India." Journal of Economic Behavior & Organization 176: 619–633.

Shapiro, Sherry Badger. 2016. "Dance as Activism: The Power to Envision, Move and Change." *Dance Research Aotearoa* 4: 3–33.

Sunalini, K. K., M. Sumalatha, Indrani Merugu, Ch. Jyostna Kumari, and V. Sharon Luther. 2022. "Transgression of 'Love Laws' and Honour Killing in Arundhati Roy's *The God of Small Things*." Journal of Positive School Psychology 6 (4): 3929–3934.

Tamalapakula, Sowjanya. 2019. "The Politics of Inter-caste Marriage among Dalits in India: The Political as Personal." *Asian Survey* 59 (2): 315–336.

2

Contact as Reframing Sociality

Rorschach Touch (2018) by Diya Naidu and "Normalizing Touch"

Touch-Gifts

The Bangalore-based Indian dancer-choreographer Diya Naidu's choreographic debut *Rorschach Touch* (2018) ends with a poignant ritual, closing the socio-physical gap between performers and audience by conjoining them as one community:

> The dancers pull everybody into a circle and intersperse themselves equally between the audience. The lights are dimmed. Everyone's nervous system is now heightened. The dancers have to work very hard in this section—to look into the person's eyes and see where they are at. Their instruction is to go and stand in front of a person, and to initiate one small touch. And then to whisper to them "pass this on." The audience member then passes this on to a stranger, and as it passes on, the initial touch changes. Then, very slowly, the lights dim out and the piece finishes. (Naidu 2022a)

Embracing the carefully shaped intimacy of the spatial proxemics that Naidu has choreographed, and maximizing their own awareness that the audience has been on a reflexive journey with them vis-à-vis the complexities that govern Indian sociology of touch along the lines of caste, faith, gender, and sexuality, as already discussed at length in this book, the performers initiate and offer these "touch-gifts" to individual audience members. These interactions vary in scale, scope, duration, and texture; but they share one thing in common: intentionality. When a performer offers the gift of touch to an audience member, the intentionality in the kind of touch initiated is crucial, and determined by close observation of the audience member, their breath, their body language, their presence. The performers study the audience members with heightened awareness, tuning into their state of being by this ultimate stage in the performance. Their gifts are directly responsive to the sensations that are palpable to them, from being in proximity with them. The touch-gifts range from walking up to someone and simply staring into their eyes and then moving on, to lifting both hands and gently cupping their cheeks in acknowledgment, to brushing their forefinger ever so gently to caress someone's face, to standing in front of them and softly but firmly squeezing their shoulders. Gradually these gifts grow—both in magnitude and scale—generating a wave of touch-gifts through the space. There is something deeply compelling about this moment—as complete strangers, many of whom have never met each other before, pass on the touch-gifts they have received from the performers to other audience members. Some are more hesitant, others rushed, others awkward, and still others deeply committed to the sharing of these gestures.

I should admit here that I am not fortunate to experience these touch-gifts on my own terms, as I am not part of the in-person gathered audience-participants. My experience of observing how these touch-gifts are offered and received is instead mediated through a video recording of *Rorschach Touch*, made on July 10, 2018, at the Shoonya Centre for Art and Somatic Practices in Bangalore, India. My analytical outsider eye therefore very likely supersedes what I can only imagine would have been a heightened phenomenological insider engagement to these gifts of touch, had I been present in the room with the community.

Naidu's choreographic impetus and intention to "normalize touch" through this piece, and "rescue touch from being constantly pinned and stigmatized as romantic" (Naidu 2022a), is in full motion by the time the lights come down on the gathering. They are now one holistic community—touched by each other. This moment is compelling to me; not just to consider the potential of healing that *may* be offered by the ritual to many in the room, but more important, because it signals the various invisible social power regimes that undergird the ritual, that undoubtedly make the experience of this moment uneven for different audience members, and that potentially run counter to and undermine Naidu's choreographic intentions. It begs the question: *is it possible for an Indian dance project to "normalize touch," without simultaneously placing at the project's core, the challenge of at least acknowledging, if not dismantling, untouchability as a founding principle of Indian society?*

Naidu's desire to "normalize touch" stems from a recognition of the complex Indian sociological codes of caste, faith, gender, and sexuality that govern touch and touching, and yet somewhere, I argue in this chapter, this recognition, at least in choreographic terms, is only partial. In his foundational work that lays bare the phenomenological principles of the Brahminical ideology and practice of untouchability, central to this book's Introduction, philosopher Sundar Sarukkai reminds us that "there is no localized organ in the body that does the job of touching," and that "the organ of touch is the skin." Naidu's choreography homes in on the skin as the locus of her project's critical inquiries, examining in dance the lived implications of Sarukkai's theoretical assertion: "if you do not like to touch something then you have to 'close your skin'" (2009, 44). Sarukkai further emphasizes the repercussions of closing one's skin:

> But closing the skin is to close the first means of contact with the world. As a variety of philosophers and biologists have pointed out, we cannot live without the skin although we can live without other senses. Simply put, the moment you close the skin you die. (2009, 44)

If touch, or its denial, becomes the fulcrum of human sustenance and care, Sarukkai's philosophical assertion of the repercussions of closing one's skin has serious consequences. Naidu and I are both interested in this notion of "closing our skin" as a socioculturally inscribed embodied state that permeates the social and psychic identity of South Asians. Where I recognize that this closed-skinned-ness is rooted in, while simultaneously transcending, the ideology and practice of untouchability, attempting to engage with touch as a broader social phenomenon, Naidu's project of "normalizing touch" lacks attentiveness to Brahminism's foundational codes governing touch and untouchability. Instead, it is this broader social phenomenon of closed-skinned-ness, such as gender, faith, and sexuality, that additionally underpin Indian stigmatization of touch, that drives Naidu's project to "normalize touch." Her attempt to examine and dismantle this closed-skinned-ness in *Rorschach Touch* is a further recognition of Sarukkai's observation that in denying oneself the ability to touch others lies "the denial of touching what is touchable within oneself" (2009, 44). The ultimate ritual of touch-gifts in *Rorschach Touch*, as described above, moves against such harmful self-denialism. However, I am curious if it is possible to transcend our closed-skinned South Asian embodiments, even within this carefully crafted dance experiment ritual, without acknowledging, and if not dismantling, the practice of untouchability that undergirds it, first and foremost.

Beyond, but interlinked with, the overlooked caste dimension of Naidu's project of "normalizing touch," I am curious too about a further question around the issue of consent, and how it is conceptualized and navigated within *Rorschach Touch*. I wonder exactly *how* Naidu's wishes her desire to "normalize touch" to manifest in the wider social world. Does it mean to touch familial and loved ones freely and without judgment, all the time? Is it being able to imagine a world where we can touch strangers, without being contained by codes of caste, faith, gender, and sexuality, and the potential of violence that arises from such touch? And where does the question of consent figure in her vision for a society destigmatized vis-à-vis touch? Is consent merely conceptualized as an individual's responsibility, and thus beyond parameters of structural critique? I am grateful here to my colleague and performance studies scholar Sharanya Murali for opening up this nuanced line of thinking through her crucial questions below on reading a draft of this chapter:

> The project of "normalizing touch" may be worth exploring in more detail, since it seems to imply a form of regulation in itself; normalizing is also a form of governance. This brings me to my question about consent: ... How does consent, as framed by neoliberal feminism in very individuated terms in the west, take up embodiment in a caste-regulated context? What does consent mean in the context of community/ensemble work across racial/gender lines? (2023)

Murali's questions are invaluable toward examining Naidu's project, which unfolds in a patriarchal society where violence, often sexual violence, against women and people of minoritised genders is the norm. Such gender-based violence is further exacerbated against women and people of minoritised genders from caste-oppressed communities, and where white women are perceived as sexually uninhibited and therefore "available." My analysis of Naidu's project therefore must be grounded in a consideration of consent vis-à-vis its often-denied relationship to sexual agency of people of all genders, as it operates at the intersections of caste, faith, race, and sexuality. This becomes even more important in relation to Naidu's cast in *Rorschach Touch* who together occupy multiple positions across the power spectrum along these social vectors.

Daniel Loick reminds us of the centrality of the discourse of consent in legal and cultural dimensions in conversations about sexual violence:

At the center of the feminist agenda against sexual violence and assault lies the category of consent. Lack of consent not only provides the legal definition of assault and rape, consent also works as a cultural norm within sexual encounters and as a central point of reference for many feminist debates (paradigmatically expressed in the slogan "No means no, yes means yes"). (2019, 1)

Loick goes on to nuance this feminist discourse with a helpful reminder that "[t]his centrality notwithstanding, there has been growing criticism of the category of consent within feminist philosophy." That while "[l]iberal feminists have used the category in order to advocate the expansion of choices for women and thus the strengthening of individual liberty and agency" (2019, 3), "[r]adical feminists, on the other hand, have questioned the usefulness of the category of consent by pointing out that women's choices take place in a situation predefined by patriarchal norms" (2019, 3). Rhiannon Graybill brings further nuance to this discourse by reminding us first and foremost that "consent is clearly vital" (2017, 175), before going on to undertake a feminist "critique, not criticism" (2017, 175) of consent through considerations of "gender, race, class, and sexuality, as well as access to sexual pleasure" (2017, 175). Graybill identifies three problems with the discourse of consent: first, that "consent assumes that we are all fully and equally able to give consent"; second, that the discourse of consent has been appropriated and made into a profiteering endeavor by neoliberal capitalism via toolkits and apps; and third, that it sets "a low bar" for pleasurable intimacy and that "sex should be more than consent" (2017, 175–176). This attentiveness to the need to consider consent as both necessary but also tied up with power asymmetries that enable agency differently for different people, in choreographic and social terms, is crucial to my chapter.

With this underpinning criticality, this chapter undertakes a choreographic analyses of selected sections of *Rorschach Touch* (2018) through an intercultural theoretical nexus that brings together two conceptual frameworks: Sarukkai's premise of touch as a moral sense that drives the socialization of Indian peoples as "closed-skinned," and Asian American dance scholar SanSan Kwan's critical intervention that "love is an essential condition of interculturalism" and that, relatedly, "we must love one another in order to connect... and, at the same time accept one another's ultimate inaccessibility" (2021, 14–15). Through this intercultural entwining of Sarukkai and Kwan's critical positions, the chapter examines Naidu's choreography to ascertain the extent to which *Rorschach Touch* is successful at moving beyond our closed-skinned-ness through foregrounding love, not just of the "hopelessly romantic" (Kwan 2021) kind, but love as a choreographic method that binds humanity and desire for human connection. It is this critical love with which Naidu places the responsibility of unpacking socialized stigmas around touch and touching on her audience members, in how they read, respond to, and interact with the touch-based intimacies that they witness in the piece. By placing on her audience members a charge of an awakening through confronting their own prejudices, desires, and discomforts, Naidu's *Rorschach Touch* offers us glimpses of "normalizing touch." In this, it builds alternative imaginaries and socialities through an, albeit partial, unmaking of Indian closed-skinned-ness.

Kwan's advocacy for love as integral to interculturalism, and its inevitable residue of loss that arises out of it, finds particular manifestations in Naidu's *Rorschach Touch*. Although Naidu's project is made and performed in India, about Indians, with predominantly Indian performers (with the exception of one white Polish cast member), interculturalism is in its very sinews. At a sociocultural dimension, the performers, and indeed very likely audience members, represent between them different identity positions, including but not restricted to, along the lines of gender, caste, faith, race, and sexual orientation. These distinct social positionalities occupy distinct cultural habitus that shapes the way they live and move through the world and encounter others.

At a dance-world dimension, for many of these performers, *Rorschach Touch* becomes an encounter between the cultural specificities and touch-refutations that frame solo Indian classicized forms that many have trained in, and the communal, touch-centered contact improvisation (CI) culture of the contemporary dance world, a derivative performance practice from the Global North within the Indian context. It is in this context that the culture of closed-skinned-ness uncritically encounters the culture of touch-driven CI. As already discussed in the Introduction, but feels important to reiterate here, Naidu's reflections on her own experience of contact improvisation training in the closed-skinned Indian context is insightful in this regard, as she brings gender dimensions into the equation:

> An experience I remember very clearly is how our bodies changed during those first months of contact improvisation classes. We were all walking around with this sense of openness, freedom and awareness, reveling in the

momentary freedom from gender. And then, when class finished, we would go outside onto the street in large groups as dance students do. Day after day, I would watch as the girls, me included, systematically and sadly closed our bodies again. The walk home would prove very unpleasant if we continued to have that sway and exuberance, indeed that inviting quality. The boys on the other hand, barely seemed to notice they had left the studio. This is something I still feel poignantly till today and it influences much of my research and work. (Naidu 2019)

In these multidisciplinary and methodological senses, *Rorschach Touch* is a fundamentally intercultural encounter, and Kwan's assertion of love and loss as integral to intercultural encounters becomes a helpful way to understand its choreographic intentions, manifestations, and limitations. The love as choreographic method that Naidu brings into her making of this intercultural encounter is what Kwan compellingly argues for as "love in the face of otherness" (Kwan 2021, 5). This love, I argue, is perhaps what drives Naidu's desire to "normalize touch," in order to create community despite and beyond social power regimes, to foster generative human connectivities. But Kwan also "acknowledges the inevitability of loss that love entails" (Kwan 2021, 5) in intercultural collaborations. In *Rorschach Touch*, this residue of loss is generated in the absence of a critique of the power regime of caste and untouchability that undergirds the very closed-skinned-ness Naidu attempts to dismantle through her choreography. It therefore makes me wonder if Kwan's conceptualization of loss entailed by love can be extended to further consider potential harm that can be its byproduct. Kwan's promise of "obstinate, continual growth, not in spite of loss but in the shape of it" (Kwan 2021, 5), however, signals the potential of self-reflexivity in artists. This in Naidu becomes an evolutionary journey as a human and as a choreographer, looking for continuous ways to grow and to un/learn how to mitigate against such harms.

Naidu and Me

Full disclosure. In understanding the loss (and potential harm) that is generated by Naidu's project, I reflect on the loss (and potential harm) I generated in my own past choreographic endeavors. Naidu's choreographic intentions in *Rorschach Touch* in 2018 echoed my own in *The Silk Route: The*

Memory of a Journey in 2004. Funded by British Council Kolkata, I traveled to India with two white male British colleagues to conduct performance workshops over a three-week period, culminating in a site-specific performance sharing at Kolkata's elite, caste, and class-privileged, colonial country venue the Tollygunge Club. We worked with brilliant and inspiring 16–25-year-old young people to devise this project.

Naidu was one of them.
This is how we met.

I worked extensively with the cast through the language of CI, and, in this, I have since realized, I was guilty of imposing this language upon them, having dangerously internalized and erased my own experiences of discomfort and harm from participating in Global North contact improvisation classes. Additionally, at the time, I had embarrassingly little to no awareness of how caste dynamics operated in India, let alone in the workshop spaces I was leading. So misplaced was my conviction that it was intergenerational tensions and specifically misogyny that drove the clear disjuncture between how these young performers seemingly embraced the language of CI without question, and anecdotal audience responses who critiqued the proliferation of touch in the performance, that I reflected on this in my first scholarly publication.

> Working as choreographer for ... *Silk Route: Memory of a Journey*, ... I was keen to ... introduce our performers to physical vocabularies and corporeal aesthetics of contemporary western performance practices. ... To achieve this, I introduced the western vocabulary of contact improvisation onto the Indian performers' bodies. The use of contact-based choreography culminated in several intense moments of physical contact and intimacy on stage, implicitly suggesting desire. On encountering these moments, the audience's response was as passionate as it was varied. While some engaged with the content and form of our work, a majority of the audience found it unsettling and controversial to witness intimacy and touch between the performers. (Mitra 2010, 561)

At the time, analyzing this disjuncture and the reasons for it, like Naidu, I argued for a feminist critique of what I deemed were conservative responses stemming from discomfort with the imposition of Western movement vocabularies onto Indian performers, particularly women. I read these responses as, and pushed back hard against such, policing of women's bodies and sexualities in performances. I argued instead, much like Steve Paxton and his generation of predominantly white practitioners, for the liberatory capacity inherent in touch. In this, I aligned with Naidu's desire to "normalize touch" in and through choreography.

> I was the *savarna* feminist.
> Oblivious to the dynamics of caste in such choreographic endeavors.
> Oblivious to the choreopower of Brahminism.
> Because there is no monolithic "woman".

Naidu and I remained in contact ever since *The Silk Route*, which became the starting point of her dance career that I continued to follow closely. The original impetus that drew us close together in Kolkata in 2004 has since evolved into a nourishing and critical bond. While writing this chapter, when I shared my self-reflexive thoughts about my use of contact improvisation in *The Silk Route* with Naidu, she acknowledged and appreciated my own self-critique, while also reminding me, that despite the problematic dynamics of CI in the workshops I led, for her, it was a turning point as a performer and as a human; that "that process with you was maybe the first time I felt seen for me, for who I was" (Naidu 2022b). This presents me with a necessary conundrum to consider through my analysis of *Rorschach Touch*: **how can we theorize choreographic touch as an emancipatory language for South Asian dancers when social touch in India is riddled with exclusionary and oppressive codes of conduct based on the caste system?**

Naidu and I share a love for dance, a commitment to un/learn from each other and others to become better human beings, and a deep investment in our own lifelong political education. It is from this shared space of critical friendship that I start my analysis of *Rorschach Touch* as an intercultural performance experiment that, led by love, generated loss and potential harm in the face of its partial challenges to social regimes of power.

Rorschach Touch and Intersecting Regimes of Power

Conceptualized as a mirror to point at her predominantly class privileged, dominant-caste, urban elite Indian audiences, in *Rorschach Touch*

112 UNMAKING CONTACT

Image 2.1 Diya Naidu, Dayita Nereyeth, and Masoom Parmar in *Rorschach Touch* by photographer Dannilla Correya

Naidu is keen to examine the relationship between Indian peoples' complex relationships with touch and the social codes that shape them (Image 2.1). She explains the inspiration for her performance's title:

> The name of the performance is stolen from the Rorschach inkblot test, a psychological test where people are asked to look at random ink blots. Based on their perceptions and certain parameters, the psychologist would be able to figure out the internal state of the mind. What interested me about this concept is that human beings have a tendency to make meaning out of something which has no meaning. I wanted to apply it to the idea of touch and intimacy, to the way that people interact with each other and how that is perceived by a third eye. (Naidu in Vakkalanka 2017)

Naidu's intention to shift the gaze from the inter/actions of the performers themselves to how audiences read them is critical here. At the heart of the piece then is its encounter between danced gestures of touch and the audience's responses to them, aimed to reveal their "tastes, tendencies, desires and prejudices" (Naidu in Vakkalanka 2017). Without their encounters with these gestures, Naidu's social and choreographic experiment would be incomplete. Thus, the audience's conceptual, emotional, visceral, and/or intellectual relationalities to these gestures, what they evoke in them, and more crucially what these responses reveal about them, are foundational to the design and intentionality of Naidu's choreography.

Thinking with indigenous dance artists and their dance-works, dance scholar Jacqueline Shea Murphy asserts that "relationality undergirds everything" (2022) and that these dance-works are premised by "human bodies coming and being and moving together in interconnection and exchange" (2022) with each other alongside non-human entities. Shea Murphy goes on to theorize an existence as "being within an expansive and felt relatedness in which these relations are kin and require upholding the responsibilities these relational connections carry" (2022). While Naidu's explorations of choreographic relationality seemingly does not extend beyond the human context, the proximity of the audience members to the choreographic world she conjures means that each body in the space, audience and performer, is bound up in an intricate and complex relational experience. This means all their individually and collectively internalized politics and stigmatizations of touch that permeate Indian sociality come alive and are simultaneously shattered and delicately negotiated through the performance encounter, which is designed on them coexisting, "being and moving together in interconnection and exchange."

In her intention to "normalize touch" by making her audience members confront their own "tastes, tendencies, desires and prejudices," Naidu's piece brings to life Sundar Sarukkai's theorization of touch in India as a moral-sense-driven activity. In placing the responsibility of unpacking their own socialized habituations and prejudices, Naidu is keen to create an experience of self-reflexivity in her audiences in a safe space, one that she curates with care.

> In India at least, touch is a loaded topic. . . . Underlying all our codes, rules and norms around how to touch or keep distance from other people is the subliminal belief that the world is not a safe space. Any experience that speaks to another possibility is therefore powerful and profound. (Naidu 2019)

I am curious though about the relationship between Naidu's claims of safety, or lack thereof, in the world at large and also in her dance studio, that she seemingly links to Indian sensibilities of social touch and the power regimes that underpin them. I am intrigued further by Naidu's insinuation of alternative and safer worlds that can come alive in choreographic experiments, beyond the constraints of such sociocultural codes, and their relationships to these power regimes. Even as she shares from her choreographic perspective that "when you watch and experience so much gentle and safe touching, your own relationship to touch changes" (Naidu 2022a), I cannot help wondering the following.

How can choreography become a critical intervention in deeply entrenched caste power regimes that forbid touch across Indian social hierarchies?
How can choreography expose deeply entrenched power regimes that result in violations of touch across Indian social hierarchies?
What are the ways in which, if any, choreography can promise us liberatory worlds beyond oppressive structures?

How can touch heal?

Can touch heal?

Whom can touch heal?

Who can heal with touch?

Whom did Rorschach Touch *heal?*

Whom did it harm?

When choreography endeavors to emancipate, this can perhaps only ever be a partial project. And we have to ask the question on whose terms is this emancipation imagined and experienced? We have already learned this from the now well-established critiques of CI that counter mythologizations of its deemed egalitarianism along the lines of race, gender, and caste, as discussed in the Introduction. In many ways, Naidu's choreographic experiment shares the same impetus as Steve Paxton's 1970s endeavor with CI, in their desire to democratize touch in movement experiments. However, Naidu's choreographic experiment goes further. I read it as a partial response to Steve Paxton's admission that perhaps oppressive structures and divides are so deeply engrained in our societies, that CI's democratic principles are not equipped to acknowledge or address these (Paxton in Mitra 2018). While Paxton arrives at this realization, Naidu starts from this premise, albeit in a partial manner in terms of the specific power asymmetries exposed by her project, and others that it invisibilizes. Where Paxton strives for a movement language that he advocates as fundamentally democratic, thereby ignoring the power regimes that are always already operating within dance practice, Naidu partially tunes into them, and places responsibility on her audiences to confront their own socialized understandings of the skin as a boundary-maintaining-moral-sense-organ (Sarukkai 2009). In doing so, Naidu places a partial wedge in the perpetuation of unequal power structures and makes her audience active participants in the discourse of social and choreographic touch in the Indian context. To understand Naidu's choreographic urge to make *Rorschach Touch*, to recognize the humanist love that shapes it, and to examine its partial engagement with social power asymmetries, it might be helpful to think through Naidu's own biographical contexts, its relationship to her performance training, and her own complex relationships to social touch.

Diya Naidu: Dancing Biographies, Choreographing Intimacies

Naidu is a Bangalore-based Indian dancer-choreographer, of mixed faith heritage, born and raised in Kolkata to a Muslim Bengali mother and a Hindu south Indian father who served in the Indian army (Naidu 2022a). Naidu describes her upbringing as deeply informed by a particular brand of secularism as championed by the Indian army, which, she believes, manifested in her father's life choices of marrying a Muslim woman and being surrounded by multi-faith, multilingual, and multiethnic peoples. While she claims that "all of this had been a big part of my identity," her own secular upbringing did not prevent her from being harassed for her part-Muslim and part–south Indian heritages in her privileged private school in Kolkata. In fact, she remembers feeling othered and reminded about "the non-homogeneity of [her] cultural upbringing and backgrounds" (Naidu 2022a) very clearly. However, she drew great strength and even fun from her multi-faith lineages, traversing between her maternal grandmother's home celebrations of Eid and her paternal grandmother's celebrations of Hindu worship seamlessly, punctuated by their annual family reunions over Christmas when her British family would visit. She recognizes that her experience of her Muslim heritage was markedly different and privileged in comparison to Muslim people growing up in socioeconomically deprived circumstances in contemporary India, or those who are having their rights to get an education at school while wearing the *hijab* stripped from them by the state, for instance.

One of the ways in which Naidu drew strength in belonging was with her swimming companions. Alongside her bharatanatyam classes in which she was enrolled on her father's insistence at the age of six, and with which she "shared a love-hate relationship" (Naidu 2016, 492), Naidu trained at school with her swimming team. She recognizes that she was likely a better dancer than a swimmer, but she "loved swimming more" (Naidu 2022a). This, she later realized, was not because she loved the act of swimming itself more, but that "feeling of being a part of a team" (Naidu 2022a), a community, unlike in her bharatanatyam classes. Further down the line, she was asked to make a choice between swimming and dancing, and much to her father's upset, "without batting an eyelid [she] chose swimming" (Naidu 2022a). She reflects on her choice and says: "what little me knew back then was that bodies need other bodies" (Naidu 2022a). Perhaps this is how she found ways to survive the othering she felt in her own skin, becoming one of many through a shared purpose.

While Naidu was clearly alert to how discriminations operated in India along lines of faith and ethnicity, she admits that she was less tuned into India's caste society:

Growing up and leaving Bengal and moving up north to Delhi, the caste thing really hit me ... the way that people talk to their domestic workers.

> It's not like such practices didn't exist in Kolkata where they will sleep on the floor, and will definitely not eat at the dining table, they'll have separate utensils ... this you can see everywhere in India. But in the north, it is as though [dominant caste people] would question their very existence.... Then I moved down south to Bangalore where I realized, oh damn ... *I* am upper caste. I had always thought, since I was half Hindu-half Muslim, that maybe ... I wasn't even aware of my own caste. But when other Naidus and Reddys would meet me in Bangalore and welcome me with a sense of pride, I asked myself "what does this mean?" I called my Dad and asked "what the hell does it mean to be a Naidu?" He didn't know. So, I called my oldest aunt and was told that Naidus are supposedly a land-owning caste. It's shameful really, because it means you are so privileged that you have never had to deal with one's own position in society. (Naidu 2022a)

Naidu's honest reflections on her late-in-life journey vis-à-vis caste-education echoes my own. The everyday invisibilization of India's caste system by and among dominant-caste people like ourselves, however, creates and sustains a gap, stopping our newfound criticality from actually changing our thoughts and actions in meaningful ways. Unless we allow ourselves to really tune in and question the core of our beings, a chasm is likely to remain in my writing and in Naidu's choreography that means that we refrain from contending with caste privilege in the way we contend with gender or racial privilege, in our lives and our works.

Naidu also identifies as a "movement artist" and she strongly believes that her movement training lends her the "primary tools for navigating the world and dealing with her own existential angst" (Naidu 2022a). She is an "ardent yoga practitioner" with a "background in kathak and bharatnatyam" and shares that if she could start her performance training career all over again, she would begin with "martial arts because the practice that changed [her] life was kalarippayattu" (Naidu 2022a) whose principles are foundational to her work. Naidu's most extensive movement training period transpired at the Attakkalari Centre for Movement Arts in Bangalore from 2006 to 2007 where she "trained in kalaripayattu, bharatnatyam, Western contemporary dance, contact work and other somatic practices" (Naidu 2016, 492), after which she stayed on as a company dancer until 2014. She reflects deeply on what her time at Attakkalari gifted her as a human, an Indian, and as a movement artist:

At Attakkalari, I discovered the possibilities of Western contemporary dance. Yet, strangely this environment was more "Indian" than any other I had been in! There were echoes of the guru-shishya relationship in our training, even as more Westernised systems of director, choreographer, dancer, employee nuanced our learning experience. It was an intense and fruitful time of my life and I learned more about being Indian and being seen as Indian, through my evolving relationship to dance practices and contemporary culture. The physical vocabulary I acquired was a unique manifestation of the Attakkalari's director Jayachandran Palazhy's training in the traditional forms of bharatnatyam, kathakali and kalaripayattu, layered with his many years of contemporary dance training in the UK. This, together with his deeply conceptual intelligence and research-driven process, produced a unique pan-Indian contemporary dance vocabulary. I loved this form and pushed with all I had to excel in it. I deeply grieved its loss when I left the company. (2016, 492).

With a keenness to explore how the rural, the global, the capitalist, and the urban coexist in Indian cities in bodily terms, Naidu set forth to make her own work, ever committed to comment on the complexities of contemporary India at these interstices. At the heart of her choreographic projects has been the urge to tackle gender politics in urban India, and her first piece, *The Red Dress Wali Ladki* (The girl belonging to the red dress), is a case in point. Through this piece, Naidu addressed head on "the violence that Indian women are subjected to in the nuanced and complex urban Indian city spaces" (2016, 493). In making and performing this piece within and beyond India, Naidu became particularly interested in speaking to Indian men in the audience, "especially the urban one, who claims empathy, shame and even hashtags and tweets his disapproval of such violence, but somehow, under the garb of political appropriateness, often remains apathetic and disengaged" (Naidu 2016, 493). Holding people in socially dominant positions to account has thus always been the driving force of Naidu's choreographic politics. But Naidu recognizes that speaking truth to power through art-making in contemporary India requires resilience:

My strategy to survive the challenging political upheavals has been intimacy. By that I don't mean having lots of sex or cuddling lots. But keeping in mind that the air we breathe in and share is intimate. Because the air I breathe out is the air you breathe in. Covid highlighted how intimately connected we are. Intimacy became a big entry point for me for me in my work. And relatedly, my other *dharma* as an artist is to listen to what is needed. I listen with my body to political and social needs around me. My body becomes the clue through which I listen to my community around me. (Naidu 2022a)

This deeply instinctual relationship with her own body and how it enables her to listen to the people is possible because of viewing her own corporeality as the one she trusts the most, because, as she recognizes, "whatever it does is truly mine" (Naidu 2016, 492). She has learned to lean in and listen to what she learns because of the body she lives and moves in, and this has enabled her to lean in and listen to the bodies of others around her.

Naidu's emphasis on listening to the needs of people around her, her sense of deep connectivity with community at a cellular level of breathing in and out, and her desire for human intimacy, not as sexual, but as modes for survival shapes the critical love she brings into *Rorschach Touch*. She recognizes, like Kwan, that human encounters across cultures are fundamentally fragile, and that they require sustained effort (Kwan 2021, 3). In *Rorschach Touch*, even as Naidu doesn't address the rootedness of closed-skinned-ness in the caste system, she reveals in her choreography an empathy for embodying "loss across translation, the failures and disappointments and sometimes the refusals, that define intercultural contact" (Kwan 2021, 3) that is the inevitable effort in listening across and between bodies and cultures. And I reiterate here, that as someone who has not experienced the performance live, but rather mediated by a video recording, it is very likely that my reading of the piece, as a nonparticipant audience member, watching the recording in 2022 in the UK, may well contribute to further layers of "loss across translation." The recorded medium, however, allows for a more nuanced analysis of the piece, enhanced by my ability to play, replay, rewind, fast forward, and pay attention to choreographic minutiae that is distinct from a live encounter. Thus, while the pandemic has hindered my chances to experience the piece live, YouTube has enabled a choreo-analysis of *Rorschach Touch* that ultimately shapes my own curated experience of Naidu's choreography, through un/making contact between my fingers and my laptop's keyboard, and by bringing my reading alive between Naidu's choreographic intentions and my own emerging knowledge of India's caste society and its strict codifications of touch. It has made the gaps between choreographic intentions and choreographic manifestations come alive. It is as though Naidu's search for intimacy and human connectivity through touch, as I witness it on my screen, is enhanced by a kind of choreographic intimacy between my screen and my fingertips. My ability to control what I see, when I see it, how I see it, and how many times I see it, transcends Naidu's choreography and becomes my own. And perhaps it is in its un/making as a choreography through my own fingertips that Naidu's love as method, and loss (and harm) its residue, really come alive.

Rorschach Touch: Love as Method and Loss (and Harm) as Residue

Naidu describes to me the material conditions that birthed *Rorschach Touch* because, she rightly insists, a dance-work "cannot be understood independently to the context and conditions in which it is made" (Naidu 2022b). After leaving Attakkalari in 2014 and in seeking ways to establish herself as an independent choreographer and dance artist, Naidu was approached by two women—friends, entrepreneurs, and dancers Sahiba and Aastha. They wanted Naidu to make a piece on them on a Rs 10,000 budget (approximately $120) in their tiny dance studio in Bangalore. Naidu accepted the invitation and started working with Sahiba and Aastha from 5:30 to 7:30 every morning, the only hours of the day when all three of them and their dance studio were available. For Naidu, this meant having to work with and around Sahiba and Aastha's energy levels after their long and hard-working days of teaching commercial dance classes. One morning the friends turned up very tired after long working hours the day before and on very little sleep. Naidu realized very quickly that she needed to change tack if she was going to make work in these constrained material conditions. She asked the dancers what they wanted to do that session, and they said that in all honesty they had nothing to give and simply wanted to sleep. So, Naidu asked them to do just so: to curl up, spoon into each other, and sleep. While they slept, or at least rested, Naidu observed them and their intimacies closely, in choreographic terms. She then slowly started to give them tiny instructions: raising a head and returning it to the floor, pulling the other back gently into the cuddle, wrapping an arm around the other, and so forth, until a little choreographic score of shared intimacies began to emerge. Exploring intimacies and play as integral to female friendships, this score developed into a twelve-minute piece titled

Raham (Urdu for compassion and also womb), which received a public showing. It is this showing that led to Naidu receiving a Rs 30,000 (approximately $360) grant from Gender Bender festival to create the next iteration of the project titled *Rorschach Touch*. For this iteration, a cast of four, two men and two women, came on board, and more permutation and combinations of gestural intimacies were choreographed into the work. Over the next few years, the piece shape-shifted into yet another iteration, still titled *Rorschach Touch*, this time commissioned by the Goethe Institute through a grant of Rs 1 lakh (approximately $1190). Naidu explains that as the budget for her project grew, the cast grew larger too and more men and women came on board. This enabled the project to also expand focus from intimacies and play to touch quite specifically. She also reflects that even as the themes of the piece expanded from the original focus on same gendered intimacies, gender and sexuality, more broadly, remained a consistent lens of inquiry in all iterations of the project. And finally, she shares that on reflection, the "rough and dirty aesthetic" (Naidu 2022b) that characterizes *Rorschach Touch* is integrally linked to the financial precarity that has been inherent in this project's birth and life. The iteration of *Rorschach Touch* that I analyze in this chapter was recorded at Shoonya on July 10, 2018, and was performed by Ajeesh Balakirshnan, Pia Bunglowala, Dayita Nereyeth, Priyabrat Panigrahi, Masoom Parmar, Nihal Pasha, Asha Ponikiewska, and Anishaa Tavag.

Rorschach Touch is more a social ritual experiment and less a staged dance performance. And its distinctive dynamic contract of intimacy with the audience are set up from the very beginning. It starts with an opening address to the audience followed by a group play of "touch-chase," laying bare swiftly the complex commentaries that Naidu wishes to make on India's vexed relationship to touch, community, intimacy, tenderness, and (social and physical) violence.

In an intimate holding space of an art studio that looks like a kitchen, the audience gathers as a poignant Malayali song filters through the space. Ajeesh Balakrishnan, the singer, meanders at a leisurely pace among the audience, smiling at them, and making meaningful eye contact. His energy is open, warm, welcoming. He walks up close to people, holding their gaze tightly with his own. He leans against the kitchen surface, placing the weight of his relaxed upper torso against the counter. He gifts them his song.

Open, warm, welcoming.

Another performer, Masoom Parmar, walks through the space with a Buddhist meditation bowl and a gong. He stands up upon an elevated level and gently strikes the bowl to command attention, and goes on to welcome the audience into the ritual that follows, inviting them to "move freely through the space as you watch, and come in really close if you choose to." He describes the space and its demarcations in the ritual room ahead, and makes clear that there is water in the space, should anyone be thirsty. Parmar's words humanize the ritual as he makes direct contact with each audience member, guiding them into a different mode of being in a performance experience. The codes of the proscenium arch are broken—the audience cannot hide behind and disappear in the darkness. The lights are as much on them as they are on the performers. Balakrishnan's melodious voice continues to fill the air as the audience is led into the performance space by Parmar, to the sound of the activated meditation bowl. Parmar opens the door to the empty studio space. He turns around one final time to the audience and offers one final provocation before allowing them into the space, "at what point does something enter your consciousness? Do you know?"

I will realize later that this becomes the haunting and foundational question that underpins everything we experience in the piece—it places heightened responsibility on how we read every detail on what we witness and experience.

As audience members start to walk into the studio with a mixture of trepidation and curiosity, performers walk up to individuals and gently pull them aside to whisper in their ears. We cannot hear what is said, but we sense from the different responses on the faces of those being whispered to that they feel safe in, and even amused by this gesture of intimacy. They listen with care. Some even walk up to the performers, wanting to be whispered to.

They yearn their whispers.
The whispers fold them into the ritual.
The ritual is now theirs and shared.

Gradually the audience settle down, positioned all around the studio space to create and frame a full 360-degree viewpoint. Their awareness is heightened toward anticipating something out of the ordinary. There is a gentle calm holding the space together.

Naidu's choreographic choices in this opening sequence foreground human connectivity and care—she choreographs contact between the audience and her performers beyond the physical dimension, seeking and establishing connections are multisensorial dimensions. She builds into this opening sequence in the most subtle and minuscule ways the intimacy she is aspiring to in her life and her art, enticing her audience into her journey. Balakrishnan's warm melody and disposition, the open and direct address from Parmar, the playful whispers into the ears of the audience, the invitation to sit really close if they wish to, all point to a new imaginary. Naidu choreographs a new space, devoid of the caution, the suspicion, the stigma, and the hierarchies that often underpin Indian social gatherings, especially among strangers; where actions insinuate intentions, words are left unspoken, and people occupy space with uncertainty and even terror; and some people are not allowed to occupy and share the same space at all. Instead, Naidu's choreography prepares us for a meditation, making us tune into our own inhalations and exhalations.

Parmar runs into the space and breaks the calm, swiftly making physical contact with a fellow performer. He playfully calls out "touch!," setting up a simple game of catch, where if they are paired up with a fellow performer then they cannot be "touched." The point of the game being to avoid being "touched." They throw themselves into this staged game of "touch-chase," with clear ground rules for engagement as the audience witness and experience them whizzing past, often very, very close to their own bodies, meandering in and around them. Some audience members clearly feel the risk and energy in the space as they shift their bodies briskly away from potential physical contact with the performers, charging through the space. The game turns intense and one of the performers even blows on a whistle to referee its intensity and ensure rules are in place.

There is as much joy in this ritual as there is a sense of edgy competition and tension.

There are patterns of collusions,
of ganging up,
of exclusions,
of belongings,
of non-belongings.
There is both comfort and discomfort.
In both those watching and those being watched.

Through this seemingly simple and harmless game of "touch-chase," Naidu invites us to become attentive to our social world of the playground, where power regimes control every tiny move and interaction. She makes a world through touch, while simultaneously unmaking our perception of it as harmless.

Watching this ritual unfold on my screen takes me straight back to the day my four-year-old daughter came home from her first year in primary school and, clearly concerned and upset, said that on the playground that day some of the boys were chasing her and her girlfriends, trying to kiss them. I asked calmly, "did you want them to kiss you?" She said, "no, definitely not!" She also said that when they went to the adult in charge on the playground and complained that their peers' behavior was upsetting them, they were told "it's only a game" and that they should ignore them. I thanked her for sharing her experience with me and for doing the right thing by seeking support from a grown-up in the space. I apologized to her that the grown-up in charge had failed her that day by not taking her concerns seriously. I wrote to the school to raise my own concerns about their irresponsibility in not teaching children about consent and bodily boundaries. Like my daughter, I too was dismissed with "they are only children," "it is all harmless fun," and "they were just playing."

But "they were just playing".
And it was harmful fun.
Consent. I told myself.
Was it her responsibility to say "stop!"?
Or their responsibility to not engage in coercion?
Or our collective responsibility as society to change the rules of this violent "game" irrevocably?

Consent. I told myself.
And agency. Her agency.
Consent. I told myself.
And power. Their power.
I raged within.
I feminist parented with more resolve.
I made it clear to my daughter that the complex power of touch is such that it can heal,
    humanize,
        communicate,
            forgive,
                comfort,
                    soothe,
                        and enable.
                                But it can also
                            violate,
                      dehumanize,
                repulse,
            offend,
        frighten,
      forbid,
    distance,
  locate,
and fix peoples and embodiments.

Naidu's choreography of the "touch-chase" exposes the seemingly democratic and simultaneously violent rituals of our children's playgrounds, revealing the power asymmetries that rip them apart. Their initial playfulness turns edgy, tense, antagonistic even. The audience watches, never intervening, just like the grown-up in my daughter's school playground, complicit in bearing witness to the regimes of powers that undergird this harmless fun ritual of "touch-chase." And all this gets heightened because the participants who get caught up in the game do so without being asked if they would like to participate in it. It is important to remember, of course, that all playful rituals, even those with fully consensual participants, teeter on the edges of risk-taking. Dance scholar Janet O'Shea's thinking on the complex relationships between play and consent seems paramount here. O'Shea asserts the centrality of consent in play while simultaneously signaling that what makes play compelling is its "potential to mess with perception, to alter perspectives, and to redefine negative, painful or frightening experience" (2019, 9). O'Shea contends that these qualities make play prone to risk-taking and exposes participants to potential danger. Naidu's choreography of "touch-chase" brings O'Shea's observations on consensual play and risk-taking alive in extremely compelling ways.

It is after all "only a game."

At one point the touch, the game, turns into a more substantial grab around the waist of Anishaa Tavag by fellow performer Priyabrata Panigrahi. Tavag distinctly vocalizes her discomfort.

Stop.
Consent.
Power.

The moment is fleeting, but chilling too. Panigrahi runs off before the moment can grow bigger and perhaps uglier.

Naidu's choreography magnifies the power implications of seemingly mechanical and harmless gestures of touching someone during play, gently or forcefully, and then running away. In the absence of consent in that moment before being touched, one's agency is stripped from them. Naidu, and O'Shea, remind us that games hoard power. Naidu exposes the fine line between the technicality of the task of touch and run, and the power that is calcified in that moment of contact, exerting itself onto the person who is

Image 2.2 Nihal Pasha and Asha Joanna Grażyna Ponikiewska Ranjan in *Rorschach Touch* by photographer Dannilla Correya

touched, and emanating from the person who is touching. In this opening game ritual, Naidu signals that an unmaking of closed-skinned-ness simultaneously requires an unmaking of power asymmetries along the lines of predominantly gender and sexuality. Other power regimes such as class, caste, ableism, are not referenced—but I am aware that they would further compound the interactions we have been witnessing.

As the piece moves on from the social dynamics of an ensemble, Naidu mobilizes duets to examine closer, and more intensely, social power asymmetries in different permutation combinations of variously gendered pairs, that stretch our imaginations in critical ways to consider what we read as intimate, what we read as familial, what we read as sexual, and indeed why we read what we read (Image 2.2). In this chapter I focus on the duets between Tavag and Panigrahi, Tavag and Asha Ponikiewska, Tavag and Dayita Nereyeth, and Parmar and Panigrahi. Following Kwan, I want to consider the duet, these duets, as an "expanded notion of partnership[s]" (2021, 15), beyond their limited associations with romantic love or sexual intimacies, even if at times they do conjure these energies. Like Kwan, then, I examine Naidu's unmaking of contact in these duets as a "feminist approach in order to advocate for the value of the intimate and the bodily, the relational and the affective, as key to intersubjective encounter in realms outside of the heterosexual" (Kwan 2021, 15). This chimes with Naidu's instinct to unmake

Indian closed-skinned-ness, beyond its stigmatized associations with the intimate, the romantic, and the sexual. My choreographic analyses operate at the intersections of Naidu's ideations and intentions, the dancers' material embodiments, and my readings of these interactions as an audience member. In this context it is important to acknowledge also that CI's original impetus had very similar aims in its wish to disassociate physical touch from romantic and/or sexual intimacies. However, the crucial difference between Naidu's and CI's intentions is the assumption in the case of the latter that bodies are somehow "neutral" in how they move through the world and devoid of both exerting and experiencing power in their interactions with each other. Naidu's duets begin their work with a keen recognition of this very reality and a desire to expose CI's pursuit and insistence on the "neutral."

After the chilling exchange of trying to grab Tavag around her waist during the heightened finale of the "touch-chase" sequence, Panigrahi runs through the space and lies down along the length of his left side, arm extended beneath him, supporting his weight. Tavag, having objected to being grabbed around her waist by Panigrahi, returns through the space to position herself behind him on the floor, and spoons herself along his spine, into an embrace, placing her chin into the crook of his waist. As he starts to move and sits up, Tavag maintains a shifting point of contact and adjusts herself so that she ends up lying with her head on his thighs. His focus is on her face, her focus away from his. He takes the longest time to gently caress her hair and turn her face to make eye contact with him. It is intimate. She gazes back momentarily before moving away, until they are spine-to-spine, and move into a contact improvisation sequence. Audience members respond to Parmar's earlier instructions and rearrange themselves on the floor to lean in, and take a closer look and experience their intimacy at close quarters. Unlike the expected smoothness and technical virtuosity that we have come to expect from contact improvisation duets, this exchange is rough in parts, jagged in others, exposing the discomfort that accompanies attempts at this seeming heterosexual partnership. It is also humanized and interspersed with moments of everyday gestures, where they touch their own bodies, mirroring each other. Tavag touches her own stomach over her clothes, exploring its contours, and finds Panigrahi moving in swiftly, his hands replacing hers on her stomach. The duet moves between intimacy, discomfort, interdependence. They test each other's ability to be there, to catch the other if and when they fall, to taunt the other toward taking more risks.

Panigrahi pulls Tavag onto his lap, as their faces come close to each other. He gently pushes her upper body away until she leans back on the floor. He inserts his hand underneath her shirt at her waist, and slowly allows his arm to travel up her midriff and between her breasts, beneath her shirt, appearing at the top of her shirt and gently pulling her back up by the back of her neck. Tavag breaks the tension of their highly erotic encounter by running, pushing, pulling—dissipating the sexual tension with frivolous play. It's a relentless game of trust-making that, for me, never seems to get there. And it is difficult to tell if Tavag feels fully like an equal in their encounter, because, choreographically, she does not seem able to exercise the same kind of power in the heteronormative power-game she finds herself in, in the way her partner, a man, can.

Kwan's conceptual and embodied understanding of the duet as relational and affective partnership comes alive in Tavag and Panigrahi's encounter.

I feel the intensity of their encounter emanate through the screen.

I feel the imbalance of gendered power choreographed into their relationality.

I feel the sincerity with which their encounter meanders
from curiosity
to play
to discovery
to risk
to the edges of violence
to exhaustion.

Perhaps Naidu wishes to expose the world of heteronormative
contact-making
for what it is;
Ever navigating gendered social norms and power,
Never in equilibrium.

The duet that follows between Asha Ponikiewska and Tavag reinforces my instincts as we witness and experience the dynamics of a close encounter of contact, this time between two women, Ponikiewska a white Pole and Tavag a brown Indian. Naidu's choreographic intentions become clearer as we find in Ponikiewska and Tavag's partnership visual and gestural echoes of Tavag's encounter with Panigrahi, but this time we become attentive to the dynamics of these gestures through this cross-racial and same-gendered pairing.

> *The gestures land so differently.*
> *The gestures read so differently.*

Naidu's choreographic strategy to position these two duets next to each other, the first between two similarly racialized people of different genders, and the second between differently racialized people who present as people of the same gender, calls out our internalized cisgenderism (Lennon and Mistler 2014) and our relationships to racial hierarchies simultaneously. We do not know anything about the genders of the performers or indeed the personas they embody in the piece. And yet we read them as man-woman and woman-woman partnerships. Simultaneously Ponikiewska's whiteness cannot not be seen as significant in the embodiment of their partnership, and impacts the ways in which we read the power dynamics between her and Tavag (Image 2.3).

Image 2.3 Asha Joanna Grażyna Ponikiewska Ranjan and Anishaa Tavag in *Rorschach Touch*
by photographer Dannilla Correya

Ponikiewska and Tavag start off asleep, spooned against each other, Ponikiewska's head nestled into the crevice of Tavag's waist, her arm gently lying across Tavag's upper thigh. Tavag rests, eyes closed, in familiarity and comfort.

They are entwined. They are at rest. They are one.

Parmar's meditation bowl gongs above them, and their peace is broken. Audiences reposition themselves yet again, around them, to get an even closer look. Tavag lifts her upper body, lifting Ponikiewska with her. Ponikiewska responds with gently returning her to the floor, back to the sleeping posture. Her arm moves from resting on Tavag's upper thigh to a full upper-body embrace, across Tavag's waist. Tavag tries again, and this time manages to sit up. But Ponikiewska remains sleepy, curled around her waist, her forehead on her upper thigh. They slowly readjust themselves around each other.

Always intimately entwined. Always interdependent. Always one.

Gestures from the previous duet echo in this one as Ponikiewska repeats the gesture of touching her own upper body, feeling for the contours of her stomach. But Tavag does not follow as her Panigrahi did, bearing witness instead to Ponikiewska's tracing of her own body. A similar playfulness and risk-taking ensues, but in this duet, the partners seem to be equals, not so much taunting each other as mutually supporting each other's energies. Tavag's disposition more assertive, less unsure. Ponikiewska more careful, less reckless. The trust seems to be more effortless. Tavag lies down on her back on the floor. Ponikiewska gently places her hand on Tavag's left knee, and then her right. The care in her hands is immense. She receives information through them, as opposed to extracting information from Tavag's knees.

The camera pans round the room, taking in the intensity and focus in the audience. Their gaze never averts, as they remain fully invested in the ritual, they are now firmly embedded in.

Naidu remains highly attentive to the gendered and racialized nature of touch and its repercussion in her choreography. And Tavag becomes the fulcrum for her commentary, shifting from her partnership with Panigrahi to her partnership with Ponikiewska, in two back-to-back duets. By choosing not to label these distinct partnerships as familial, romantic, sexual, or expressions of friendship, Naidu unmakes contact by placing the responsibility of engaging with what we are experiencing and witnessing on us at the audience, forcing us to question how we interpret these partnerships, why we interpret them the way we do, and more important, what it says about our own prejudices and stigmas within in the ways in which we read touch in social interactions, and the power

134 UNMAKING CONTACT

regimes we reinforce through these readings. For instance, if we read Tavag and Panigrahi's duet as primarily expressing sexual intimacy, and Tavag and Ponikiewska's partnership as primarily familial, perhaps that says more about our own constrained ways of thinking of gendered and racialized interactions in our social worlds. Perhaps the idea of a queer interracial duet between two women, full of tenderness, is more unsettling to us than the idea of a heterosexual couple where the man remains the dominant partner, mirroring social gender roles. The equilibrium of power I feel emanating from Ponikiewska and Tavag's same-gendered partnership finds a very different manifestation in two simultaneous duets that follow between Parmar and Panigrahi—two men, and Tavag and Dayita Nereyeth—two women.[1]

Generating an air of levity and flirtatious playfulness, Tavag and Nereyeth engage in an endless exchange of air kisses accompanied by sounds and gestures of smacking and pursed lips, and whose interaction ends with Tavag excitedly extracting Nereyeth's blown-up bubblegum with her mouth. The gesture is intimate, cheeky, funny, playful, sexy, and takes Nereyeth by total surprise. Tavag exercises a flirtatious power over her partner, coming incredibly close to her without actual making physical contact. Indeed the gesture of eating the bubble of her bubblegum out of her mouth is in many ways far more powerful and invasive than Panigrahi's meandering hand on her upper torso under her shirt, which builds steadily over time.

As Nereyeth catches her breath, unsure of what to make of Tavag's flirtatious and invasive move, another same-gendered encounter ensues between Parmar and Panigrahi and the expanse of a wall. Mirroring Tavag and Nereyeth's closely held mouths for the extraction of the bubble gum, Parmar and Panigrahi sit intimately entwined, eyes locked, their lips viscerally close to kissing, hovering erotically against each other. They are talking to each other, smiling, laughing, teasing by maintaining a thin layer of distance that keeps their lips from locking. Unable to contain the building sexual tension, Parmar pulls Panigrahi up to standing by his t-shirt at the neck and pushes him up against the wall, walking right past and grazing the shoulder of a man in the audience. Their desire is mutual and their power symmetrical, leading to a charged eroticism that verges between tenderness and violence. The intensity of their erotic encounter is situated right next to audience members who cannot take their eyes of Parmar and Panigrahi, while also deeply uncomfortable to be bearing witness to it. This charged queer eroticism is dissipated by Tavag and Nereyeth, who both watch the men from the other side of the room, and pretend to copy their intimacy, accompanied by giggles of embarrassment (Images 2.4 and 2.5).

Image 2.4 Priyabrata Panigrahi and Masoom Parmar in *Rorschach Touch* by photographer Dannilla Correya

Image 2.5 Priyabrata Panigrahi, Masoom Parmar, and Diya Naidu in *Rorschach Touch* by photographer Dannilla Correya

I am left wondering if this is Naidu's attempt to expose societal homophobia against partnerships between men, by making Tavag and Nereyeth embody what many in the audience might well be feeling. And if so, then in this attempt, what are the risks she is taking of reinforcing homophobia itself against not only partnerships between men, but also intimacies between two women?

As Parmar and Panigrahi's erotic encounter finishes with Parmar walking away, Tavag and Nereyeth's kissing game returns, and this time, taking

Nereyeth by surprise yet again, with no bubblegum in the way as a protective layer, Tavag plants a kiss directly on her lips. And giggles. Nereyeth smiles and then returns the kiss, with more intention, savoring it with more time. And they walk up to a man in the audience and Nereyeth asks "you want?" and he, with joyous glee, responds with "why not?"

Through these two duets that are placed alongside each other, Naidu forces us to think in the most expansive ways about queerness, as not just pertaining to homosexual desire and expression but also non-normative with regard to gender norms. Naidu's choreography exploration of queerness mirrors Los Angeles–based Black queer artist Diedrick Brackens's thoughts on queerness in an interview with TK Smith, on being asked what a queer relationship might look like:

> I think I am trying help broaden my own understanding of what queerness looks like without thinking about sex.... I would like to imagine that I could be intimate with a broad range of folks who don't identify as queer, in the same way that I would be with people who do. That's a very complicated space to access, especially with other men. I'm often thinking about making an image where the two bodies could be thought of as lovers, as brothers, as father and son, but knowing that reality doesn't quite exist. That queerness gets read into those images is something I'm really excited about because I think it expands the idea of what queerness is in nonromantic relationships. To be a straight man and have this moment with a son, if that's coded as queer, then what potential is there for queerness to be this thing beyond sex—to be familial—is what's interesting to me. Queerness could save the world on some level. (in Smith 2019)

In the spectrum of queerness that we witness in the distinct encounters between Tavag and Ponikiewska, Tavag and Nereyeth, and Parmar and Panigrahi, Brackens's conjuring of queerness in nonromantic relationships comes alive, pushing the boundaries of queerness beyond romantic love into familial love and friendship intimacies.

Afterthoughts and Reflections

Through these carefully choreographed partnerships that unmake contact, Naidu joins the dots between her own survival instinct of seeking out intimacies, and her social critiques of the one-dimensional ways in which India's closed-skinned-ness pathologizes and stigmatizes such intimacies and touch. In this endeavor, *Rorschach Touch* teeters between successfully critiquing power regimes along the lines of gender and sexuality and, at times, bolstering them as dominant social forces. It is forthright in its choreographic choices, never dancing around them to bring queer intimacies to life. The piece is confident in its intentions to confront audiences' predispositions and prejudices and makes no excuses for providing us with palatable ways to admit to our own internalized biases. It does not pander to lulling audiences into complacency or even zones of comfort. It confronts Indian closed-skinned-ness vis-à-vis gender and sexuality head-on, placing the responsibility of processing any discomfort that arises from the performance encounter on the audience. Its choreography wants to unmake how we connect in our social interactions, by asking us what we read into our interactions, and how and why. Naidu's love for human connectivity is undeniable, and as Kwan reminds us, her choreography reinforces too that while "the motivation for intimacy can be love, ... loving is not always the same as intimacy" and that "sometimes the act of loving requires distance, not knowing, not connecting" (2021, 18). Her choreographed duets in variegated forms as analyzed above embody Kwan's call for uncertainty, "as ongoing, always stumbling, *acts of loving*" (2021, 18). But as Kwan continues to argue, these loving acts of stumbling inevitably generate loss, and I argue, potential harm, because "engaging across difference is unavoidably imbued with the failure to apprehend" (Kwan 2021, 18).

The harms I argue that are potentially generated through the inevitable loss that becomes the residue of working across difference, transpire at multiple levels. First, the very power regimes of gender and sexuality that *Rorschach Touch* takes on are, in moments, potentially crystallized and reinforced in these duets. The fine line between inviting an audience to confront their own prejudices via their encounter with non-normative gender presentations and sexualities, and the reinforcement of dominant representations of gender and sexuality, is a risk that the piece takes. And it sometimes does not pay off. Second, and relatedly, the piece's engagement with gender politics remains partial in its reach. Although we do not know the gender identities of any of the performers, the piece reinforces a binarized gendered world of men and women only. This becomes a missed opportunity to consider how contact is made and unmade between and across gender-nonconforming and non-binary peoples. Naidu's challenge to the audience to question our own inherent cisgenderism is not held up in her own choreographic choices. Third, in her choreographic embodiments of queer intimacies, Naidu both makes space for depicting the ways in which contact is made and unmade between queer subjects. However, envisioned through her own cisgender and heterosexual positionality, these depictions are inevitably limited, even as some queer subjects occupy these pairings. Consequently, their queer embodiments are mediated via Naidu's own non-queer aesthetic, sensibilities, and lived reality. Finally, and most important, Naidu's understanding of Indian closed-skinnedness disregards its rootedness in the caste politics of untouchability. This becomes an unfortunate oversight to acknowledge that the very stigmas that code Indian touch and touching, that she is so deeply invested in questioning and dismantling, are Brahminical in essence, and shape our everyday social codes and moralities. Thus, the moral policing of touch and contact, via the surface of our skins, is a boundary Naidu inadvertently and partially upholds in *Rorschach Touch*. However, as I signal earlier in this chapter, Kwan's offering of the evolutionary potential in artists of "obstinate, continual growth, not in spite of loss but in the shape of it" (Kwan 2021, 5) is visible in Naidu's *Hands and Face Project* (2017). In this work, Naidu takes on the stigma against, and denial of, cross-gender, class, and caste contact-making and intimacy-building that constitute urban Indian sociality. In this beautiful film Naidu places her own *savarna*, multi-faith, class-privileged womanhood in intimate interaction with a series of men from across class, caste, and faith locations, in different Bangalore city locations. The film traces Naidu's journey of staring into the eyes of these men, one at a time, and in some rare instances offering them a tough-gift akin to the gestural offerings we see at the end of *Rorschach Touch*. At times, Naidu's gestures are returned with sincerity and care. At other times, they are received but not reciprocated. The carefully crafted touch-gifts in the dance studio between the audience and the *Rorschach Touch* performers find, in this project, a very different manifestation and generates very different meanings. There are social risks involved for all participants—Naidu included—for such flagrant and public dismantling of social codes around touching and being touched by total strangers. As the film develops, Naidu's contact making expands to stare into the eyes of women. And interestingly, the dynamic of these same-gendered encounters are more unsure, more hostile, more awkward. Naidu's *Hands and Face Project* further reveals the complexities of touch within India's social landscape. In taking on gender, class, caste, and faith in her choreographic dismantling of the stigma of touch in India in the public and urban space, Naidu's intentions come closer to Akila's anti-caste choreography through inter-caste intimacies as discussed in Chapter 1. *Hands and Face Project* offers us glimpses of Naidu's growth as a human and a choreographer in the shape of the loss generated by *Rorschach Touch*, guided by love and un/learning.

Thus, despite its shortcomings, *Rorschach Touch* is a milestone inquiry that locates in Indian contemporary dance a crucial challenge to Indian society to confront and dismantle its stigmatized relationship to touch and touching. In interacting with it, it thus necessarily requires us to confront our closed-skinned-ness, and lean into the challenges Naidu poses through her choreography—vis-à-vis the many power regimes that constitute Indian socialities. In this, it is a call for "loving over loss and of learning how to connect, impossibly" (Kwan 2021, 31).

References

Graybill, Rhiannon. 2017. "Critiquing the Discourse of Consent." Journal of Feminist Studies in Religion 33 (1): 175–176.

Kwan, SanSan. 2021. Love Dances: Loss and Mourning in Intercultural Collaboration. New York: Oxford University Press.

Loick, Daniel. 2019. "'. . . as if it were a thing.': A Feminist Critique of Consent." Constellations 27: 412–422.

Mitra, Royona. 2010. "Living a Body Myth, Performing a Body Reality: Reclaiming the Corporeality and Sexuality of the Indian Female Dancer." In The Feminism and Visual Culture Reader, edited by Amelia Jones, 560–570. London: Routledge.

Mitra, Royona. 2018. "Talking Politics of Contact Improvisation with Steve Paxton." Dance Research Journal 50 (3): 6–18.

Murali, Sharanya. 2023. *Informal comments on chapter draft*. Unpublished.

Naidu, Diya. 2016. "Essai: Dancing for an India That Has Seen the World." Theatre Dance and Performance Training. Special Issue: "Intercultural Acting and Actor/Performer Training" 7 (3): 492–492.

Naidu, Diya, 2019. *Personal communication via email with the author*. February 28.

Naidu, Diya. 2022a. *Interviewed by the author via Zoom*. June 9.

Naidu, Diya. 2022b. *Personal communication with the author via WhatsApp*. October 7.

O'Shea, Janet. 2019. Risk, Failure, Play: What Dance Reveals about Martial Arts Training. New York: Oxford University Press.

Paterson, Mark, and Martin Dodge. 2016. Touching Place, Placing Touch. Abingdon: Routledge.

Sarukkai, Sundar. 2009. "Phenomenology of Untouchability." Economic & Political Weekly 44 (37): 39–48.

Shea Murphy, Jacqueline. 2022. Dancing Indigenous Worlds: Choreographies of Relation. Minneapolis: University of Minnesota Press.

Smith, TK. 2019. "Queer Intimacy: A Conversation with Diedrick Brackens." Art Papers. Accessed June 1, 2022. https://www.artpapers.org/queer-intimacy-a-conversation-with-diedrick-brackens/.

Vakkalanka, Harshini. 2017. "The Perception of Touch: Diya Naidu Wanted to Apply the Concept of Touch and Intimacy to the Way People Interact with Each Other." The Hindu: Lifestyle. Accessed June 1, 2022. https://www.thehindu.com/life-and-style/the-perception-of-touch/article19187501.ece.

3
Contact as Ecological Relationality

Mirror Within (2022) by Nahid Siddiqui and Shakila Maan and Touch without Tactility

It's 2001 and I am sitting in the Purcell Room at the Royal Festival Hall in London. My anticipation knows no bounds as I wait to watch the British-Pakistani kathak maestro Nahid Siddiqui live, for the very first time, in Scene Unseen *(2001)*, described as a homage to the four cosmic elements of air, earth, fire, and water. Earlier in the year I have discovered Siddiqui's dance-art while studying for my MA in performance at a UK university—exploring a curriculum so steeped in white-US-Europeanness—that I find myself seeking out racially minoritized dance artists of Global South heritages. I am yearning to learn from other ways of knowing, being, and moving as I find myself really missing kathak, the dance that I trained in from a young age in India. I am particularly mourning my relationship to kathak because, through my undergraduate and postgraduate studies in performance in the UK, in many instances when I have drawn on kathak in my performance work, I have been discouraged from, even disparaged for, doing so. I can sense that my university learning spaces are undergirded by asymmetries of power. They not only hierarchize the relationships between us learners and our educators, but also uphold the erasures of knowledge systems that we learners bring into the space, in favor of those that our educators want to impart to, impose upon, us. The latter is always deemed as more valuable. These carefully crafted contractual contact junctures in the performance studios, between us as racially minoritized students and a white dominant and dominating faculty and curriculum that does not reflect our realities, are unsettling and demoralizing, to say the least. So, sat in the Purcell Room that evening, I know full well that, on this occasion, I am seeking solace and growth in the dance I know, and love, and miss within my sinews. What I do not know, however, and could never have anticipated, is the extent to which I shall encounter kathak anew in Siddiqui's art. When

I finally leave the experience that night and walk along the South Bank, I am transformed. And yet, I cannot quite put into words what it is that I have experienced.

It is drizzling as I walk along the Thames;
that British drizzle that is soul-destroying for those of us who grew up in warmer climes;
that British drizzle,
like British racism,
that soaks through your layers and chills you to the bones;
that British drizzle that is incessant, and that I usually avoid at all costs.

And yet that evening, as the drizzle continues to moisten my hair and face,
I feel alive and alert.
I don't want the drizzle to stop.
It is as though the drizzle on my skin, as I walk outdoors,
is the drizzle of rain that Siddiqui conjured within the auditorium;
the drizzle that graced her skin.

As though my drenched face and arms outdoors are nothing but an extension of Siddiqui's dampened face and arms indoors.
As though, in invoking rain within, Siddiqui had invoked rain without, over the London skyline along the Thames.

But it doesn't take me to walk out of the Purcell Room and into the London night to actually feel the rain on my lips. Sat in my seat that evening, I feel the droplets vicariously through Siddiqui as she summoned the rain on her skin,
her face,
her spine,
her arms,
her hair,
her hands
in her dance.

As Siddiqui worked intimately with an evocative sound composition of rain, I shall never forget experiencing her undulate her spine, ever so subtly and joyously, to register the first drop of imaginary rain that made contact with her body. As she continued to allow different parts of her body to register more and more drops of rain, I experienced what can only be described as an illusory torrential monsoon downpour within the auditorium, brought to life through intimate and sensual interactions between Siddiqui's body and the rain-sound composition. But this was no Sridevi's rain-dance-sequence in Mr India, *as discussed at length in the Preface to this book.*

> **This was, instead, a meditation,**
> **a prayer,**
> **a du'a.**
> **To rain.**
> **And to all life it brings forth on earth,**
> **in all its complex relationality.**

More than two decades later, undertaking research for this book, during an interview with myself, Siddiqui mentions that perplexed UK audiences, with their disdain for rain, often ask her why she repeatedly conjures this natural phenomenon in her dance (Siddiqui 2023). And finally, I understand why her invocation of rain was as impactful as it was, sat in the Purcell Room in 2001. Because, she says, the arrival of rain on the arid terrains of Central Asia, where she locates her journey and knowledge-making of kathak, is a moment of sheer joy and gratitude for its people.

Indeed, it is these same parched landscapes that are evoked in the opening scenes of *A Thousand Borrowed Eyes* (1995), a documentary on Siddiqui by the British-Asian filmmaker Shakila Taranum Maan.[1] Shot from above, looking onto an outdoor location in a quarry in Birmingham (UK) that is reminiscent of sun-scorched desertscapes, and framed by the life-affirming presence of a green branch of a tree that dances in the wind at the bottom of the screen, Siddiqui completes incessant *chakkars*, the spins that characterize kathak, to the lyrics of an Urdu song, in praise of thunder and rain. It is the arrival of rain that creates an ecological balance in these parched lands, bringing forth more greenery, and thus life itself. As Siddiqui whirls, her spinning shadow on the dry landscape creates an illusion of multiple moving peoples. Somewhere, her gyrating form, the dancing green branch of the tree, and the barren desert lands are in intimate conversation—each a manifestation of life on earth that must remain in symbiotic contact with each other to survive and thrive. The documentary ends on a contemplative image of Siddiqui looking up to blue skies, while grounded firmly on dry terrains, as her voice-over makes clear the entwined connection between her own life force and her art:

> There were some questions in my mind.
> Why ... why do I dance?
> I only know how to live through this.
> I have to live, so I will breathe.
> And my breath is dance.
> So I will go on. (Siddiqui in Maan 1995)

Her image gradually morphs from being present within the arid lands, where she began her journey, willing rain, onto an expanse of golden yellow mustard fields of Elstree (UK), made possible by rain. She moves through the fields at a meditative pace and in complete coexistence with her environment and her ecological companions. As I watch this documentary on a loop for my research, I finally start to understand the ways in which Siddiqui's intimate relationship with nature and her surrounding ecosystems interlock firmly within her intimate relationship with dance, and the two are always found in synergistic dialogue in her art. This ecological relationality that is so central to Siddiqui's art is in deep, if unconscious, conversation with the concept of relationality that is central to indigenous studies and thought, as I have already signaled in Chapter 2 through the words of Jacqueline Shea Murphy, where the connection between human and non-human entities is theorized as undergirding everything (2022). In this chapter I argue that Siddiqui's art does not just embody such ecological relationality between humanity and its non-human companions, but more important, it signals the unraveling of ecological harmony and balance when such relationality comes under threat. In this, Siddiqui's art speaks to the thinking of dance scholar María Regina Firmino-Castillo in her writing on the Mayan "Kaqchikel concept of 'ruximik qak'u'x' ("the binding of hearts")":

> It is a theory of an always and already present relationality between humans and other beings, both material and immaterial, who demand recognition and reciprocity, and who, when not attended to, can make themselves

seen, heard, and felt in ways that can be disruptive, and even dangerous. (2020, 32)

Firmino-Castillo continues to explain that when as human beings we "are not engaged in these corporeal enactments of reciprocity, the beings we are inescapably entangled with feel ignored; they become louder, manifesting as illness, ecological devastation, social violence, and death" (2020, 33). Siddiqui's art is attentive to this need to both acknowledge and work toward sustaining this human–non-human interdependency and ecological relationality, without which, she tells me, climate catastrophe is inevitable (Siddiqui 2023). While clearly in dialogue with indigenous knowledge systems in this regard, Siddiqui embodies this philosophy in her art via Sufism. Her art responds unconsciously to Firmino-Castillio's questions to dance-makers:

> With what acts do we acknowledge—or not—the inextricable ties that bind us to the abject, the strange, the toxic, and the viral near us, around us, and within us? What forms of corporeal dialogue do we enter into with these beings with whom we are entangled, and who are here to stay? Finally, what worlds do we bring forth with our acts? (2020, 34).

A Thousand Borrowed Eyes effortlessly captures Siddiqui's Sufism-informed embodied provocation to the kathak world in the documentary when she proclaims "when you harmonize with nature, then you are doing kathak" (in Maan 1995). And it is this provocation that is the starting point of my chapter, catalyzing me to examine Siddiqui's unique embodiment of kathak as an ecological meditation, resting on a complex and beautiful relationality between the interiority of her womanhood, the exteriority of the environment in which she dances, and its connections to non-human living beings at large. As I process Siddiqui's words that signal this fundamental relationality—a contact, between nature, and ecosystems, and kathak—I realize that in all my time I have encountered kathak as an audience member and/or a student, I have not been made to consider the form's ecological dimensions. Indeed, my experience of kathak has been predominantly shaped by Hindu mythological narratives of divine characters and/or human stories of desire and love. In all these contexts, the human form, the human story, the human existence has always prevailed, taken up the most space. Siddiqui's approach unsettles kathak's focus on such human supremacy, and invites us to necessarily consider humanity's ecological relationality in and to the non-human world. Aligned with Sufism's foundational practice of caring for, protecting, and living with the environment (Qudosi 2010), Siddiqui's own desire "to connect to the sky and the earth at the same time, feeling the core of my existence at the centre of the Universe as my navel" (Siddiqui in Sadler's Wells 2022) comes alive in this chapter's subject of analysis, the dance-film *Mirror Within* (2022). Commissioned by Sadler's Wells with a surprisingly low budget of £3,000–4,000 that Maan describes as symptomatic of "an afterthought," and yet another example of Siddiqui's continued minoritization in the British South Asian dance sector (Maan 2023), this is the second collaboration between Siddiqui's choreography and Maan's filmmaking. I examine this dance-film at the intersections of feminism, ecology, and Sufism, arguing that Siddiqui's anti-patriarchal choreography emerges at the junctures between her own selfhood and its relational synergies with her ecological surroundings.

I come to this chapter as an outsider at many dimensions, in many ways echoing my relationship to *Theenda Theenda* in Chapter 2, but for very different reasons. My dialogue with Siddiqui and Maan over their dance-art and film-art respectively, their feminist and ecological politics, and their Sufism and agnosticism respectively, is intergenerational, even as we share spaces and struggles in the British South Asian diaspora. I am a first-generation immigrant in the UK and moved here from India in the late 1990s for my university education. Siddiqui is a first-generation immigrant in the UK and moved here from Pakistan in 1979, in her twenties, as an exile. Maan is a first-generation immigrant in the UK and moved here from Kenya in the 1970s with her family whose ancestry traces back to the Punjab region of north India.[2] Our experiences of immigration are thus distinct. As an Indian-heritage woman, my analysis of *Mirror Within* and its call for gender and ecological justice does not, and cannot, embody Siddiqui's perspective as a Pakistani woman and her experience and critique of Pakistani patriarchy, or Maan's British-Pakistani experiences of racial and gender-based discriminations. While we all share an understanding of spirituality as divorced from organized religion, Maan's inherited understanding of Sufism as an agnostic is distinct from my own perspective as a person of non-faith, and I have come to encounter and engage with Siddiqui's Sufi practice in her kathak from a place of complete ignorance. My sustained engagement with Siddiqui's embodiment of kathak as relational to ecology has opened my eyes to the importance of intimate relationships between art and nature, and between human and non-humans, in ways I had never considered before. To think with Siddiqui's decentering of human supremacy in her art has been transformative. And so, to close these gaps of embodied understandings on my part, in this chapter I foreground Siddiqui's voice, the perspectives of Sufi scholars and ecologists, and the scholarship of Pakistani feminists as leading lights in their fields.

Dancing Her Father's Calligraphy: Siddiqui's Childhood and Dance in Pakistan

Nahid Siddiqui was born in 1956 in Rawalpindi in Pakistan to actor and singer Talat Siddiqui and government civil servant Mohammad Bashir Siddiqui. Her childhood, which she describes as "something out of a film" (Siddiqui 2020), prepared her for the many adversarial circumstances she would go on to face through life, while fighting for her right to dance in her own country. She reminisces viscerally about her childhood calligraphy lessons with her father, to whom she ascribes her aesthetic and somatic sensibility, that enabled her to cultivate her own supple, strong, and upright spine. The conceptual and embodied connection she draws between her strokes of calligraphy on the page and her own moving spine and limbs as she dances, she claims, is the earliest foundation of her kathak through which she "dances [her] father's calligraphy" (Siddiqui 2020) to life. She equally remembers being humiliated in front of her class by her primary school teacher, who read aloud her essay where Siddiqui wrote that she wanted to be an actress like her mother when she grew up, because she was her role model. She remembers too her mother meeting with the school principal to complain about the incident, to "give the teacher a piece of her mind" (Siddiqui in Ahmed 2007). Eldest of her three siblings, Siddiqui was inspired by her mother, a strong woman who found herself supporting her family through challenging and unforeseen circumstances:

> I remember seeing my mother as a very strong woman. When I was about seven, Ayub Khan came to power and my father, a government servant, was sentenced to jail for 10 years because he had allegedly printed material against martial law. . . . At the time that my father was imprisoned, my mother used to wear a burqa. She was educated till about 5th grade. Our neighbour was a news reader at the time, Shakeel Ahmed. He suggested that my mother, instead of going to relatives for financial help, give interviews at the Radio Station to see if she could sustain her family by her own earnings.

She liked this idea and passed the station tests for singing and acting. She became a star. (Siddiqui in Ahmed 2007)

These unsettling years during her childhood led her to become "very quiet and mature" (Siddiqui 2020), as Siddiqui watched her mother take on the roles of both primary carer and earner at once for three children, while absorbing the absence of their father. She is certain that "this incident had a lot to do with my dancing, because I could not express myself in other ways" (Siddiqui in Ahmed 2007). Siddiqui continues:

When my father was released from jail after two years, I remember he was shocked to find my mother's face on billboards. He could not adjust in the beginning and they came close to leaving each other. But he quietly appreciated my mother for not approaching anyone for support. His world changed. My mother was now the breadwinner. Her work brought us to Lahore in 1969. (Siddiqui in Ahmed 2007)

In Lahore, Siddiqui enrolled herself onto a degree program on her mother's request and started her *seena baseena* (one-on-one) kathak training with her guru Maharaj Ghulam Hussain. She claims that once she started her immersive education with Hussain, "everything else became meaningless" (Siddiqui in Ahmed 2007), as she was absorbing not only the technique of the art form, but more important, Hussain's underpinning philosophy of love and compassion as her friend, guide, and pedagogue. Siddiqui describes her training with Hussain as "holistic and expansive" (Siddiqui 2020) and admits that while this made her understand the arts in the most capacious of ways, she did crave a more disciplined approach to training. This led her to seek his permission to travel to India to continue to finesse her kathak artistry with Pandit Birju Maharaj.[3]

Siddiqui's kathak trajectory in Pakistan needs to be understood within the context of Pakistani culture's apathy toward dance as a worthy art form, which continues into the present day. Pakistani dancer-activist Sheema Kermani historicizes this cultural contempt for dance in Pakistan as it manifests in contemporary society and argues "that the policies followed by Pakistan result in making its cultural wealth vulnerable and endangering the life of its cultural exemplars," resulting in dance "being pushed to the edges of precarity" (Kermani 2022, 56). Siddiqui echoes Kermani's despair at the continuing disparagement of dance, especially for women, in present day:

> In Pakistan I am still dealing with hierarchies. They have taken this impression of Islam that women should not be dancing. The problem with hierarchies is that their notions are so fixed. There is only mediocrity. Dance is such a subject that it is not even seen as a subject. It is seen as entertainment. Nobody is going to take it up as a serious profession. There are no platforms. They will come and watch my performance, they will bring their daughters, but they will never consider enrolling them in classes. It will only ever be a hobby. (Siddiqui 2023)

In an interview with Siddiqui in 2022, Pakistani television presenter Sophia Khan maps the devaluing of dance in Pakistani culture further:

> As Pakistanis we have failed to embrace [dance]. I want to talk about dance, particularly its struggles in today's Pakistan. Dance, as I call it, the stepchild of the arts in Pakistan has taken a beating since the inception of the country. (Khan S. 2022).

In this interview, Khan goes on to trace the position of dance in Pakistani culture, immediately post-independence in 1947 and into the twenty-first century. She reminds us that soon after independence, the arts were actually held with reverence, dance academies existed, and children were encouraged to be immersed in singing, dancing, and musical instrument lessons. In the 1970s, broadcaster, producer, and director Zia Mohyeddin was appointed as director of the PIA (Pakistan International Airlines) Arts Academy. He invited Siddiqui, at the time a student of Hussain, to join the academy and thus placed dance at its heart. In 1976, the first national televised broadcast of kathak performance in the history of Pakistan took place. Siddiqui featured in the thirteen episodes that were filmed, but only six were broadcast, before shifting political landscapes in Pakistan resulted in General Zia-ul-Haq taking over with his military regime in 1979. Under this regime, all dancing was prohibited, and thus the remaining episodes were banned from being aired. The regime's "Islamization agenda" led to a 1980s legislation that "banned any woman from wearing *ghungroos* and dancing on stage" (Khan S. 2022). The impact of these legislations continue to manifest in Pakistani culture today. Nadia Khan writes in conversation with Pakistani dancer Nighat Chaodhry that these legislations that banned dance led to a particular phenomenon in and vis-à-vis Pakistan:

> On an international stage, many would presume that there is no dance heritage in Pakistan, which could not be further from the reality. Despite the strict edicts from those in power, it has not been an easy task to eradicate dance and expression; and Pakistanis continue to dance with folk dances being extremely popular. (Khan N. 2021)

Alongside these folk dances, a whole other underground layer of dancing continued to proliferate with the commercialization of *mujras*—a genre that became the domain of working-class women's entertainment, as captured evocatively in Saad Khan's recent documentary *Showgirls of Pakistan*, "deemed too vulgar, sexualized and lowbrow according to the middle-class morality standards and for the elite" (Khan Sa. 2017). But the lack of state patronage and proactive vilification of dance as un-Islamic, and thus potentially too Indian, resulted in the dance as an art form being associated through patriarchal discourse with immorality and cultural impropriety.

Siddiqui describes the injunctions that were placed upon dance in Pakistan during the military regime, and indeed on her own movements within and without the nation, during this time:

> The minister of culture at that time came to the television studios and said that this is not Muslim culture, or Pakistani culture. That a woman should not be dancing and it is not a good example for our younger generations. Then I really couldn't even practice dance in Pakistan.... I was not allowed to go out of the country also. And they said—your name is on a black-list. They made me sign a document that I will not dance anywhere in the world, unless the government of Pakistan wants me to. (Siddiqui in Khan S. 2021).

Caught in an impossible political bind in her own country, and enabled by the mobility afforded to her by her class privilege, in 1979 Siddiqui sought refuge in the UK, which she has since made her home. For the next two decades, while living in exile from Pakistan, Siddiqui would not be able to dance publicly in her home country except under very "adversarial circumstances" (Khan S. 2021), enabled by the support of her art patrons. She would only return to her first openly public performance in 1997, after the end of the military regime, to a very emotional homecoming performance.

Written into the sinews of Siddiqui's relationship to kathak, then, is an embodiment of dance born of struggle and resilience, seeking liberation from intersectional shackles of patriarchy and a deeply conservative, nationalistic, interpretation of Islam. By having resisted the idea of being relegated to "the kitchen—or most probably in purdah" as a Muslim woman, and taking up dance seriously as "work," Siddiqui has put her own body on the line repeatedly (Siddiqui in Maan 1995). This has made dance for her a fundamentally political and simultaneously an anti-fundamentalist act. It has inculcated in Siddiqui an understanding of dance beyond boundaries:

> I don't want to have anything to do with boundaries of any culture or religion. I don't want to ever be a rigid person. Fundamentalists? I am not one of them and I don't approve of them. So, I have to take risks, put my life at risk. I have to go on dancing. (Siddiqui in Maan 1995).

It would have been so easy for Siddiqui's relationship to kathak to be one of resistance alone. And yet, it is much more about harmony and healing, as this chapter will go on to demonstrate. Yes, Siddiqui's kathak is distinct because it carries within its sinews the art of putting her body on the line. Yes, she understands the risks involved in doing so. Yes, she understands that some factions of her own society are deeply threatened by the act of dancing. Yes, she understands the needs to keep dancing despite such oppressive forces. And yet, she also simultaneously knows the healing that can be derived from dancing, not just for herself but also for the environment in which she dances. To her, kathak is much less an exhibitionistic display of virtuosic skill, and much more a meditation on the human condition in dialogue with her environment.

Dancing kathak in the UK in the 1980s presented its own challenges for Siddiqui, as she found herself among kathak artists who did not share or understand the particularities of her own journey with the form. I ask Siddiqui what she thinks distinguishes her art from that of kathak dancers of predominantly Indian heritage in the UK. She says, firstly, it is her existential approach to the dancer as a holistic entity whose actions have consequences on their environments beyond the stage, and who are not distinct from their art, "because you are what you do" (Siddiqui 2023). Secondly, she recognizes that moving to the UK required her to find her own kathak, as she found herself in a landscape led by predominantly Hindu Indian women who did not share Siddiqui's ancestry, faith, or lived reality. She felt dissonance between her own embodiment of kathak rooted in calligraphy, Islam, and political struggles, and her peers' Indian embodiments of kathak steeped in Hindu mythology and Brahminism.

Siddiqui reflects further on these dissonances and contextualizes her continued experiences of related minoritizations within the British Asian landscape as symptomatic of larger contexts of Islamophobia in the UK, not just within the South Asian dance sector itself, but also at the hands of the British state, its policies and its "hostile environment". She shares, for instance, that in 2019 when she was invited to perform *Stories of Thumris* at UK's annual South Asian arts festival Darbar, her own Pakistani musicians were denied visas to enter the UK, leading her to have to adapt her work with local British Asian musicians, overnight, for her performance. At the very same time, Siddiqui equally recognizes the simultaneous marginalization that she faced at the hands of fellow British Pakistanis who were not comfortable with the Sufi content and *qawwali* form of Siddiqui's kathak, which they deemed a threat to their own practice of Islam (Siddiqui 2023). Maan echoes Siddiqui's sentiments and recognizes the sociocultural and systemic marginalizations experienced by British-Pakistani artists who do not conform to the expected mold of British South-Asianness, a narrative that is over-determined by the British Indian diaspora (Maan 2023).

These multiple discords and barriers could have led Siddiqui to give in to the pressures of assimilation into the dominant British South Asian dance sector aesthetic and politics. Instead, they reinforced for Siddiqui the need to catalyze her own distinct journey in kathak further, as she turned to Central Asian philosophy and aesthetic:

> The other thing is, which I feel now more than before for sure, is the Central Asian influence in my work. It is what makes my kathak different from Indian kathak. Because you know the Central Asian belt is very rich in philosophy and aesthetic. So I come from a place where I had to dig out what kathak is. Actually I had to dig out for myself the meaning of kathak. I didn't grow up with Indian mythology. When I first came to England, everyone was doing *vandana*, everyone was doing *bhajan*. I saw that and I thought I should also do that. So, I did try and I didn't feel like it was coming from within a deeper core. Then I realized that if I am not steeped in that culture, why am I trying this? This is what led me to start experiencing identity problems in the UK—I had to ask myself "where am I coming from"? And this is what forced me to find my own kathak. (Siddiqui 2023)

Visually, she has over the years developed an aesthetic that unsettles the classicized rendition of Indian kathak through the "grammar of whirling dervishes" (Siddiqui in Maan 1995). Philosophically, her embodiment of kathak has been informed by Sufism, drawing on the poetry and teachings of the thirteenth-century Persian Islamic scholar and poet Jalalu'ddin Rumi. Inspired by his open-heartedness to practice love without boundaries and embracing his whirling as "a very individual way of praying" (Siddiqui 2020), Siddiqui has nurtured a kathak that is an embodiment of her childhood calligraphy lessons with her father, enhanced and formalized by her study and practice of Sufism, dancing her father's scripts and Rumi's words to life.[4]

Gesture by gesture.

Word by word.

Stroke by stroke.

But there is much more to Siddiqui's kathak than its formal aesthetic. What distinguishes her art for me, and draws me to her expansive and philosophical vision of kathak, is the emphasis she places on the relationality between the dancer, the human, and the non-human ecosystems within which she dances, and that sustain her. This interconnectedness, this interdependency, this ecological companionship, she seeks and sustains in her dance, is to me her contact making as a Sufi with her environment.

Kathak to Siddiqui is ecological relationality.

Kathak to her is contact.

Siddiqui's Kathak, Sufism, Environmentalism, and Feminism

The Islamic-Hindu dual heritage of kathak as a dance form, originating in what is now northern India, is long established in dance studies and ethnomusicology (Chakravorty 2008; Walker 2014; Saraswat 2019, among others). Despite its dual heritages, however, what is undeniable is kathak's "Brahminical revival in the twentieth century through its classicization as part of the Indian nationalist project, and the resultant violent erasures of the often, though not exclusively, Muslim, socio-economically marginalized and caste-oppressed women kathak dancers whose artistries were written out of kathak's Indianized master-narratives, in favour of the form's legitimization through a search for its Brahminical patriarchal lineages" (Patel and Mitra forthcoming 2025). It follows, then, that kathak's Indianization, Brahminization even, has happened at the expense of many layers of minoritarian erasures, particularly along the lines of faith, caste, and gender. Unsettling this dominant narrative, this chapter focuses specifically on kathak's philosophical Sufi dimensions as embodied in Siddiqui's art.

A lot has been written about the mysticism of Sufism, but perhaps the most helpful way to understand Sufism is as a "fluid and shapeshifting phenomenon" located between being regarded as "the spiritual dimension of Islam" and a "religious movement with practices, doctrines, and structures" (Piriano and Sedgwick 2019, 1). Its contested relationship to Islam is also an important consideration in understanding Sufism, with many Sufis not drawing a distinction between Islam and Sufism, some even considering Sufism as "the only true Islam," while others considering its roots to share both "Islamic origins and exogeneous influences" (Piriano and Sedgwick 2019, 1). What is central to all these understandings of Sufism is its "expression of religious heterodoxy" (Piriano and Sedgwick 2019, 2), manifesting in an unbounded relationship between the human, her environment, her ecosystem, and the divine. This rests on the principle of the singular Divine Unity, of which every living being is an equal fragment, thus binding an anti-discriminatory principle into the heart of Sufism. This infinitude and unboundedness toward all divine creation is often captured most poignantly in the words of Jalalu'ddin Rumi:

> Come, come whoever you are
> An unbeliever, a fire-worshipper, come

Our convent is not of desperation.
Even if you have broken your vows a hundred times,
Come, come again. (Rumi in Friedlander 1992)

An important component of the Sufi pathway to liberation is through the practice of *Sama*, a "specific liturgy, composed of prayer, litany, singing, music and sometimes dance" (Lewisohn 2012, 1). *Sama* is a congregational ritual that leads to the experience of an aura of ecstasy, a heightened dimension of reality, and an embodiment of "contemplation in action" (Seker 2007). According to Mehmet Seker, while originally music and singing characterized the invocation of *Sama*, "with time, people started to accompany the musical harmony with swaying and larger movements" (Seker 2007). This is how "contemplation became the union of the soul, sound, and motion, as both the heart and body achieved a state of meditation, overcoming all physical and intellectual interference" (Seker 2007), and dance was placed at the heart of *Sama*. In her foreword to *The Whirling Dervishes*, Annamarie Schimmel notes that dance was an integral part of Sufi practices from as early on as the ninth century AD and that the "whirling dance can be interpreted as everything created around the central Sun of Divine Love" as well as a reenactment of "death and resurrection" (Schimmel in Friedlander 1992, xvi). Dance was thus central to a Sufi understanding of the cosmos and humanity's place within it, and as Shems Friedman describes below, the material body of the dancer was seen as a fractal of nature itself:

> The body is like the earth, the bones like mountains, the brain like mines, the belly like the sea, the intestines like rivers, the nerves like brooks, the flesh like dust and mud. The hair on the body is like plants, the places where hair grows like fertile land and where there is no growth like saline soil. From its face to its feet, the body is like a populated state, its back like desolate regions, its front like the east, back the west, right the south, left the north. Its breath is like the wind, words like thunder, sounds like thunderbolts. . . . Its motion and act are like motions of stars and their rotations. Its birth and presence are like the rising of the stars, and dots death and absence like their setting. (Friedman 1992, 18)

The body's moving relationality to the cosmos thus places dance at the heart of the *Sama*, through which "the creation of the universe; the creation of human beings; our birth into the world; the progress of human beings after the realization of servanthood, as supported with the love of God; and our escalation towards the ranks of perfected human (*insan-i-kamil*)" were all stirred into consciousness (Seker 2007). As the Sufi dances, "his arms are wide open, with his right hand turned towards the sky as if praying, ready to receive honor from the Divine One, and his left hand turned down, transferring the bounties that come from the Lord to those who are willing to receive them" (Seker 2007). Shems Friedlander reminds us that although movement in some form or another featured in Sufi ritual, it is Jalalu'ddin Rumi who "began the whirling dance and established the dervish order known as Mevlevis. Since his passing in 1273 the Mevlevis have made their *dhikr* in a whirling fashion which was stylized by his son Sultan Veled on the basis of the movements established by his father" (Friedlander 1992, xix).

Siddiqui maps the similarities in gestures, lines, energy flows, and spiritual immersion between the whirling of the dervishes and that of kathak, as she notes that in kathak too "we put our right hand up and our left hand remains parallel to the shoulder line" (Siddiqui in Maan 1995). In our conversation she quotes Rumi's immortal words "Come, come whoever you are," inviting and embracing people into prayer, regardless of their backgrounds. She is inspired by his unboundedness to love, and desires in her own art to embody a similar sense of love and compassion beyond boundaries. I ask her to describe who constitutes a Sufi:

> Sufi is someone who has a vast heart, who embraces, who loves. Sufism teaches you to love without boundaries. You really expand and grow like a tall tree. Free from the notions handed to you in childhood. Sufi is just someone who practices ... you have to become a better person first. Self-realization is the biggest part of Sufism. If you are not connected with your own self, you cannot connect with anybody else. You have to know your own identity, and then you know, you also have to forget it. That's the most important thing. (Siddiqui 2023)

Siddiqui, with her life experiences of state censorship by politicized Islamic nationalism and patriarchy in Pakistan and Islamophobia in the UK, is understandably drawn to practicing such "love without boundaries." She makes clear that in order to love others without boundaries, one first has to connect with oneself. But that this too is only the beginning of a Sufi's much more expansive relational journey that connects them to their ecological companions. She shares too that becoming a Sufi is a life's journey. Wirajaya et al. describe the spiritual Sufi pathway as consisting of three stages: *takhalli* (emptying stage), which consists of draining oneself of arrogance, envy, prejudice, and other negative energies; this is followed by *tahalli* (filling stage), which consists of replenishing oneself with the positive energies of love, sincerity, compassion; and this manifests in *tajalli* (embodiment stage), which consists of putting exterior actions out into the world that embody love and compassion (Wirajaya et al. 2021). They continue to explain that Sufism not only "focuses on ethical and aesthetic relationship between human and god" but also focuses on the same "between human and other ecosystems" (Wirajaya et al. 2021, 4).

This ethical dimension of existence is what drives Siddiqui's kathak. While Indian and Indian diasporic circulations of kathak tend to focus selectively on the aesthetic relationship between human and god, and mostly ignore the relationship between humans and non-human other ecosystems—very little attention is placed on its ethical dimensions. In response to the recent #MeToo movement, the Kathak Kendra and Kalakshetra, Indian-government funded institutions for the nurturing of kathak and bharatanatyam respectively, that revere and implement the *guru-shishya* model of dance training have had several cases of sexual, emotional, and physical abuse allegations lodged against their pedagogues and teachers. Anti-caste activist and hereditary dance-artist Nrithya Pillai writes about the need to examine all the different and intersecting power asymmetries on which these institutions are built, such as Brahminical heteropatriarchy, in order to address these allegations, and dismantle these historic abuses of power at these institutions (2023). While positioned differently on social power spectrums to Pillai, Siddiqui too critiques this lack of ethical considerations in the deeply entrenched pedagogic system of the *guru-shishya* training model, for instance, which proliferates in Indian and Indian diasporic dance sectors, and which is open to well-established and troubling abuses of power. She criticizes the system as dehumanizing, where students remain in servitude of the *guru* who demand unconditional respect without necessarily earning that respect through kindness and compassion, and without investing energies in the building of mutual trust and confidence. Furthermore, Sufism's emphasis on nurturing awareness about the relationality between humans and non-human ecosystems is mostly absent from predominant kathak artistries in India and the Indian diaspora. Siddiqui believes that such inner consciousness-raising within the dancer, the human, is ignored at the expense of an emphasis on "exhibitionism of skill" (Siddiqui 2023). Dancers and their training thus fail to look within themselves, let alone desiring to acknowledge and make contact with their environment. Siddiqui uses the example of the listless gaze of the dancer as indicative of self-absorbed artistry, with little consideration for how their artistry impacts their environment. She describes the need to find a balance between a dancer's inner and outer gaze:

> When we are looking inside us, we are not really looking at our intestines, etc. We are looking into our inner world, the world that is unseen. But this is hard. Instead, we are so used to our eyes looking out all the time. I have actually witnessed dance gurus directing the eyes, the gaze of their students, by saying "look here, or there." They are actually guiding them in the wrong way. As far as I am concerned, you don't follow the eyes, you have to know instead when and how the eyes should be at play and when not. When does the internal eye opens, and when the external eye opens. And when do they both merge. This is an important lesson for the dancer. (Siddiqui 2023)

The merging of the internal and external eye requires the dancer to be fully cognizant of and attuned to the ecological systems—both human and non-human—that they are a part of, that sustain them, and on whom their actions have material consequences. It echoes Maria Regina Firmino-Castillo's invitation and warning to dance-artists to take responsibility of caring for and sustaining the fundamental relationality that keeps these ecologies alive and healthy, and recognizing how ignoring their sustenance leads to irreparable damage and destruction (2020).

Siddiqui's astute critique of the vacuous and self-absorbed outer eye that merely seeks validation of the ego, without any recognition of the ecology in which their dance exists, is in critical dialogue with dance scholar Ranjana Dave's ableist critique of the famous Natyashastra quote by Bharata "Where the hand is, eyes should follow" (Dave 2018). Thinking deeper about the relevance of Siddiqui's reference to the internal and external gaze through the lens of Sufism, we understand that the dancer exists within an interconnected ecological system:

> Existence is a system. That is casually human beings cannot exist before the existence of other forms, including minerals and soil, plants and animals. Understanding the spiritual system of existence will lead a person to

be closer to his Creator and to become wiser in his behaviour. (Wirajaya 2021, 5)

Thus, to consider the dancer and their dance as distinct from this ecological system in which they exist is a dangerous fallacy, and only serves the ego. Siddiqui insists that the dancer's inner eye has to transcend the anthropocentric ego in order to merge with humanity at large and the ecological system in which they exist, while simultaneously focusing on the outer eye that makes them alive to the ecological system itself (Siddiqui 2023).

Siddiqui's kathak, with its emphasis on the dancer's place in her ecological system, embodies Sufism's call on the need to forgo the ego in search for a peaceful coexistence between human and other ecological companions, as a pathway to the divine. Writer Shireen Qudosi explains the foundational interconnectedness between Sufism and environmentalism, in its call to move beyond the material world:

> Initially rising out of a reaction to materialism and over-indulgence resulting from excess wealth and power, Sufis are mystics at heart, lovers of the natural world, inclined towards heterodoxy in a culture in which ego and possession is norm. The key aim of any Sufi is to separate themselves from the material and seek enlightenment by way of serving God, achieved through an internal process that shifts perspectives away from the ego and towards the divine. (Qudosi 2010)

Siddiqui finds this interconnectedness with the ecosystems in which she dances through her footwork, which brings into an intimate conversation with the Earth; through her *chakkars*, which allow her to experience the equilibrium of gravity in the universe; through reaching the *sum* of her *tatkar* as she taps into the metaphoric pulse of eternal cosmological time; and through invoking the chirping of birds in her *ghungroos*. Her kathak is deeply entwined and in conversation with nature and the ecosystem that sustains her and, she says, only when we are able to achieve total immersion in this interconnectedness, this ecological contact, do "our eyes become Sufi, our heart becomes Sufi" (Siddiqui 2023).

It is in this larger spiritual and philosophical context that I want to examine *Mirror Within*, a dance-film that I argue is the very crystallization of Siddiqui's vision of kathak, and what she has worked toward throughout her entire artistic trajectory. When I ask Siddiqui if she agrees with this description, she nods vehemently but nuances it with the Urdu word *nichod*—the action of wringing water out of a piece of fabric—as the metaphoric process that has led her to this point, squeezing out every last drop of her life's learning into the new knowledge-making process of the dance film (Siddiqui 2023).

Mirror Within (2022): A *Nichod*, a Meditation, a Du'a to Kathak

The act of making *Mirror Within* is a *nichod*, a wringing out, a distillation of Siddiqui's life and artistry. To understand what this means in material terms, I take a towel and place it in my bath at home, full of water. Once fully wet, having absorbed water beyond its saturation point, I lift the now heavy towel, its weight reminiscent of the weight of Siddiqui's expansive life journey through kathak. I start to twist the fabric between my hands, turning my wrists rhythmically to face away from each other, squeezing the liquid out of the towel.

> *My nails dig into my palms.*
> *My knuckles feel the pressure of the twisting motion.*
> *My forearm muscles tense up. My elbows stick out.*
> *My shoulders start to accentuate.*
> *My spine accentuates in its curvature.*
> *My heart starts to pound.*
> *My breathing gets quicker.*
>
> *My whole body is engaged in this act of nichod.*

When every last drop of water has been wrung out of the towel, I wipe my cheeks on the fabric and bury my face in it in relief. I can only imagine the neurological, muscular, skeletal, sensorial, and emotional effort that it took for Siddiqui to squeeze out this profound residue, this dance art, this prayer, this *du'a* to kathak into the world that Maan describes as both a meditation on "the sustainability of aging selfhood" and a "lamentation of youth" (Maan 2023). In this, Maan suggests, that *Mirror Within* signals both the ecological relationality that Siddiqui shares with her environment that exists outside of her, and also to the ecological relationality that exists within her own body, as she navigates the arid terrains of an aging dancing body and health as her own parched lands within, intimately linking her own organic and fleshly membranes to that of her ecological atmosphere (Maan 2023).

A close camera shot focuses on Siddiqui's feet adorned with ghungroos as they start to quiver with the gentle weight of her tatkar. The camera moves to a shot of the top of a lush green tree, and as the sound of the ghungroos builds in volume and pace, they appear to disperse a huge assembly of birds sitting on its branches into the sky. The flight of the birds makes the branches appear to explode into life and expand into the atmosphere, until there are no birds left to grace them.

Siddiqui's feet and the birds' flight are intimately connected.

Every ecological companion in the shot appears so beautifully in sync, in a forever dance with each other.

Stillness graces the screen, much like the stillness that precedes and terminates the Sufi's dance of contemplation (Lewisohn 1997); much like the calm before a storm. It alters our experience of time, making us home in on every small detail in nature as captured through Maan's eyes. The camera settles on an image of Siddiqui's silhouette. Filmed from the ground and looking up, she appears as the connecting force between the backdrop of the sunlit skies, and the yellow-green fields in which she exists. Or is she, in fact, connected to the earth by the expansive skies and lush fields? Perhaps they are all in equilibrium, connected to each other. She is upright and her arms paint swift strokes through the air, as though of calligraphy from the pages of her childhood. Her limbs move deftly, precisely, economically, and purposefully. There is no excess in her motion. She looks up at her own extended arms as her hands twirl, scripting gestures in the air, framed by the golden yellow halo of the sun. The film morphs in and out of the negative image of the film, as though she continues to exist in the terrain into the night's darkness, until the sun rises again. She appears to exist in this eternal rhythm, intimately connected to and at one with her environment (Image 3.1).

Siddiqui describes this deep connection between her limbs, her core, her gaze, her spine, and the natural environment around her as the same connection a painter's limbs shares with their brush and palette. This connection is contact. She reminisces that a painter friend of hers once said that when they observe dancers they experience the deep love with which dancers connect to their moving limbs, a love that enables them to weave geometry and emotion and send it out into the environment in which they exist (Siddiqui 2023). This is the great and overpowering Sufi message of love that I see that

Image 3.1 Nahid Siddiqui in *Mirror Within*
by photographer Nabila Mujassam Maan and film editor Shakila Taranum Maan

connects Siddiqui's limbs to her core, linked by her gaze as she sends out her actions into the natural world, open and receptive to all she receives back from her non-human companions.

The film moves back to the trees as Siddiqui reaches out to touch them and her voiceover explains:

> When we enter the physical world, we take individual forms.
> But our connection to the womb always remains. (Siddiqui in Maan 2022)

Shrouded completely in a turquoise blue wrap that makes her faceless, Siddiqui moves at a meditative pace in the forest environment. And although she moves with great stillness and precision, unlike the fast whirling of Sufis, she evokes the image of a Sufi, a human in deep and meditative contemplation who has found their own pace and pulse in moving toward ecstasy to merge with the Divine, the nature around her. Perhaps Sufism's relationship to time, both faster than human time and slower, is integral to achieving a heightened state of consciousness. Like a Sufi's flowing jacket, the fabric in which she is encased moves in the wind and choreographs gestures of its own. Siddiqui's pace of movement is hypnotic, her ever moving stillness exquisite. When her face is finally revealed, framed by the branches of a willow tree, it is reminiscent of the opening seen of Maan's Thousand Borrowed Eyes, *where Siddiqui dances in the arid desert landscape, framed by a singular green branch that breathes life into the frame. Siddiqui's moving existence is nothing without the movement of nature itself. With her back to the camera, Siddiqui's undulating spine draws the subtlest and slowest of lines through the air, accentuated by her extended arms and twirling wrists above her head. Siddiqui's voiceover continues:*

> *To me, dance is about evoking the mirror within.*
> *To see and feel the lines, shapes and geometry of the body.* (Siddiqui in Mirror Within)

Siddiqui reflects critically on the use of mirrors in dance training in the UK, where the emphasis on form and lines and geometry is achieved by looking at one's own reflection in a mirror in a dance studio. The mirror, she explains, used in this way becomes a corrective and disciplinary tool, and she argues that such an outward emphasis on how a dancer looks reduces the art of dance to the visual realm only. She speaks instead of her own kathak training with its emphasis on nurturing one's inward artistic eye, not to stroke one's ego, but to reach into one's inner human journey and become one's mirror from within. This inward reach toward the selfhood of the dancer, she insists, is a manifestation in her art of her journey with Sufism (Siddiqui 2023). This inward reach through her Sufi practice has enabled her to nurture and sustain her own "mirror within."[5]

With such a deep awareness of her inner landscape and its intimate connection with her non-human ecological companions surrounding her, the geometry of her limbs extends out into the forest as a gift. She knows that her movements are in fact meaningless without the forest's green contours and textures. She is in a deep meditative dance with her environment, in relational coexistence with nature. Her voice-over reminds us about the materiality of the aging body while noting that "the soul is limitless and forever young" (Siddiqui in Maan 2022).

The film cuts to yet another silhouette of Siddiqui, this time a shadow reflection of her dancing form onto the surface of water. She dances with her mirroring shadow, her companion created by the surface of the waterbody over which she stands. The length of her spine, her extended arms, and the curvatures of her upper body create calligraphy like shapes, woven into and upon the water's surface (Image 3.2).

Image 3.2 Nahid Siddiqui in *Mirror Within*
by photographer Nabila Mujassam Maan and film editor Shakila Taranum Maan

I see the moon
cradled somewhere in between the curvature of her arms,
held,
and revered
from the surface of the earth.

The human and the non-human
embodied and reflected
in each other.

Together a holistic whole.

Siddiqui tells me that she was keen to choreograph with shadows and silhouettes created in conjunction with the natural environment. This is yet another echo of the dancing shadows in *A Thousand Borrowed Eyes*, but in this dance-film it reaches a heightened and more sophisticated and complex form. She shares that all the while that she danced over the waterbody, she was immersed in the act of staring at her own silhouette reflected on the water—that her silhouette instigated the way her fleshly self moved, as much as her fleshly movements manifested in the movements of her shadow on the water. This intimate and relational conversation between her human self and her non-human shadow is the *nichod* of her ecofeminism—a deep dance of relationality between her human form, and its reflection upon the surface of water, catalyzed by the light of the sun and its casting shadows. She describes this sequence as a duet with her own silhouetted reflection that made her want to "merge into water" (Siddiqui 2023) such that Rumi's poetry comes to mind, "like a shadow I am, and I am not." I am reminded of her relationship to water from way back when in *Scene Unseen*, and how, like water itself, it is an amorphous choreographic connection that she carries deep within her body through her career.

Perhaps at some dimension, she does merge with the water, as it is impossible to tell the quivering of the water's surface apart from the quivering of Siddiqui's meditative gestures. They become one and the same, each influencing and enhancing the other. At the bottom of the screen, yet again, appears Maan's signature gesture toward ecological coexistence; a green plant swaying in the breeze, its own shadow reflected next to Siddiqui's. Siddiqui's homage to water, in deep dialogue with it, is a reminder of its life-affirming force when in harmony with it. We see her raise both her palms up above her head, facing her, in a position of prayer, of dua, as she gently bends her spine backward and lifts her face toward her palms. The water is both her mirror within and without. It enables a pathway toward her own selfhood, while simultaneously allowing her selfhood to extend into an ecological relationship with her surroundings: a poetic reminder that we as humans do not exist divorced from, but rather in a relational dance with, our natural environments. And that, moreover, when our dance is interrupted or even worse blocked, there are consequences that are borne out in our ecological systems.

168 UNMAKING CONTACT

The camera returns to the dense forest greenery, slowly panning across plants, trees, water surfaces. Siddiqui's arm and hands movements get faster as she finds herself located in its intimate midst. Framed by a gap between branches of dense green bushes, Siddiqui performs what appears at first to be sringara, the mimed ritual of adorning oneself with jewelry and makeup, invariably evoked in kathak recitals by women getting adorned for their lovers, usually men (Image 3.3). Looking straight into the camera, with not a trace of the characteristic coquettishness in sight, she places the tika across her forehead with her forefinger, she applies color to her lips with her little finger, she smears kohl under her eyes as her voice-over explains:

When one paints with her body
The lines extend beyond the horizon
Exploring the canvas of nothingness. (Siddiqui 2022)

As she puts on her invisible bangles and starts to twirl her wrists against each other, the camera shifts backward, and we get a glimpse of Siddiqui's arm and left shoulder, as though the moving form we have been looking at all along was in fact her reflection, and that she is staring at nature, her mirror, preparing

Image 3.3 Nahid Siddiqui in *Mirror Within*
by photographer Nabila Mujassam Maan and film editor Shakila Taranum Maan

herself for none other than her own awakened selfhood and its relational love affair with her non-human companions.

It is possible to read this unsettling of the *sringara* ritual in multiple ways. The first, a woman preparing herself, for herself, on her own terms—beyond the heteropatriarchal framing that usually accompanies this kathak ritual.[6] The second, as Siddiqui explains, unlike the conventional *sringara* where a thin space is maintained between the dancer's fingers and her face as she pretends to touch her own face, Siddiqui actually touches her own skin; she makes physical contact with her own human form; she connects with her own materiality, her own humanity. But she also and simultaneously journeys beyond her own materiality as she signals through her gestures an existence beyond her corporeality, in contact with her surrounding ecology. And in this she brings to life Rumi's words, "I am not his hair; I am not his skin; I am the soul that lies within." Siddiqui's physical touch of her own skin is distinct from most classicized dance's renditions of *sringara*, as described in the Introduction to this book, where the bejeweling of oneself happens through mime, and without physical contact. Siddiqui unsettles this convention by making contact with her own materiality and womanhood. Finally, in a conversation with me about the dance-film, Siddiqui nuances the complexity invoked in this physical contact with her own face by saying, "I am not touching someone else, but I am not touching me either. It's humanity I am in contact with" (Siddiqui 2023). She summarizes that this contact becomes the premise of her "biggest lesson of self-realization," about her place within humanity and her relationship to non-human components of our ecosystems at large (Siddiqui 2023).

And now at last adorned in her own awakening and self-realization, she walks into and through barren, brown, and sun-scorched fields. No longer the lush green and gold mustard plains of A Thousand Borrowed Eyes, *but elsewhere, in another manifestation of our earth's environment.*

In our devastating current reality of climate crisis, which we already know is impacting racially minoritized and indigenous communities in the Global South more profoundly and violently than its white Global North counterparts, Siddiqui's sustained relationality and coexistence with her ecological companions remind us:

> The world is not a problem to be solved; it is a living being to which we belong. The world is part of our own self and we are a part of its suffering

wholeness. Until we go to the root of our image of separateness, there can be no healing. (Vaughan-Lee 2021, vii)

Siddiqui recognizes that the only way to counter the ongoing neocolonial, capitalist, and racist violence that threatens our planet's survival is to locate her own existence in relationality and entwine herself with the non-human dimensions of her ecology that are at threat. Her choreographic entwinement with the natural world in *Mirror Within* is a poetic reminder that humanity's "separation from the natural world may have given us the fruits of technology and science, but it has left us bereft of any instinctual connection to the spiritual dimension of life—the connection between our soul and the soul of the world, the knowledge that we are all part of one living, spiritual being" (Vaughan-Lee 2021, viii). Siddiqui forces us to contend with the reality that "our way of walking on the Earth has a great influence on animals and plants" (Hanh 2021, 33).

But the actual physical location of the natural world in which she dances is just as significant to this analysis as the natural world itself. Filmed in the countryside and forests near Southhall, in the west of London, Siddiqui's gendered and racially minoritized presence within the countryside environment that continues to be dominated by white demographics is a disruption, an intervention, an intrusion. Siddiqui is a space invader (Puwar 2004) as her dancing presence marks "the arrival of women and racialised minorities in spaces from which they have been historically or conceptually excluded" (Puwar 2004, 1). I note here of course the history of urban cityscape of Southall itself as a historical home for Black and brown British peoples in London and the locus of 1970s London's protests against race-based discriminations and violence and advocacy for race equity, led by solidarity movements between Black, South Asian, and other racially minoritized communities. The urban parts of Southall, to this day, continue to be home to diverse racially minoritized communities. However, the forests and countryside surrounding Southall are differently occupied, akin to much whiteness-dominated environments of English countrysides. In this, the struggles against racisms as carried in the sinews of urban Southall, spill into its surrounding rural landscapes where the violence of whiteness lurks. The whiteness of English country landscapes is a well-documented phenomenon that initiatives such as "Decolonising Green Spaces" (2023) by education and feminist scholar-activists Geeta Ludhra and Giuliana Ferri are trying to undo. Ludhra speaks of the experience of occupying space in the English countryside as a racially minorized Indian-heritage woman who lives and walks in the Chilterns in Southeast England. And while the Chiltern landscapes are distinct both in its racial demographics and in its architecture to the forests around Southhall, where the *Mirror Within* was filmed, the experience of being a "space invader" in these distinctly racialized spaces spills over.

> I remember moving into the Chilterns and worrying about racism and feeling "othered." I knew communities were close-knit and supposedly kind, but would they be the same with me and my family? Would we always be "the other" family? I've always felt "that othered gaze" and apprehension when entering countryside pubs with my family, and that made me feel unwelcomed. Repeated visits changed this in some spaces, as connections were built through conversations over time. I remember walking the Chilterns Hills on a cold foggy morning in 2020, meeting an older woman who said: "We don't see many of you around here." I paused, responded politely, but carried that "you-ness" for many days. I have made the effort to connect because I want to change the narrative of countryside spaces for me and future generations. I have met some beautiful souls who kind of get where I'm coming from now, but the labour of connection generally comes from me. I belong as much as "they" do, and I'm not walking away, but will continue walking this space as a gentle activist "changing perspectives." (Ludhra 2022)

In her efforts to cope with the hostility of the whiteness of the Chilterns, and to make the English countryside a more expansive space for Black and racially minoritized communities, Ludhra set up the "Dadima's Walking Group" (Grandmother's Walking Group) in 2018. Initially this was designed for people around Slough and Windsor "as a simple way of encouraging local communities and interested people to connect with nature for physical, mental and spiritual wellbeing" (2022). Ludhra notes how this Sunday morning initiative "quickly became a safe space to talk and share stories, learn from each other, and offer encouragement (and accountability) for regular outdoor movement" (2022). However, after she moved to the Chilterns in 2020, Ludhra's efforts to restart the group were filled with much "greater apprehension" (2020) because she "didn't see [her]self represented or reflected in the Chilterns countryside" (2020). Walking with fellow South Asian heritage women over the years has built a community for Ludhra and others to contend with racism in the countryside, to find communion and solace in each other's company, and to heal in and through nature. Ludhra's efforts in the Chilterns find intimate and moving echoes in Siddiqui's poetic and synergetic presence within the forests and fields surrounding Southhall. Even as they are not explicitly connected in their endeavors, they are conjoined in their desire to implicitly stake a claim not just for their gendered and racially minoritized presence within English countryside and nature, but to remind us more capaciously of the need to "examine the position of women in relation to nature and colonialism" (Ludhra 2022), patriarchy, indigeneity, whiteness, and indeed Sufism, each a much-needed feminist intervention in their respective fields of practice.

The Feminisms within *Mirror Within*

In her paper "Women in Sufism," Rukhsar Hussain argues that despite the foundational roles that women have played in the Sufi movement from its inception, their contributions have been erased at the expense of superseding patriarchal narratives (Hussain 2022, 2). Hussain reads "the invisibility of female Sufi lives and their poetic compositions as a structural erasure by patriarchal forces" (Hussain 2022, 3). In her work she builds on similar endeavors by Annemarie Schimmel (1982) and Margaret Smith (1984), to provide a corrective to this established and gendered historiography, by centering the theological and literary contributions of women Sufi saints. Hussain reminds us that the saint Rabi'a al-Adawiyya of Iran who lived in the eighth century AD, was for instance, the first Sufi to introduce the concept of love to Sufi poetry as a delinked phenomenon from life's materialities. Yet, it is Rumi, who lived in the thirteenth century, to whom this greatest poetic and philosophical achievement is historically attributed.

In undertaking this feminist historiography of women Sufi saints, Hussain asks the following questions:

> [W]hat does the presence of female Sufi saints tell us about Sufism? How does it disrupt the dominant narrative where men are always seen as saints? How have female saints survived over all these years in the deeply patriarchal societies where they have lived? How does sainthood connect to everyday lives of these Sufi females and finally, how does it connect/divide with the lives of "ordinary" women of the times? (Hussain 2022, 3)

Despite Sufism's underlying anti-discriminatory principles, its gendered historiography has thus continued to shape our understanding of Sufism. Additionally, it is important to note that in its focus on ecology and environmentalism, even though this chapter does not engage a caste-critique of Sufism, Sindhi-Muslim scholar Ghulam Hussain's (2019) and political sociologist Julian Levesque's works (2016), among others, have unsettled dominant liberatory narratives of Sufism through examining caste hegemonies in Sufism in the context of Sindh in Pakistan (2019). This chapter has tried to understand Siddiqui's Sufi practice in her art, as contextualized against the stronghold of patriarchy within Pakistani culture at large, and opens up scope to consider how this might also intersect with a caste-critique. Siddiqui's kathak, with its roots in Sufi philosophy and her commitment to living life as a Sufi and a Pakistani woman, disrupts these patriarchal narratives in important ways. By bringing her womanhood in conversation with Sufism's founding principles of nurturing and sustaining ecological companionship with humanity, Siddiqui's kathak is both feminist and environmentalist at once. However, such a combined ecofeminist analysis of *Mirror Within*, made, performed, and circulated in the UK, needs to be understood through the particularities, nuances, and critiques of ecofeminism as it manifests also within the Pakistani and the British-Pakistani contexts.

In her materialist approach to ecofeminism, Indian ecofeminist scholar and environmental activist Vandana Shiva names the cause of our climate catastrophe and threats to planet Earth as the "capitalist patriarchal world system" (2014). She follows the "central contention of ecofeminist political philosophy that the oppressions of women and nature are linked" (Kings 2017, 70). Shiva writes that that this system emerged through sustained "colonization of women, of 'foreign' people and their lands; and of nature, which it is gradually destroying," links the project of modernity to the degradation of the natural world, and identifies that women have always been the first to protest against such devastations to natural habitats (2014). To nuance her generalization of the category of womanhood in this claim, Shiva does clarify that "some women, however, urban, middle-class women, find it difficult to perceive commonality both between their own liberation and the liberation of nature, and between themselves and 'different' women in the world" (2014). While Shiva's materialist approach to ecofeminism is a helpful way in, it falls short on some dimensions. A more explicit articulation of how, for instance, race, faith, ableism, and caste, among other social vectors, intersect with, complicate, and hierarchize the category of womanhood, and thus women's liberation, is necessary to understand the shortcomings of ecofeminism. To understand ecofeminism as a project undertaken by women who occupy positions of power by virtue of their whiteness, and/or their class privilege, and/or their dominant caste status, in different social and national contexts, is a helpful and necessary nuance here. A. E. Kings signals precisely this necessary move in ecofeminism toward intersectional considerations of feminist praxis in the context of environmental activism (2017). Kings writes:

> Intersectional ecofeminism builds upon this foundation by further postulating that the "freedom" of humanity is not only reliant on the freedom of nature and women, but it is also reliant on the achievement of liberation for all of those at intersecting points on along these fault lines. (2017, 71)

But perhaps this intersectional approach has played out more in some world contexts more than others. In her rightful critique of the whiteness of the field of ecofeminism, Neelam Jabeen proposes the concept of the "postcolonial ecofeminism" to theorize what ecofeminism might mean for the postcolonial context of Pakistan. She argues that ecofeminism both problematically conceptualizes womanhood as a monolith, and attributes to women an ability to relate to nature through a "relationship of care and compassion" that is either innate or socialized (Jabeen 2019, 355):

> Postcolonial ecofeminism still rests in the basic ecofeminist assumption that there is a connection in how one treats women and the environment and all feminized and naturalized entities. However, it contends that to explain the women–nature relationship, especially in the South Asian, post/neocolonial Pakistani context, it is important to consider the material realities of women (and men) that are directly related to their status as members of post/neocolonial societies. This relationship is neither an outcome of women's innate quality of care and compassion for nature and life in general (as cultural ecofeminists would believe), nor because of women's socialization as nurturers and caretakers (as constructivist ecofeminists would assert). Instead, the women–nature relationship is determined by women's material realities, which include the sociopolitical and religious conditions of their societies. (2019, 356)

Siddiqui's intimate, entwined, and material presence in nature in *Mirror Within* must be resisted, then, as being framed through the lens of mainstream white ecofeminism, as an innately compassionate image of women-nature relationships. It must also be resisted as representative of a monolithic experience of either Pakistani or British-Pakistani womanhood. Jabeen's argument is that, in fact, women-nature relationships are varied and complex, and reliant on the particularities of women's material realities. It is this complex understanding that is crucial to a feminist reading of Siddiqui's *Mirror Within*.

Siddiqui's staking her claim to British landscapes through which she moves is complicated by her immigrant and racialized identity in a nation caught up in anti-immigrant rhetoric and government legislations, at the time of writing. This relationship to stake her claim on this land is made even more complex by her experience of becoming an exile from her own Pakistani lands in the 1970s and 1980s. And finally, as Jabeen reminds us of the deeply complex relationship between women and land within patriarchal societies like Pakistan, where patriarchal subjugation of women leads to the commodification of their bodies, "their connection with and treatment like land provides a logic of domination to the oppressor" (Jabeen 2020, 1098–1099). Jabeen continues to explain this analogy further:

> [S]eeing land as woman's body gives a similar sense of authority over land, where every virgin piece of land is thought to be waiting to be "husbanded." Oppression and exploitation on the basis of the embodiment of women and nature—land in this context—is so complex that rejecting this woman–land connection as essentialist might do more harm than good. (Jabeen 2020, 1098–1099)

Seen in this light, Siddiqui's feminist and postcolonial claims to the natural lands and environments surrounding Southall are a nod at multiple oppressive systems at once, operating in the UK, in Pakistan, and in the spaces in between. While her material presence intervenes with the white-dominant British countryside that remains hostile to her presence, she simultaneously challenges Pakistani heteropatriarchal narratives of womanhood through her self-sufficiency and agency. She speaks her particular truths as an immigrant Pakistani-heritage woman in the UK with tenuous and complicated ties to her homeland and culture. She does not claim to speak for all of womanhood, or all of Pakistani womanhood, or even all of British-Pakistani womanhood. And yet her feminist truths do not transpire in a vacuum—it is necessarily in transnational conversation with her homeland and sits alongside the truths of the millions of young people who are driving forward Pakistani feminism's fight toward self-determination.

I ask her
    in my interview
        whether she identifies as a feminist—

        and she respond
            instantly
            and
                without a shadow
                of a doubt,

    "Yes, absolutely!" (Siddiqui 2020)

On March 8, 2018, to visibilize a collective struggle for women's rights, the first Aurat March (Women's March) came into being in Pakistan. Since its inception, this annual event has "remained persistent in taking up women's issues and ridding them of many discriminatory laws ranging from domestic violence to honour killing" (Saif 2022). Its feminist and anti-patriarchal commitments have been deemed a threat to Pakistani values and principles by fundamentalist factions of society. In a published interview essay with dance scholar Priyanka Basu, dancer and feminist activist Sheema Kermani, a leading figure of the Aurat March, reflects on its intentions, its challenges, its implications, and its future aspirations:

> It has now been more than 5 years since we started Aurat March. The initial idea was borrowed from all the marches that were taking place in other countries such as in the USA and Europe; we felt why shouldn't Pakistan have a women's march of its own? However, it was not an easy task. To get women out on the streets in Pakistan is very tough. Firstly, there is a huge resistance to this concept. Secondly, there is resistance to the fact that women are coming out into the domain of politics and not restricting themselves to smaller niche places such as conferences and seminars.... I think Aurat March has been a very big move for Pakistan. It has brought the dialogues and discourses on women's issues to the mainstream of life where everybody is talking about it.... While this has been a huge step forward, we have also faced many attacks. Last time we were charged with blasphemy when there weren't any other issues to slam against us. Our videos were manipulated and doctored (other words were put into our mouths) to hold us guilty of being blasphemous. It has been a struggle to continue with the march.... The point now, however, is that where does Aurat March go from here and what is its future. The idea for most of us was that at some point women would become part of the mainstream politics, administration and governance of the country. Sadly, we are still nowhere near any of these. In fact, gender-based violence has increased hugely in Pakistan in the last many years.... Although we make such a noise about it, we protest, we come out on the streets, it is written about, there is no improvement. Actually, the state has to implement the laws and see to it that the perpetrators are punished. Unfortunately, that does not happen. Those who are the perpetrators of violence on women, they hardly ever get punished. They always seem to be able to get away with it. The last time the Prime Minister of Pakistan, Mr. Imran Khan, made some remarks about women; comments such as if women wear

short dresses they will be raped. If the leadership is so misogynist, obviously then these ideas penetrate the society hugely and it becomes more and more difficult. I think we still have a very long way to go regarding women's rights issues and for equality for women. But at least, the discourse has started and every family, home, kitchen talks about Aurat March—why are these women marching, what do they want? Bringing this discourse at the forefront has been a huge step in itself. (Kermani in Basu 2023, 6)

Kermani speaks critically too of the patriarchal forces that have weaponized Islam to subjugate women from dancing. Journalist Rubina Salgol, in her overview of Pakistani feminist activism, writes of the current generation:

The new wave of feminism includes people from all classes, genders, religions, cultures and sects without any discrimination or prejudice. The young feminists are diverse, yet inclusive, multiple yet one. There are no leaders or followers—they are all leaders and followers. The collective non-hierarchical manner of working and the refusal to take any funding is similar to the functioning practised by WAF and represents continuity with the past. But the entire framing of the narrative around the body, sexuality, personal choices and rights is new. The young groups of women say openly what their grandmothers could not dare to think and their mothers could not dare to speak. They say what women have known for centuries but have not been able to voice. They have broken the silences imposed by various patriarchies in the name of religion, tradition and culture. They have torn down so many false barriers including the four walls of morality built to stifle their selves and curb their expression. (Salgol 2019)

The focus of twenty-first-century Pakistani feminism is distinct from the focus of twenty-first-century feminist activisms in the UK—and Siddiqui's *Mirror Within* is a simultaneous nod to both these divergent and convergent gender justice and liberatory efforts in her country of heritage and her country of residency.

Afterthoughts

Siddiqui's deep connectivity to nature, relationality between human and non-human ecologies, and unwavering challenge to heteropatriarchy through the embodiment of self-sufficient feminist agency in *Mirror Within* (2022) can be traced back to *A Thousand Borrows Eyes* (1985), and later on in *Scene Unseen* (2001). But, by being in deep and relational conversation with her non-human companions in nature, it is also a simultaneous critique of the anthropocentric tendencies of valorizing humanity over our non-human counterparts. It is a response to Maria Regina Firmino-Castillo's questions to dance artists, with a deep recognition that without reaching, nourishing, and sustaining a relational equilibrium between humans and non-human components of our ecologies, there are serious and devastating consequences. Siddiqui, thus, simultaneously critiques both heteropatriarchy and human supremacy in *Mirror Within*. This is most astutely embodied in her unsettling of *sringara*, where we see a necessary aesthetic and philosophical collapse between contact as physical touch and contact as relationality. The first dimension of contact as physical touch, as embodied in her own hands touching different parts of her face, recognizes and asserts her own womanhood on her own terms and beyond the realms of heteropatriarchy. She exists beyond its regime. The second dimension manifests in the form of contact as relationality and is embodied in Siddiqui's adorning of herself by engaging with her own imagined reflection in nature, reaching out to her non-human companions in a relational dance and conversation with them. This slippage, back and forth, between contact as touch and contact as relationality together embodies Siddiqui's ecofeminism as informed by her Sufism, and necessarily places her own existence in equilibrium with nature and the environment that sustains her. She not only rejects the idea of dressing up for a lover, a man; more importantly she undermines the narrative of anthropocentricism that dominates kathak recitals, by adorning herself for her self and her non-human ecological companions.

Siddiqui's kathak, again and again, emphasizes her Sufi and ecofeminist-inculcated interrelationship between humanity, nature, and our ecological companions. In this she stands distinct from her fellow kathak artists' obsession with the human story on human-only terms. Siddiqui is an anomaly for having withstood and resisted multiple dimensions of exclusionary politics through her life and art: heteropatriarchy in Pakistan that banned her from dancing; a Hindu-dominant South Asian diaspora in the UK that meant finding her own Sufism-inspired kathak at odds with the kathak of her predominantly Hindu and Indian peers; white supremacy of the UK landscape itself with its anti-immigration hostility and racism; and a male-dominated kathak community in UK's South Asian dance sector with multigenerational artists such as Pratap Pawar, Akram Khan, Aakash Odedra, Jaivant Patel, Shyam Dattani, and others.[7] It is no wonder that Sufism's call to love beyond boundaries, to focus beyond the human paradigm, to search beyond our egos, to challenge any form of discrimination, to embrace our ecological companions as equals, and to live in harmony with nature speaks intimately to Siddiqui's expansive heart. At a time when so much of kathak in the British South Asian diaspora has come to be valued for its speed, technique, virtuosity, tenacity, and flair, Siddiqui's immersion in kathak's meditative and contemplative dimensions to reveal and revere what lies beneath its surface to advance humanity in conjunction with our ecological companions is a gift to our survival.

It is a homage to our burning earth.

It is a prayer to our relationality with every living organism,

human and non-human.

It is a d'ua to contact.

References

Ahmed, Imaduddin. 2007. "I Remember—Nahid Siddiqui." Accessed March 1, 2023. https://imadahmed.com/2007/02/06/i-remember-nahid-siddiqui/.

Basu, Priyanka. 2023. "Dance, Gender, and Activism in Pakistan: Interview with Performer-Activist Sheema Kermani." Feminist Encounters: A Journal of Critical Studies in Culture and Politics 7 (1): 1–10.

Chakravorty, Pallabi. 2008. Bells of Change: Kathak Dance, Women and Modernity in India: Calcutta: Seagull Books.

Dave, Ranjana. 2018. "'Ability' and the Spectrum of Performative Possibilities: Dismantling Notions of the 'Perfect' Dancing Body." Firstpost. Accessed on 22 March 2022. https://www.firstpost.com/living/ability-and-the-spectrum-of-performative-possibilities-dismantling-notions-of-the-perfect-dancing-body-4562181.html.

Firmino-Castillo, Maria Regina. 2020. "RUXIMIK QAK'U'X: Inextricable Relationalities in Mayan Performance Practice." Conversations Across the Field of Dance Studies. Special Issue: Decolonizing Dance Discourses. Special Issue: "Decolonizing Dance Discourses" 40: 31–35.

Friedlander, Shems. 1992. The Whirling Dervishes. Albany: State University of New York Press.

Hanh, Thich Nhat. 2021. "The Bells of Mindfulness." In Spiritual Ecology: The Cry of the Earth, edited by Vaughan-Lee, Llewellyn, 33–36. Point Reyes, CA: The Golden Sufi Centre.

Hussain, Ghulam. 2019. "Understanding Hegemony of Caste in Political Islam and Sufism in Sindh, Pakistan." Journal of Asian and African Studies 54 (5): 716–745.

Hussain, Rukshar. 2022. "Women in Sufism." Accessed March 1, 2022. https://strathprints.strath.ac.uk/79586/.

Jabeen, Neelam. 2019. "Women, Land, Embodiment: A Case of Postcolonial Ecofeminism." Interventions: International Journal of Postcolonial Studies 22 (8): 1095–1109.

Kermani, Sheema. 2022. "The Unchanging Reality of Male Dancers in Pakistan." South Asian Dance Intersections 1 (1): 52–59. https://journals.charlotte.edu/sadi/article/view/1474/1231.

Khan, Nadia. 2021. "Keeping Kathak Alive in Pakistan." TRTWorld. Accessed March 1, 2023. https://www.trtworld.com/magazine/keeping-kathak-alive-in-pakistan-50652.

Khan, Saad. 2017. "Pakistani Commercial Mujra—The Working Class Women of Pakistani Lowbrow Entertainment." Medium. Accessed March 1, 2023. https://khajistan.medium.com/showgirlsofpakistan-e015b7926105.

Khan, Sofia. 2021. "Nahid Siddiqui Guru of Kathak in conversation with Sophia Khan: Struggle of Arts/Dance in Pakistan." Mango Prime. Accessed March 1, 2023. https://www.youtube.com/watch?v=52zd5S7CcBo.

Kings, A. E. 2017. "Intersectionality and the Changing Face of Ecofeminism." Ethics & the Environment 22 (1): 63–87.

Levesque, Julian. 2016. "'Sindhis Are Sufi by Nature': Sufism as a Marker of Identity in Sindh" In Islam, Sufism and Everyday Politics of Belonging in South Asia, edited by Deepra Dandekar and Torsten Tschacher, 212–227. London: Routledge.

Lewisohn, Leonard. 2012. "The Sacred Music of Islam: Sama' in the Persian Sufi Tradition." Institute of Ismaili Studies. Accessed March 1, 2023. https://www.iis.ac.uk/media/uibjnzcy/the-sacred-music-of-islam_pdf-366408512.pdf.

Ludhra, Geeta. 2022. "Changing Perspectives in the Countryside: Dr Geeta Ludhra." The Museum of English Rural Life. Accessed March 1, 2023. https://merl.reading.ac.uk/blog/2022/03/changing-perspectives-in-the-countryside-geeta-ludhra/.

Maan, Shakila Taranum. 2014. "Gods and Daughters." In Women Against Fundamentalism: Stories of Dissent and Solidariity, edited by Sukhwant Dhariwal and Nira Yuval-Davis. London: Lawrence & Wishart.

Piraino, Francesco, and Mark Sedgwick, eds. 2019. Global Sufism: Boundaries, Structures, and Politics. London: Hurst & Co.
Puwar, Nirmul. 2004. Space Invaders: Race, Gender and Bodies out of Place. Oxford: Berg.
Saif, Uzma. 2022. "Is Reconciliation Possible Between Pakistani Feminism and Religion?" Centre for Strategic and Contemporary Research. Accessed March 30, 2022. https://cscr.pk/explore/themes/social-issues/is-reconciliation-possible-between-pakistani-feminism-and religion/#:~:text=The%20struggle%20for%20women's%20rights,domestic%20violence%20to%20honour%20killing
Salgol, Rubina. 2019. "The Past, Present and Future of Feminism in Pakistan." Herald. Accessed March 1, 2022. https://herald.dawn.com/news/1398878#:~:text=The%20new%20wave%20of%20feminism,are%20all%20leaders%20and%20followers.
Saraswat, Shweta. 2019. *"Constructing Diasporic Identity through Kathak Dance: Flexibility, Fixity, and Nationality in London and Los Angeles."* PhD thesis, University of California Los Angeles. Accessed March 1, 2023. https://escholarship.org/content/qt8st886mh/qt8st886mh_noSplash_887e60c87af15c52676c7e45ad9ff998.pdf?t=pskl9n.
Schimmel, Annemarie. 1982. "Women in Mystical Islam." Women Studies International Forum 5 (2): 145–151.
Seker, Mehmet. 2007. "Mevlana's Path of Love and "Being Freed" by the Sema." Islamic Research Foundation International, Inc. Accessed March 1, 2022. https://www.irfi.org/articles/articles_1651-1700/mevlana.htm.
Shea Murphy, Jacqueline. 2022. Dancing Indigenous Worlds: Choreographies of Relation. Minneapolis: University of Minnesota Press.
Shiva, Vandana, and Maria Mies. 2014. Ecofeminism. London: Zed Books.
Siddiqui, Nahid. 2020. *Interview by the author.* October 13.
Siddiqui, Nahid. 2022. *Interview by the author.* May 1.
Siddiqui, Nahid. 2023. *Interview by the author.* February 14.
Smith, Margaret. 1984. Rabi'a the Mystic and Her Fellow Saints in Islam. Cambridge: Cambridge University Press.
Vaughan-Lee, Llewellyn. 2021. "Introduction." In Spiritual Ecology: The Cry of the Earth, edited by Vaughan-Lee, and Llewellyn, iii--xi. Point Reyes, CA: The Golden Sufi Centre.
Walker, Margaret E. 2014. India's Kathak Dance in Historical Perspective. Farnham: Ashgate Publishing Limited.
Wirajaya, Asep Yudha, Bani Sudardi, Istadiyantha and Warto. 2021. "Eco-Sufism Concept in Syair Nasihat as an Alternative to Sustainable Development Goals (SDGs) Policy in Environmental Sector." IOP Conference Series: Earth and Envionmnental Science 905: 012081.

4
Contact as *Adda*

Critical Encounters in *#KaateNahinKatte* Instareel (2020) by LaWhore Vagistan and Digital Touching

Adda: From Interviews to Critical Encounters

If Chapter 3 shone a light on contact as ecological relationality between humans and non-human dimensions of our world, this final chapter returns us to examine interactions between people who occupy different and overlapping social and professional positions vis-à-vis each other, and alerts us to the need to re-evaluate such contact as critical encounters. One such mode of critical encounter might be conversations. This book hinges crucially on long, in-depth, back-and-forth, convoluted, expansive, and critical conversations that my artist-interlocutors have generously and graciously agreed to enter into with me—conversations that, I hope we all now realize, have no ending. And yet, so far in the first three chapters, the terms of these conversations as a means to one of my methodologies have been almost entirely mine—and in truth have been shaped more like semi-structured interviews. Even as I have heavily quoted their words on the pages, weaving my own through the trellis of their thoughts and ideas, the terms of our conversations have not been truly equitably distributed. While, during our interviews, I have had multiple opportunities to answer their questions and remained accountable to them, these moments have not necessarily been captured in the book.

This seems a little disingenuous of me.

In this final chapter, I examine the Instareel of *#KaateNahinKatte* (2020) by US-based drag queen artist LaWhore Vagistan, a remixed rendition of the same love-dance sequence from *Mr India* (1987) that opened my Preface, as a critical encounter between queer and non-queer communities online. I use this final case study to theorize critical encounters, mobilizing critical encounter as a method in itself. I do so to address the gap in this book by offering an *adda* (defined below) as method; a holistic and three-way critical conversation between LaWhore Vagistan, Kareem Khubchandani and myself, and our queer and non-queer selves. This *adda* exposes the power-laden hierarchies that are inherent in artist-scholar interviews, shifting the terms of the conversation from a one-way, often extractive process, that is usually controlled by the researcher, to a back-and-forth critical dialogue between LaWhore, myself, and Khubchandani, where all parties get to shape the trajectory of our exchange, and share the uncertainties of its paths. In this, I theorize *adda* as contact: between scholar-artist-scholar positionalities (scholar Khubchandani, their drag-artist persona LaWhore, and my own scholarly self), between queer and non-queer subjects, and between the formal essay interjections and the more informal conversational modes that this chapter explores. This chapter is thus a contact-dance between multiple layers of choreography, mirroring the ways in which #KaateNahinKatte creates, touches, and sustains communities on Instagram.

I want to recognize here, too, the temporality that frames LaWhore/Khubchandani and my *adda*: we are witnessing a terrifying rise of anti-LGBTQ+ movements across the United States, the UK, and other parts of Europe under right-wing authoritarian regimes, creating a dangerous and hostile environment for our trans and queer siblings. We are witnessing, too, a steady rise of coordinated and transnational anti-drag sentiments and protests, with drag artists coming under attack across both sides of the Atlantic. Writing in an opinion piece on LGBTQ+ rights for the British newspaper *The Guardian* in June 2023, during Pride Month, Tom Squirrel writes:

> More than 50 family drag events in the UK were targeted by protesters from June last year to this May, according to data gathered by our researchers at the Institute for Strategic Dialogue (ISD). Ten shows were cancelled or postponed before they even took place. At the ones that did go ahead, small groups (rarely more than 12) using abusive and confrontational tactics routinely accused parents who were taking their children to the events of supporting paedophilia, or threatened to perform "citizen's arrests" on the drag queens performing at them. (Squirrell 2023)

Writing from New York in March 2023 also on the same issue, Olivia Empson writes that "drag story hours are no longer simple in the US" (2023):

> They have been targeted by Republicans and the far right with protests and threats of violence and wild conspiracy theories around grooming

and abuse. At the same time, there has been a concerted legislative push to erode LGBTQ rights in state legislatures across the US, an effort to remove LGBTQ literature from public libraries and rising acts of violence against the community. (Empson 2023)

Entering an *adda* with LaWhore/Khubchandani as a cisgender and non-queer woman researcher comes with responsibilities and accountabilities at all times. But these are particularly heightened in this moment, against the backdrop of the toxicity and hostility that is being aimed at LGBTQ+ communities. I lean in and listen carefully also to Khubchandani's words on the "Queer Everything" podcast as they talk about this very hostile temporality aimed against drag artists, and how it needs to generate nuanced discussions and recognize the crossovers between the personal and the political:

> We have to be complex about talking about drag right now, because the right wing is insisting that drag is sexual. That is a misnomer. But for me in particular, it *is* sexual. It is a very concerted effort to access a sexuality that me and people like me are often denied or exoticized for, and to work with sexuality on my own terms. (in Queer Everything 2023)

Our *adda* thus necessarily makes me cognizant of my role, and the role of all cis and non-queer people at large, from our places of privilege, in the ongoing and intensified fight for LGBTQ+ rights. And the immense urgency for me to really, and truly, and deeply listen and, more important, act is not lost on me.

An *adda* is a "distinct Bengali speech genre" (Sen 2011, 521) and refers to "both a place of assembly and an art of conversation (Dutta 2022, 150), mostly associated with urban settings (Sen 2011, 522). Legal scholar Debolina Dutta expands:

> In the context of a Bengali post-colonial life, *adda* belongs to an artistic and literary genre where it is neither solely text-based nor only about public or published texts, but is embedded in a linguistic tradition in the form of the oral or *moukhik*. *Moukhik*, in Bangla, refers to that which is tied to speech and what is spoken, as well as the expressional. In other words, *adda* is as much about the content of speech as it is about the style, manner, gestures or conduct of its participants. (Dutta 2022, 148–149)

Cultural studies scholar Debarati Sen identifies its distinctiveness:

> Adda is a kind of informal social talk in Bengali, among friends and colleagues, but its content is always of intellectual significance, addressing issues such as local/global politics, art, literature, and music. Casual conversations and gossip are common in many societies, but the creative performance of this genre by Bengali elites made adda a marker of an urban middle-class identity, especially in response to the cultural hegemony of British Imperialism. (2011, 521–522)

Developed in the nineteenth century as a resistive anti-colonial practice against British colonialism, the *adda* became a mechanism through which the Bengali *bhadrolok*—the middle- and upper-class, dominant-caste, elite Bengali man—could "cope with one's westernized status within British supremacy and its effects on the dignity of the westernized Bengali middle class as a whole" (Sen 2011, 524). The Bengali cultural exceptionalism attached to the *adda* was mobilized to "specify Bengali cultural identity vis-à-vis other Indian forms of identity" such that both "Bengalis and Bengaliness [wa]s being made and remade through *addas*" (Sen 2011, 527). Sudeep Chakravarti notes that while it may have laid its roots in Kolkata, "over time āddā travelled to other places, Dhaka and beyond into Greater Banglasphere, taking wing wherever there were well-to-do hosts and a ready gathering of local worthies from pundits and poets to politicians on the make" (Chakravarti 2017). He goes on to note, too, that despite its beginnings in Bengali dominant caste-class-masculinist elite circles, "it has since travelled well down to the bottom of the socio-economic pyramid" (Chakravarti 2017).

> Āddā is by now function-agnostic, taking in a gathering that can range from intense discussions at the residence of a publisher or, say, young movie director to a weekend gathering of modern-minded working friends catching up over food (and, possibly to the horror of āddā purists, including women, often women who work jobs away from home, women with minds of their own supercharged by independent incomes); even an āddā triggered by the visit of an old friend; to the determined everyday āddā. (Chakravarti 2017)

Journalist Tania Banerjee notes too that the *adda*'s social trajectory now operates across caste-class-gender lines, and that it is "no longer an exclusively male activity, though men are still the dominant gender. Adda is also no longer a strict domain of the upper class or educated—people from all strata are seen enjoying this interaction, although members of an adda tend to belong to the same socioeconomic status" (Banerjee 2021).

In her article that theorizes *adda* as method, Debolina Dutta offers her critical reflections as a participant on a gathering between a panel of researcher/activists speaking on sex workers' rights and their research participants, the sex workers themselves. She describes a moment when, during this gathering, the conventional power dynamics between researchers and their subjects shifted viscerally:

> [A] majority of the women in the audience who were sitting at the back left their seats and came and sat on the floor at the front. The distance between us shrank, both materially and metaphorically, as we engaged in a conversation in close proximity, speaking to and with each other. The sheer symbolism of the shift in the landscape of the sitting arrangement in the room was fascinating—we (the panelists) were no longer facing the audience and imparting knowledge; we were sitting in a circle and had assumed roles as both speaker and listener. We were collectively expressing and exchanging our disparate views on the legal regulation of sex work. This shape-shifting materialised a form of knowledge about sex workers' lives and law that seemed to be founded on reciprocity, as opposed to hierarchical talk. What I was witnessing was not an outburst of subaltern-speak that was meant to drown the privileged academic into silence; it was meant to draw her in as a participant. Our panel became a place for an engagement like no other, carrying an emotive and affective charge, as we engaged in an appreciation of life and law. Such joining of multiple voices created a chorus of ideas about law and how it is lived and known, akin to the Bengali literary tradition of *adda*. (Dutta 2022, 148)

Dutta describes here a modality of collective speaking and listening where she experienced a shift, as a researcher, from "speaking to others" to "speaking with others" (2022, 152). She recognized in that shift the power of the *adda* as "a means of experiencing knowledge production and gaining a worldview by engaging in mutual speaking and listening that is physically and emotionally pleasurable" (2022, 152).

Pratistha Singh recognizes too the latent and transformative power of the *adda* as she locates it in the resistive mode of the women of Shaheen

Bagh, in New Delhi, and their December 2019 protests against the Indian government's non-secular immigration policy that disproportionately impacted Muslim peoples. She notes that "The women decided to sit outside their homes, by the side of a big road and began talking to each other about it. It was started by ordinary Muslim women but soon, it was joined by people from a cross-section of religions, gender, caste and social status" (2020, 100). Singh continues to describe how the protests embraced the agitative and reparative mode of the *adda*:

> The adda became their life. I spoke to many women in Shaheen Bagh and they said they liked this idea of being close to one another, not only was it great to talk freely about things, it also gave them a sense of security. They were not alone anymore. And every time I went to Shaheen Bagh, I felt this sense of safety was not just limited to the CAA-NRC. The women felt safe because they were talking about themselves and their idea of India, they felt safe in their self-realization through that historical protest. For weeks, speeches were made, poems recited, songs sung. The Preamble to the Constitution was read aloud in chorus. Political parties made attempts in between to oust the protesters; a man called Kapil Gurjar fired bullets at the gathering in Delhi; communal violence broke out. But the protesters stuck to the rule-book definition of non-violent agitation. (2020, 101)

Both Dutta and Debolina signal ways in which the *adda* can, and must, be unmoored from its Bengali roots and exceptionalisms, by homing in on the speech form's emphasis on growth, critique, and transformative, mutual, and collective knowledge-production. It is *this* quality of the *adda* that I advocate for as a form of contact, as a space of critical encounter and the unmaking of knowledges and worldviews. Furthermore, its looseness and lack of rules, its encouragement to embrace unpreparedness and open-endedness, and its emphasis for the need to both listen and speak allow for an emergence of messy and brown and distinct femininities to coexist, in mutuality and solidarity across different social positionalities, in a white majority, cisgenderist, masculinist, and heteronormative Global North academia that is waiting to inflict violence at every turn on minoritized peoples. It is also not lost on me that the very messiness and uncontrollable spillages of the communication style embodied in the *adda* are in direct and welcome tension with the clean, controlled, and contained aesthetic of contact improvisation as a movement and danced communication aesthetic that is supposedly premised on spontaneity.

But the COVID-19 pandemic meant that during lockdowns, we had to seek out new ways to engage in *adda*.

Zoom, Zoom, Zoom: *Addas* during the Pandemic

It is the summer of 2020, and we are in the very thick of a global lockdown, courtesy of the COVID-19 pandemic. Endless days turn into endless nights turn into more endless days of anxiety, boredom, despair. I am privileged enough to be spending these terrifying times in a home with more than one room, high-speed internet, a garden, and co-habitants—a loving partner and our dazzling daughter. My daughter is in primary school and aged eight. My partner and I suddenly find ourselves at the heart of our respective employing organizations' COVID-strategy teams. We spend every moment of our waking day staring at our computer screens in meetings after meetings. They are now all back-to-back with no break, hearing people repeatedly asking others to "unmute" themselves.

"What an ableist term!"—I say to my colleagues.

We process the extent of preexistent social, racial, health, inequities that the lockdowns have suddenly brought to the fore. We are supposed to also home-school our daughter. Yeah ... that ... that hardly ever happens, except between gulps of tuna sandwiches that she prepares for us and leaves at our desks. We hug her to say thank you, and because we are the fortunate few, in this unimaginable situation, who can actually still give and receive hugs.

While those living alone crave human contact.

There is no clear demarcation between work and home time anymore—it all blurs into one, big, blurry, toxic, mess. And even when work stops, our way to socialize with, and check in on loved ones—whether thousands of miles away in India (as with my elderly and clinically vulnerable parents), or a ten-minute walk away (as with dear local friends)—is still on Zoom. My daughter comes to understand swiftly that on some evenings, Mama drinks wine with her friends from all over the world, late into the night. She thinks it is on FaceTime.

Zoom/Facetime/WhatsApp Video, what does it matter, right? They are all vital portals that are our only ways to connect with other humans.

So, she makes me a poster for my door that says:

MAMA IS ON ~~FACETIME~~ WINE

AND THE ANSWER IS:

IN THE LAUNDRY /

I ATE THE ICECREAM /

DOWNSTAIRS /

GO TO BED/

ASK BABA /

SEE YOU TOMORROW /

NO.

I don't know whether to laugh or cry at its accuracy of sentiments. I put it up on my study door, where it remains to this day.

With no theaters, no cinemas, no local parks, no shopping centers, no pubs, no bars, no restaurants, no friends' homes, no street corners, or gardens to gather in, I turn to social media.

#MISTAKE101.

> *Facebook is toxic.*
> *Twitter is a raging mess.*
> *Thank fuck I am not on Instagram.*
> *And what fresh hell even is Tik Tok.*

Everyone's insecurities and fears and uncertainties are fully on display, and no one comes out looking good.

Yet, the irony is, these digital and social media platforms provide ways for people to connect, to be nurtured and sustained by, and in community with each other—something that lockdown has disabled. We crave community—healthy or toxic—and we find it in #hashtagtivisms and online addas.

The digital is all powerful too. It mobilizes resurgence of global #BlackLivesMatter protests after the murder of George Floyd, an African American man, at the hands of a police officer in Minneapolis, USA. This is turn ignites a much-needed parallel mobilization of the #DalitLivesMatter movement by Dalit rights campaigners in India, who lend their support to the #BlackLivesMatter movement while foregrounding the urgency of caste annihilation.

Thanks to the power of open access social media, Indian dance/studies experiences a seismic shift as we are made to confront its casteist foundations by crucial interventions, made for the first time in the history of our field by anti-caste and hereditary dance-artists like Nrithya Pillai, forcing many of us to reckon with our own complicity in this (Kedhar 2020; Banerji and Mitra 2020).[1] The tactility of social media in these social justice movements is palpable and brings about irrevocable changes.[2] Reflecting on her journey from feeling futility and despair during the pandemic and questioning the relevance of dance studies in the larger scheme of a broken world, dance scholar Munjulika Tarah shared with me in personal communications how she slowly got to grips with the purpose of researching under such despairing circumstances, "because everything as we know it was shifting, it gave us energy and perhaps clarity to focus on and hold on to things that we felt are important to bring to this new post-pandemic world" (2023).

Artists turn to digital platforms for making and marking their work. In October 2020, Akram Khan Company marks its twentieth anniversary via a screening of The Silent Burn Project, slicing and curating together the work and words of artists, thinkers, collaborators that the company has worked with over its two-decade journey. Footage of dancers working across continents appear interwoven into a beautiful, fragmented blanket—desperately seeking each other out, to be whole again.

Our teaching too responds to these bizarre circumstances of isolation, as I find myself delivering choreography lessons to my students on Zoom. And for all my anxiety of these classes failing even before they have started, by the end of the term, these young and vibrant humans blow my mind with their solo dance-films. Shot on their smart phones, edited on their laptops, their endless creativities conjured via their stunning movements, are underpinned by searing commentaries, and lonely and uncertain existences.

My research journey necessarily adapts to this new norm also. No longer sitting in studios watching the subjects of my writing make their art, or interviewing them over lunch and coffees, Nahid Siddiqui and I connect via Zoom. And we talk every Monday evening for several months—across timezones and borders—as we get to know more about each other's work. I similarly contact Akila on email, and we too find a connection on Zoom.

I learn, slowly and reluctantly, to appreciate and embrace the power of the digital. And this totally changes the entire direction of this book.

And then one evening, scrolling through my phone trying to fall asleep at night, stopping myself from entertaining the terrifying "what ifs" about the pandemic, and closed borders, and elderly parents, I stumble onto the total treasure trove that is LaWhore Vagistan's Instagram page.

There, staring straight at me is LaWhore looking glorious in an electric blue chiffon sari with a border of exquisite gold thread embroidery, a sleeveless gold blouse, a chunky gold necklace with the same blue stones, her black and wavy hair cascading over her shoulders and framing her impeccably made-up face, highlighted by the most stunning gold and black eyes and brown lips. She holds a mobile phone in her hand, making it clear that what I am staring at is a photo of LaWhore staring into the mirror at her own reflection. Keyed up with anticipation and hoping that this is an Instareel of LaWhore channeling Sridevi in #KaateNahinKatte *from* Mr India, *I click "play."*

Dancing Slippages

LaWhore Vagistan is the drag queen persona of performance studies scholar Kareem Khubchandani (any pronouns), who is associate professor in the Department of Theatre, Dance and Performance Studies at Tufts University. Her pronouns are she/her/auntie and her social media profiles remind us that she is "everyone's favorite over-educated *desi* drag auntie." In a recent episode of the "Queer Everything" podcast, when asked about the role and experience of doing drag in academic spaces, Khubchandani replies:

> I think academic spaces are hungry for a different kind of academic body. I think the researcher's/professor's body is a masculinized white one. . . . Doing drag in the academic has been about insisting upon and experimenting with what a kind of messy brown femininity can do in these spaces as well. When I show up to class in drag, which is not often, . . . if LaWhore shows up to the classroom instead of me, she is tripping over her sari. My body is not used to moving in the space dressed like that with that much jewelry and wigs and makeup and whatnot. So it's not this graceful, powerful femininity. It's a playful messy one. It allows students and colleagues to see me differently and to see the space differently. It transforms the space. And my students take it really seriously. They will call LaWhore, Dr Vagistan. They will talk about Kareem in third person in those times. There is room for play in the classroom. (in Queer Everything 2023)

LaWhore herself has famously been in conversation with Kareem on these topics in a published essay titled "Lessons in Drag: An Interview with LaWhore Vagistan" (Khubchandani 2015), has delivered her own TEDx Talk on "How to Be an Auntie" (Vagistan 2020), and has written the "introduction" and "outroduction" to Kareem's book *Decolonize Drag (Decolonize That!)* (Khubchandani 2023). These playful and critical slippages between LaWhore and Kareem, as humans, as artists, as writers, as thinkers, illustrate the (un)making of contact points between gender identities and embodiments; between performativity and materiality; between social and the corporeal.

> *RM: Thank you so much for agreeing to be in this* adda *with me. It strikes me as significant that while in this final part of my book I focus on*

LaWhore, I am actually having this adda *with Kareem. Can you tell me more about these critical slippages and overlapping points of embodiments, and thinking, and being, between LaWhore and Kareem? What do you think are the traces that you find of each other in each other as you move between and embody both personas?*

LV/KK: *Yeah ... erm ... (long pause).... I think I like to say ... that to say that LaWhore is Kareem after two vodkas.*

(*Laughter from RM*)

So, there is a kind of ease and a dropping of façade perhaps? There is a looseness that LaWhore can embody. Whether or not I have had the two vodkas, an ease and comfort that she gets to have, that I don't always give myself permission to. But that said, LaWhore has been a way of creating a place for me? You know, like just in the name of LaWhore Vagistan as someone coming from a Sindhi Merchant diaspora. Who has and has not had attachments to the subcontinent, but also being someone with family from Gibraltar and Ghana. All of these things have actually allowed for Vagistan to actually be a place for me. A place to think with in terms of holding multiple histories. And so, she is ... she is a way of reckoning with some of my own travels. And the travels of my own family and history and identity. So that's just in the name alone.

And then in terms of performance, she allows me to perform forms of dance I haven't been allowed to perform, right? You know ... "don't dance that way!" But she also gives me permission to try out new forms of dance. The year I started performing as LaWhore was after a year of being on a competitive Bollywood dance team. Where the men and the women rehearsed separately, and I was like "oh but the women's steps are so much better and why can't I do them?!" And I would copy them while they were doing their sections....

RM: *... so you were doing the men's sections?*

LV/KK: *I was doing the men's sections. And all of that also meant like having to do lifts and jumps and things that I did not have the strength to do. And didn't really want to do. I mean this is classic dance theory right? The men were there to lift the women—and I didn't really want to find myself in that position. So LaWhore gave me permission to just do the moves and steps that I have never given myself the permission to do. So she just created more repertoire in my body at a very technical*

level. And so when you ask me what does she allow me to embody, it has to be a certain set of movements that have been really held back or I have not allowed myself to try on me. And I remember actually in my very, very first performance as LaWhore, I did the steps from the women's choreography from the dance group. There was like this little dance movement that they did that I loved, and I took that on.
(KK smiles as they reminisce and share their memory).

So, I guess there is all the psychic stuff around history and identity and Vagistan and all. And then there is the literal and embodied movement. And then she has allowed me to be a different kind of teacher and researcher in many ways. LaWhore brings research to Kareem because people talk to her about things they might not have talked to me about. She allows me entry into spaces, gives me a certain kind of legitimacy. So... embodying this drag queen has been a way of negotiating my way through the academy and through research fields.

And so I have the diva, drag queen, aunty personas—that allow me to negotiate the various demands of being an academic and a performer, and also help me negotiate being a person of color in the academy as well. I feel like it would be great to hear from you also about what different personas might do for you? I wonder if and how personas function in your teaching/research/writing/performance/administrative work? Do you have another persona? Are there other Royonas? Who are the other Royonas who we perhaps don't see, or see a lot of, in this book?

RM: So...

(RM exhales)

This is such a moving question, and I have a slight gulp in my throat as I try to respond to it, because I don't think I have ever allowed myself the time or space to consider this question. And yet, in different ways, navigating a majority white Global North academy as a racially minoritized woman is, and has been, challenging. And hearing you talk about the "looseness" that LaWhore enables in Kareem, is really powerful because I don't think I have ever allowed myself looseness.

So, being asked this question has made me pause, as I have never thought about the possibility of coexisting Royona personas. But before I respond to you, I want to firstly reflect on something else.

You asking me this question is a stark reminder that conventional interview processes between researchers and our subjects of research more often than not allows the power to sit with the researcher—and that very much shapes the way in which a conversation unfolds. What I really appreciate here is, that I am hoping that this adda *modality enables a permanently shifting power dynamic between the two of us. So, your question is an urgent reminder of what it is actually like to be in such an* adda. *Until you asked me this question, I had only theoretically set up this* adda *model of exchange between us and not felt, at a bodily psychic level, what this actual shifting of power, of shifting between the one asking the questions to the one responding to them, really means. And I am so glad that we are doing this.*

So, going back to your question. I think I identify myself into different categories: there is like "the educator Royona," "the researcher/writer Royona," and then there is the "administrator/senior manager/Ass Dean Royona." And in some ways I feel like the roles blur. There are common ways in which I move through all of these roles and spaces, but there are also qualities that are quite distinct. And where and how they are distinct is determined by how I perform each role in relation to different power structures in any given situation.

There's the classroom power structures, there's the dance studies/performance studies field power structures, there's the institutional power structures. And I think what all of these Royonas hold in common is perhaps an urge to agitate; whether it's agitating hegemonic learning environments and dismantling what that means; or whether it's agitating dance and performance studies; or whether it's agitating university structures and institutional practices. And what I am coming to realize is that in each of these agitative acts, I operate in different modes.[3]

In the classroom I think my agitation manifests as a vulnerable person who is also very held together. I am reminded here of your recent podcast where you talk about the unraveling of yourself through LaWhore to become more clumsy and chaotic. I have never allowed myself to unravel in appearance, but I think I allow myself vulnerability and a little bit more clumsiness in my words and actions within the classroom space. I feel like in order to be taken seriously as a racially minoritized woman in our majority white academy, I can't afford to let go of the held together outer appearance. But I allow myself to expose my vulnerabilities or to share experiences with students in hope that it encourages them to consider how power operates in classrooms, even though as an educator I do hold power in those spaces.

Then there is the Associate Dean Royona, and perhaps also the researcher Royona, and I feel this is the Royona who asks questions. The agitation is done through incessant questioning. It's asking questions of the institution, it's asking questions of the field, it's holding myself accountable both as a human and as a scholar. And constantly reminding myself and others that we all occupy social positions in which we simultaneously hold privileges of some power systems, while also being marginalized by other power systems. That we can both harm and be harmed at the same time. And that by asking questions, and sharing examples of instances where I am causing harm to others, I can get others to reflect on their own actions and words vis-à-vis power.

And then there is the Royona who listens—and she moves through all three spaces also—and this Royona comes out of an awareness that listening is a skill that we do not really instill or value in the academy and our institutions. We are all trained to talk, we are trained to write, we are trained to take up space through communicating our own thoughts constantly.

But we are not really trained to listen.

How do we nurture and bring up a generation that knows how to really listen. And how can I listen with more active attentiveness? Because I can tell that my fellow senior managers around me are not really listening; they allow people to air their thoughts and then they hope these people are going to go away and not come back.

Because truly listening requires commitment to change.

I am also very aware that the questioning and the listening Royonas are contradictory personas. One takes up space, and one is committed to not take up space. So that's like a constant juggle. So yes, my personas are very different to the ways in which you describe yours, but perhaps I think of them as different and holistic set of skills I bring to my work as an educator, a researcher, an administrator, indeed a human.

And all these Royonas are present in abundance in this book and they seamlessly morph into, call upon, and enable each other. And it makes me want to ask you that although you so beautifully articulated how LaWhore enables Kareem, how does Kareem enable LaWhore?

LV/KK: I think in a lot of ways I wouldn't have a drag practice without research. If LaWhore is the creative end of me, then Kareem is the researcher, the curious end of me. The one who pushes me beyond my comfort zone and asks questions beyond what I know. Instead of just making, making, making, Kareem is the person who says, "ok but you can't make without these grounding tools." And this is not to say that drag artists are not researchers. The drag world is very full of socially, and critically, and pop-culturally aware performers. But I think Kareem the scholar gives me a certain kind of grounding to make performance in a way that feels, for lack of a better term, intellectually sound. That all the fun and joy are situated somewhere and are not simply "ok let's have fun!"

RM: That's so spot on. That contact point between fun and criticality is so beautifully interwoven and so present in the interactions between Kareem and LaWhore. I know Kareem and LaWhore have been in addas with each other. In those adda sessions what did Kareem and LaWhore learn from each other about these crucial contact points between fun and criticality?

KK/LV: Erm ... (long pause and intake of breath). This was really an exercise in writing and learning how ... well. LaWhore taught me to write in a different way. I published that interview with LaWhore very soon after graduate school. But graduate school training taught me to write in a very particular voice: "where is your argument? Are you evidencing your claims? Why is this valuable?" etc. And I came out of a performance studies program at Northwestern that really advocated for performative writing, but I think that writing a dissertation was so enormous that I lost the kind of play that I was offered.

So, forcing myself to write in a different voice, in LaWhore's voice ... to find a voice for her ... at a time in my drag career when I hadn't gotten on the microphone very often ... so this was a way of harvesting a language for her by writing in her voice. But it also gave me room as a scholarly writer to again find looseness, make jokes. And I think having to do the back and forth writing—the scholarly and the drag-artist—was really a rehearsal in another kind of writing. And like I said, gave LaWhore words at a point when she didn't have any. And since then, my Decolonize Drag book has an Introduction and an Outroduction by LaWhore...

RM: "Outroduction"—love that!

KK/LV: So she gets to have the first and the last word instead of me. It's not that... you know... I am living this split psyche... it's that I think that scholarly writing is very useful and productive and careful, and that other creative forms of writing are also useful and productive and exciting. And I wouldn't want to compromise one for the other. And I am sure there are people who are skilled enough to weave both... but for me rehearsing these two very different kinds of writing feel very helpful.

RM: It is so reassuring to hear you say this, because one of the things I have been trying to do with this book is to make words look different on a page to how we have been trained to write at graduate school, like you say. Instead, I want the words themselves to look like they are moving on the page. So, it's not exactly the same as what you are describing in terms of your performative writing in LaWhore's voice, but I guess I also trying to unsettle and liberate myself from conventional academic writing modes. So, it's exciting to hear about your journey through this terrain.

KK/LV: Right... I guess it is also important for me... because I often get this pushback from students, especially graduate students and other scholars, that "scholarly writing is a writing of privilege and it is jargony and difficult, and my grandmother can't read it, is it really useful" etc.? All of that kind of discourse can sometimes undermine the quite radical work of discipline-based knowledge, that is steeped in technical language. And we don't have similar critiques of the sciences working in technical language....

RM: Absolutely....

KK/LV: It's always the humanities and the arts, and the thing is that when we are articulating complicated ideas, we can lean on those "big words," because sometimes we are speaking to our peers to push their knowledge. Things like terms like "performativity," right? It's actually a phenomenal word that can teach us about how power replicates itself, when it's understood in its genealogy. It's a really phenomenal word to think with. But to say "it's a big word don't use it" is also really limiting, right? So, being able to work in both modes is to me really important.

RM: Yeah... it feels as though it is an opening up of possibilities and not a shutting down.

KK/LV: So yes, doing this sort of multiple work with LaWhore has got me there. You know there is a point in the interview I published with

LaWhore, where it sort of falls apart that they are in fact these two people in this interview. But it is working with the very familiar format of like the scholar interviewing the artist. And I know that interview is very important to the way you do your work. You work closely with artists and learn their biographies and research everything they've made and written and talked about. But then you actually sit and talk to them as yourself.

(RM nods in agreement vehemently)

KK/LV: And I want to ask you what is at stake in speaking with artists in order to write about them or us and how does conversation, whether long-term discourse over time or one-time interviews, shape your or our role as cultural critics?

RM: This is such a valuable question because it helps me to sit with something that perhaps I have romanticized over my career that I have built as a dance scholar who works very closely with artists, like you say, prioritizing their words, their works, their critical biographies and how they feed into each other. And I think it's one of the reasons why I don't think I could ever be a dance historian, because in my work it is incredibly important to be in conversation with someone who is alive and making work, and whose works are unfolding the same time as my thinking. This is particularly true of my body of work on Akram Khan, whose dance career trajectory happened the same time as my own scholarly trajectory unfolded. So I have premised my career on the fundamental belief that I cannot think and write about the dance-art I am engaging with without being in conversation with the artist concerned. Erm...so...

(long pause and exhalation from RM)

RM: In this current book project, I have engaged in these long and detailed interviews with my artist-interlocutoes, written the chapters about them, integrated their words into my writing, and then gone back to them many times, back and forth, to ensure that our exchanges don't stop at the interviews. But rather to seek their thoughts and to ensure that their words have been accurately reflected into my writing. So they have turned into long-term invested conversations with each of my artists. I guess this way of working signals something that I am invested in, perhaps something that I romanticize, as a kind of co-production of knowledge.

> *So I work hard to ensure that I am not speaking on behalf of the artists in my book.*
>
> *I am conscious of how power-laden those conventional modes of working are with artists, and try to resist and unsettle them.*
>
> *And yet ... and yet (RM laughs nervously) ... the word that really sticks out to me in your question is "what is at STAKE?" in this mode of working. I think the importance of your question lies in an acknowledgment that despite all of these ethical commitments and intentions, I guess the main question in these artist-scholar conversations that I ask of myself is "ultimately, who's benefiting from these exchanges?" Within the academy, as we both know, resources are so tight. I'd ideally like to offer fees to artists who are in these conversations with me, and yet I can't acknowledge their labor and expertise in material terms. So much of this work is built on good will. So much of this work is built on trust that something good will come out these exchanges that will be mutually beneficial. Even "benefit" is the wrong word ... perhaps that is mutually ... erm ... erm ... generative. And yet perhaps there is truth here too in the word "benefit" because these exchanges are happening on the terms of my academic career. The book I write will lend me further social, cultural, and academic capital. But ultimately, what is in there for these artists who have so graciously and generously given their time and expertise to me and my project?*
>
> *So I don't know if I have a direct and clear answer to your question, but what it does is to alert me to the engrained power-dynamic that is inherent to artist-scholar exchanges.*
>
> KK/LV: I mean I hear you and I also think will this conversation in your book lead more people to my Instagram account?
>
> RM: True ... yes.
>
> KK/LV: I mean we know that academic books don't necessarily have that extensive reach, right? But if students are reading this, will the professors assign the work? Will all the interviews that you do after the book comes out about the book, and all the talks you give, create life and work for the artists? So I guess when I write about artists, I am also trying to give their work platforms, in whatever capacity. I think there is something redistributive about it.
>
> RM: That is really helpful to think that way. Thank you.
>
> KK/LV: And your writing—well it teaches me how to watch Akram Khan's work, for example. You're giving people language and

epistemes actually with which to understand someone who is now a canonical dancer, right? Who is choreographing for global events. To teach people how to look through his own words and yours, I think is actually very useful to me, at least, is what I want to say.

RM: Thank you for saying this, it's so helpful to hear. Because yes, it is of course our intention as scholars to give platforms to artists and their works. It is all really complicated, and I am acknowledging the complexity of these artist-scholar exchanges as I think with you.

But I guess at another level what is at stake is when I am in conversation with artists who are differently located to myself on social power spectrums, I think I need to be really attentive to not reinforcing my ways of knowing and moving through the world through my own social positionings, in the ways in which I write about their works. So that's something really at stake, and something that I need to have a heightened awareness of.

Even in our email exchanges leading up to this adda, I have become aware that if I am not fully tuned in to the need to unsettle my own dominant social positions at every dimension of my writing, my thinking, my communication processes, it will reassert and foreground itself in insidious ways. So that's at stake and a risk I really need to be tuned in to and consciously working to mitigate against.

So yes, what's at stake is ensuring I do not reinforce artist-scholar hierarchies, that conventional extractionist models of knowledge acquisition are not present in my work and a constant awareness that none of us is immune to these practices as researchers. So what's at stake is that we are all working constantly to mitigate against these real possibilities of inflicting harm.

I say all of this with the awareness that those who are the loudest and more vociferous about being committed to social justice in our sub-field of South Asian dance studies are also often the people who end up reinforcing and upholding power in their practices and inflict harm. So, I just want to remain alert to that in my own work.

KK/LV: Right, and I think this is where Auntie becomes helpful. So, you need to ask, "which kind of auntie do I want to be in this situation?," regardless of gender. As we grow into administrative roles and we are editors and deans, we become the auntie, right? We become the figure who is around, and orbits and watches . . . who curates. So this opens up the space for us to thinking about the auntie I want to become *rather than letting auntie just happen. And since you talk about power structures and being disciplinarian, I am actually always invested in not being of discipline. So how do you then be the auntie that undoes rather than reifies?*

RM: *Exactly this. That's such a beautiful way of putting it because the idea that you can make proactive choices to become a particular kind of auntie who enables, who dismantles as opposed to reifies and harms, is everything! It liberates you from thinking, "I am just going to fall into an auntie trope and I can't stop that from happening to me." I want to realize that this is something I am allowing myself to do and become, and I can stop it and shape the Auntie I aspire to.*

And it makes me question further, what is then the relationship between aunties and uncles, at the expense of reinforcing gender binaries. It's striking to me that, in your Mr India *Instareel, you evoked both LaWhore and Kareem. Sridevi and Anil Kapoor were both conjured. So what led you to create that Instareel where LaWhore and Kareem worked together to evoke both Sridevi and Anil Kapoor?*

Between Sridevi and Kapoor: LaWhore, Kareem, and #*KaateNahinKatte* (2020)

She stands in front of a door frame covered with a red bordered chiffon sari, dusted with gold chumkis that hangs over it like a curtain. Kareem dressed as Anil Kapoor appears from the bottom of the screen and stands in front of the curtain. With their gaze and forefinger directed straight at me, the camera, their Insta audience, Kareem lip-synchs to the lyrics: "lo aaj mei kahta hoon.... I love you" (So here I am to tell you today.... I love you) to a remix version of the 1980s hit track from Mr India (Image 4.1).

They are dressed in a stone-colored linen jacket over a turquoise and pink block printed shirt, and a stone-colored matching hat, detailed with a yellow and pink striped ribbon around the rim. Kareem also wears their own version of a signature Anil Kapoor mustache. Their eyebrows dance provocatively to the rhythm of the song, gazing directly at me. They point their forefinger at the camera to emphasize the "you" of the infamous refrain

Image 4.1 Kareem Khubchandani in *#KaateNahinKatte* Instareel by videographer and editor Kareem Khubchandani

"*I love you*"—as though directing their words at every person engaging with their Instareel.

This includes me. And I giggle appreciatively at this direct address from Kareem/Kapoor.

Multiple Anil Kapoors appear on screen until Kareem morphs into LaWhore and becomes Sridevi (Image 4.2).

The very first moment we see her appear is like watching her split reflection through a mirror. She is dressed in that blue chiffon sari with gold embroidery, a sleeveless gold blouse, a chunky gold and turquoise necklace and earrings and bangles. The wavy pitch-black wig frames her face bountifully. Her eyes, eyelashes, and eyebrows stand out from a mile, highlighted with a cream-gold eyeshadow over the lids and beneath the eyebrows. Her lips are defined with a brown shade, and on the right cheek a black beauty spot (Image 4.3).

Her arms are hairy. A stark and magical reminder that this is Kareem in their drag persona of LaWhore playing Sridevi, and a welcome critique of the obsession of hairlessness as a marker of South Asian femininity.[4]

The reel uses a filter that makes little white hearts rain across the screen, as though they are the same raindrops falling from the sky that drenched Sridevi's blue chiffon in Mr India. She uses the width of the hallway, framed by the walls on either side to twirl and shimmy and throw and catch her weight on the walls. She stands between the two walls with each hand against them, using their groundedness to pivot and gyrate and swivel backward and forward— her focus always directed straight into the camera (Image 4.4).

Loose, wayward, out of control.
But also so very much in control.

All the while her gaze never leaves the camera—her Instareel audience. She echoes Anil Kapoor's gesture of emphasizing "*you*" as she mouths the lyrics: "*Koi nahi bas tum ho paas, kehni thhi tumjhe so dil ki baat*" (No other person here but you, and I wish to share with you the words from my heart). And then she repeats Kapoor's refrain: "*Lo aaj mei kahta hoon.... I love you*" (So here I am to tell you today.... I love you).

As I watch the reel, transfixed, on a loop, I am reminded that in the original video Sridevi and Kapoor aimed their words at each other. But in LaWhore-Kareem's rendition these words, and their gestures, are aimed at me, at us, at every Insta audience member who chooses to watch the reel. Their gaze and pointed forefinger touches each of us personally, drawing us into their Instareel.

Image 4.2 Kareem Khubchandani in *#KaateNahinKatte* Instareel by videographer and editor Kareem Khubchandani

Image 4.3 LaWhore Vagistan in *#KaateNahinKatte* Instareel by videographer and editor Kareem Khubchandani

Image 4.4 LaWhore Vagistan in *#KaateNahinKatte* Instareel by videographer and editor Kareem Khubchandani

*Her eyebrows, too,
dance seductively,
as she cups her face in her bejeweled hands
and stares into the camera* (Image 4.5).

*There are multiple Sridevis as she morphs into many and one through
skillful and sensual editing* (Image 4.3).

She is one and she is many, and she speaks to so many of us.

Image 4.5 LaWhore Vagistan in *#KaateNahinKatte* Instareel by videographer and editor Kareem Khubchandani

LV/KK: So that reel was made in the summer of 2020, if I am not mistaken, in the heights of the pandemic lockdown. Also, June of 2020 was Pride Month in the US, and there were all these digital drag events that were emerging. And specific South Asian party planners and folks who had had to go online for their events started producing digital drag shows. There was a variety of formats: some of them were livestreamed, and then there was the other format or making performances, recording them, editing them, and presenting them as a music video. So I would get into drag for those events and videos and realize that I had spent two hours getting ready to film a five-minute thing—and after that there was no one to hang out with, no one to have a drink with. I started to wonder how I could make this labor do something.

I started making these digital videos and a lot of them were LaWhore and Kareem playing these feminine and masculine parts and counterparts. I did a Drake and Rihanna, I did a Raj Kapoor and Nargis, and then also a Sridevi and Anil Kapoor reel. But this song in particular and Sridevi in particular comes out of my research, right? It goes back to your question what does Kareem do for LaWhore. In my fieldwork for Ishtyle, Sridevi and Madhuri Dixit showed up as these core figures in shaping queer dance in the nightclub and elsewhere. And regardless of my general familiarity with Bollywood that was definitely shaped by 90s liberalization and aesthetic of the Kuch Kuch Hota Haye, Kal Ho Na Ho, Kabhi Khushi Kabhi Gahm—that set of films, I grew up in Ghana hearing these songs but not seeing the videos of the 1980s films. These videos didn't circulate in the same ways. But it was my research with these queer South Asian folks who said, "no, you have to have a diva and you have to research her and you have to hold onto her aesthetic and you have to think about what she does for you, how she teaches you how to move, and feel, and you need this costume and that costume." And it brought me back to the things I did know about Sridevi and Madhuri.

RM: So you didn't watch the videos until you were much older? You had just heard the songs?

LV/KK: Yeah, so, I saw Mr India once when I was a kid and then we sang the songs, but it wasn't Kaate Nahin. It was the one with the kids, right? It was joking about Mogambo. So there were other memories that were not about the diva, that were not about her. I hadn't seen

Hawa Hawai until I was much older, although I knew the song. But, and this shows up in my other work, what I had seen was all my aunties performing these songs. So, that I think was actually really valuable to return to also. So as I talk about LaWhore letting me try on steps that I had never let myself, it was also returning to these auntie choreographies. But the aunties would do the men's and women's roles. They did Anil Kapoor and Madhuri Dixit doing Dhhak Dhhak and they were sexy with each other. I saw them in the living rooms rehearsing and giggling. So, you know, I have seen drag Anil Kapoor growing up and I have seen drag Sridevi and Madhuri. But it was in these intimate spaces and not the screen. So filming these videos in my house also works in that genealogy of home-style performance.

RM: And also already mediated by so many other bodies that you had seen perform these sequences.

LV/KK: Yes, exactly right. And I guess, even the digital format also changes so many things.

So the algorithms are also doing their own kind of work. I made this video in Covid conditions, and algorithms are shaping how it circulates and what it is, what it's called. But these were all opportunities for community making in a digital pandemic context. And you're thinking about touch and virtual performance and caste politics and touch and dance in pandemic times. How are you thinking about this digital mode in relation to your work on touch and dance and caste and movement in and beyond pandemic times?

RM: Yeah . . . so . . . if I am honest, I was already starting to have these thoughts as a pedagogue and researcher even before the pandemic. In many ways I have internalized the very principles of contact improvisation and the ways in which touch operates in, let's say, predominant Global North dance contexts, long before I started critiquing any of it. This was even as I knew there were layers to this work that I was uncomfortable with, that did not sit easily with me. I knew they needed questioning, but I just didn't feel I had the tools or the right headspace to start doing that. So in the meantime, I started operating in exactly those same ways as an educator. I have taught contact improv and touch-based practices in my classrooms. And then, when I finally felt able to enter the right headspace to start interrogating those practices, the first thing I realized was to recognize the hypocrisy in my emerging *thinking and my pedagogic practices. So, long before the pandemic hit, I had already realized and acknowledged this dissonance.*

I felt in those moments, that the only way in which I could remain true to my emerging sense of inquiry was to stop engaging in touch-based practices between humans in my teaching. So, I was already starting to explore physical points of contact and interactions between walls, and surfaces, and props, and costumes and individuals. I had already started to explore these possibilities before the lockdown. And in a way when lockdown happened and I was suddenly having to teach choreography online overnight, it was tough as it was for everybody, but I was able to draw on the mechanisms I had already started to explore in being expansive about how I thought about contact within my teaching. Such that the principles of contact improv could be expanded to explore interactions between human and non-human contact. Students were obviously in their own bedrooms or living spaces during these classes making solo work. And this bizarre situation that we all found ourselves in allowed for these incredible dance-films made in solo capacities, where my students showed me the multiple ways in which contact can be made in choreography, that neither the sector nor I had really imagined or tuned in to.

When I find moments of dissonance in my life between what I am starting to reconsider and what I have historically done, I stop the doing until I can figure out a way of moving through the doing in a different way. For instance, over the last few years I have become alert to the casteist roots of Hindu festivals like Holi or Durga Pujo. While I am a person of non-faith, I have leaned into Durga Pujo socially and have certainly celebrated Holi. But as soon as I started to learn about their inherent casteisms, I stopped marking these festivals. And maybe I shall never figure out a way to celebrate these again, in which case this pause becomes crucial to my development as a human being.

So similarly, as soon as I felt able to, and was ready to take on the power regimes that frame contact improv and other touch-based movement practices, I stopped engaging with them as an educator until I could figure out alternative ways forward. But I do want to note that until this point in my thinking, many of my former students will have been taught contact improv by me and may well find its critique in this book a contradiction. So that contradiction is something that I am living through within myself, acknowledging that it's flawed and messy. But also that this messiness has enabled me to move forward and unravel and reflect on my own past pedagogy.

And, of course, now that I am back in the classroom in person, I have carried through those practices that I was really starting to learn from my students by working with them online. I've introduced solo practice as an option for those who wish to work on their own, I've introduced working with props and surfaces and costumes as alternative ways of discovering contact-making in choreography. And I am starting to explore with students what contact might look beyond physical touch, in line with what my book does, which is to theorize contact in different ways that moves beyond tactility.

The final layer of this massive and important question that I am trying to address through my book and my pedagogy is that we want to move to a world where touch-based practices are not oppressive and harmful. We want it to be a harbinger of a liberated society. And yet we can't get there until we actually dismantle the oppressive systems that make touch-based practices oppressive, whether its race, or gender, or caste, or faith, or sexuality. So I feel as though we are sitting on the cusp of realizing its liberatory capacities, but also knowing that we are nowhere near as a field, as a sector, as a society, to actually dismantle those systems so that in can take us to a place of liberation.

LV/KK: And I think that's been so valuable for me to think about the fact that the digital is not the ultimate equalizing place—there are power structures in the digital space as well—it is often categorized as the fake or the not real, the virtual or the "not yet here." But in fact it is a very real place for disabled people, people who are in the closet, people who are socially isolated in a variety of ways. It allows people to try on identities that are not theirs and experience what other ways of living in the world can be. For instance, the internet was a well-established place for disabled artists, well before the pandemic. So even as we glorify touch and contact as "the real" and authentic, virtual spaces are spaces of touching, making emotional contact. People who have not had the same kind of access to public spaces, not just because of the pandemic but because of a variety of precarious conditions that makes being out in the world unsafe... have found homes in digital spaces.

RM: Absolutely, and that is actually what my students taught me through their solo dance-films that there are so many different ways in which

> to expansively think about touch and contact beyond tactility that we had limited ourselves from and denied in the live classroom. And not to bring those learnings from the digital classrooms into the live classroom now would be ridiculous and irresponsible.
>
> One of the reasons that I was drawn to that particular reel that you made is because it is digital, and it makes me wonder what the digital platform did for LaWhore to embody the emergence of Sridevi as an auntie through drag?

Genealogies and Technologies of Choreographing Auntie Sridevi

In an interview with Kshiti S.V. on the *India Culture Lab*'s "The Meme Project," Khubchandani talks about the genealogy of aunties and describes the auntie label as "capacious" and the auntie figure as "an aesthetic, a figure, a cipher, an idiom, and ethic" (in India Culture Lab 2020), identifying the "aunty as aesthetic" as their most enjoyable auntie-mode. They describe the aesthetic of the auntie as one of excess with "big eyes. Big body. Big gestures. Always wearing prints. Excessive, fun, cool. Accented" (in India Culture Lab 2020). To understand aunties as excess means to understand that they also offer "too much food, too much advice, too much information" (Khubchandani quoted in India Culture Lab 2020). This lineage of excess in aunties can be linked to the aesthetic of the camp and more specifically to the aesthetics of many "women of colour, trans folks, Indian heritage performance communities" (Khubchandani quoted in India Culture Lab 2020) who are historically written out of white genealogies of camp aesthetics, and takes a very particular culturally specific form as it amalgamates the Indian dramaturgical codes of *abhinaya*: a lexicon that codifies human emotions through hand gestures and facial expressions. Khubchandani says that they share much more affinity with *this* manifestation of the camp, a *desi* camp, as opposed to the white gay male aesthetic of the camp that they have been exposed to in their drag art and studies. They cite Sridevi's pouted lips and big, startling eyes, often embodied and replicated in their own aunties from their children, as part of the genealogy of their drag, in which they honor *this desi* aunty aesthetic, sharing that they "lean into the auntie aesthetic as a way of not forgetting histories . . . as a way of saying that the cool things I do come from somewhere" (Khubchandani quoted in India Culture Lab 2020). Conjuring Sridevi as conduit and precursor to *desi* camp auntie aesthetic in LaWhore then serves the important role of "carry[ing] that aesthetic but not the politic and conservatism" that can also come attached to aunties who can also harm, while being harmed themselves. (Khubchandani quoted in India Culture Lab 2020).

LaWhore's Sridevi comes alive at the intersections of multiple components: her makeup, her facial expressions, her costuming (Mitra 2019), and the complex layer of choreography that emerge between her "danced-gestures" (Khubchandani 2020), her repetition, the physical place of filming, the camera, the Insta filters, the editing, and the digital world-making they collectively engender. I should clarify here that in this chapter I mobilize world-making in this context; I am attentive to Thomas F. DeFrantz's critique of the concept in queer studies as discussed in the Introduction, and therefore do so, to argue that the world-making that is discussed in the chapter embodies the spirit of unmaking as a method, a politics, and an emancipatory mode of birthing new and more just worlds.

All these components come together to what LaWhore refers to below as an "approximation" of Sridevi, and not Sridevi herself. A particular potent part of this heady mixture is LaWhore's wayward, chaotic, seductive, and unruly movements and the constancy of her direct gaze at the camera. The repeated and circulatory flinging of her body from one end of the wall to the other, framed tightly by the length and breadth of the corridor, creates a sense of willful and sexy abandonment, illuding a lack of control while, ironically, being in impeccable control of both her own movements and our desire to emulate them. She takes me back to my childhood days of dancing in my Ma's chiffon sari under the shower, throwing myself between the wall on one end and the glass screen on the other. It is in the repetition of this "danced gesture" to control and be controlled that harbors our desires to make and unmake contact, for queer and non-queer peoples, on our own terms.

> KK/LV: *So I guess I have already mentioned that I grew up watching aunties do Sridevi. But there is also, I think the ways in which my research interlocutors led me to her work, led me to study her artistry. I know Saroj Khan has choreographed a lot of her work and we don't credit the dance director in our study of film-dance, but Sridevi is also an exceptional artist in herself. And she does a kind of Bollywood*

heroine embodiment that we just don't see, and that's like high comedy? Like she commits to movement in a way that is not about being sexy, but there is still grace, and there is still skill and technique and care. Like she does the big open eyes, she pouts her lips, and she is goofy. And so I think she is a different form of embodiment that I don't think we see much of any more. Or that has been coopted into certain kinds of neoliberal aesthetics. So being able to do her silly dances ... like literally her in her Mr India choreography she is dancing with an invisible person. And she is swinging around and there are posts online that laud her ability to move chiffon. But it is also ridiculous....

RM: Yes, it totally is....

LV/KK: And it's not about hitting the beats and creating precision ... it's more about the ways in which she occupies space and manipulates the garment and practices her imagination, right of this invisible man dancing with her. So to think of her as an auntie is to think of her as a dance ancestor, a "dancestor"—whatever ... I am not going to make that word up—we don't need it....

(RM and LV/KK both laugh spontaneously)

LV/KK: But it's the way she gives us options for dance that I think we have lost that makes her stand out for me. Ramon Rivera-Servera has this essay called "History in Drag" (2017) that is about how older queens in Latinx nightclubs perform slower songs and ballads, things that slow down and drag the speed of the club, but also drag us into the past, into like the wrong repertoire for dancing. So, like, I should be doing Deepika Padukone, but instead I am doing Sridevi. Right?

RM: Right ... yes I see what you are saying....

LV/KK: So this is the kind of auntie-drag that isn't about the coolest new steps, but is about these other kinds of movements that are not at the center of our popular culture, in this moment. And Sridevi is a complicated character to embody, you know? She died early ... complicated conditions with a lot of rumors attached to it. In one of her later movies English Vinglish, she plays an auntie, she plays the immigrant auntie, who actually in the film is too shy to dance. She gradually kind of lets go of that. And a lot of our favorite 80s and 90s stars, as they age in the industry, also become conservative, in a variety of ways right? About dance, about modesty ... so to go back to that version of her feels refreshing and fun and is an opportunity to dabble in the wrong ways of ... of being.

RM: So true. When I watch you do that move of swinging from one end of the corridor to another? It takes me back to the thing I talk about in the Preface to this book, about putting on my Ma's blue chiffon sari and dancing under the shower. It takes me back to replicating exactly the same movements ... it's kind of like the ... waywardness of losing control and yet so impeccably in control ... as you describe so beautifully that tussle in her embodiment. Where she is performing a loss of control, when she is so fully in control. Watching you in the reel really took me back to my own childhood.

LV/KK: I mean, I am wearing my mom's blue chiffon sari when I am doing that, and there are like food and oil stains on the sari from whatever wedding she wore it to, that are impossible to get out....

(RM and KK/LV laugh gently and acknowledge together a precious moment of intergenerational nostalgia)

LV/KK: I am wondering what your childhood relationship with Sridevi that you talk about ... erm ... I haven't seen your reel of Sridevi yet....

RM: Haha—no there isn't one ...!

(RM laughs nervously)

KK/LV: So ... how does that relationship extend into the present?

(RM swivels on her chair and a long pause follows)

RM: I mean it's so complex, and it's a bit like the complexity with which I have had to reassess my own pedagogy. As is evidenced by the fact that this monograph is book-ended by Sridevi, right ...? So I clearly am instinctually obsessed with her as a dancer. She drives the beginning and ending of this book. And through this journey, I have come to realize that my historical engagement with Sridevi's work has always been quite sensorial, quite sensual, and has existed at the levels of acknowledging and appreciating a model of femininity that is sexy and exuberant and confident and fun in the ways in which it is able to take up space. It goes back to a memory I have of my Ma as a child, who is now 80, but at the time would probably have been about the same age as me, maybe even younger in her later thirties–early forties. And my memory is waking up in the morning and drinking milk and watching this beautiful woman with really long hair, choreographically sweeping her hair up into a bun every morning. And I would watch the grace with which her hands would work and dance to create this bun—of a very held together femininity. And I always wondered even as a child what it would be like to watch her loosen, *and let go, and even be chaotic. This reminds of our earlier discussion about what does LaWhore enable in Kareem . . . so, for me, coming back to Sridevi, watching this video of* Kaate Nahin *made it possible for me to imagine a loosening up of femininity on its own terms, even as it conjures this heteronormative relationship with an absent Anil Kapoor. But really, she occupies screen space on her own for most of the song. So it's always been this kind of sensual and empowering engagement with femininity, and thinking about the possibilities that Sridevi offers for myself and others as a young woman.*

And now, I think my engagement with Sridevi's dance has become a much more complex question. It doesn't mean those previous sensual and sensorial ways of understanding her work have disappeared—they are very much still present. As I said earlier, as I watch LaWhore mediate Sridevi's exuberant and abundance of throwing herself across the corridor, there is something in me that is reignited. But I guess the sharpest shift in the journey has been about moving away from thinking about what the dance is doing for me to thinking about what it is doing for all these other people in the world who have always engaged with this video. The fact that it's still iconic, the fact that you are not going to Deepika Padukone, but you are going to Sridevi as the auntie to conjure in that reel. You know, what is it doing to a diverse range of people with a diverse range of social positions and their embodiments. And how has she inspired and impacted all these different people? So that's one question.

But I guess I am also questioning, for all the people she has empowered and inspired, who are the people whose femininities and embodiments might be excluded from her depictions of femininities? So, I guess Sridevi and her dance in Kaate Nahin *becomes this fulcrum through which I start to engage with the lack of intersectionality in the idea that I repeat in the Preface as a refrain—"She is alone and she is enough." I start with that and then go on to demonstrate how that in itself is a flawed monolithic statement. And then toward the end of my Preface I start to consider the fact that "Yes she is alone. And she is enough, but whose humanity is she denying as a consequence of her taking up space."*

So yes, I guess my more recent engagement with Sridevi becomes a way into a more intersectional feminist analysis of that moment that stands out to my childhood me as this is what I aspire to when I am older.

KK/LV: Yeah, you know it's funny that . . . I think you write about Hawa Hawai *and the use of blackface . . . ?*

RM: *Yes, I do, very briefly in the Preface.*

KK/LV: So yes, there is that critique of the blackface in the background of that number. But you know there is one way we can critique her move into Bollywood away from South Indian cinema, but there are a lot of South Indians who will go on to say "but did you know she came out of South Indian cinema?" and will actually hold on to that piece. And they will go even further back in my drag historiography and say, "actually there is another piece to her that you don't know." So, just the way people hold on to different parts of a public figure's history and persona, to go back to persona which is where we started, right, how people use the star is interesting. So she becomes for you a fulcrum for critique, for others it becomes a kind of regional identity. I just think the kind of multiplicity she offers complicates any singular telling of her that I think is really powerful thing to think with.

RM: *Yeah . . . I think you are right. It's not like the intersectional critique overrides all the other ways of reading her work. Absolutely not.*

KK/LV: Right. . . .

RM: *For me it just becomes an awakening of my own ways of thinking about her work. Which rests and is located in parallel ways of reading her work. Which are empowering and are fulfilling different purposes simultaneously.*

KK/LV: Right . . . exactly . . . yes.

RM: *And I guess because of the multiple ways in which she can be conjured, I am curious to ask how you choose to conjure her in the reel. What are the kinds of technologies of LaWhore's drag art that you draw upon for this particular manifestation of Sridevi? How do you choreograph Sridevi in all her multiple layers?*

LV/KK: Erm . . . you are making me remember something that I had maybe blocked out or haven't mentioned to you before, but I have this short performance piece I do called "Bollywood Divas 101." It's a lecture performance and I don't know if there is footage of it. I do Sridevi as a comedy queen. So I actually pigeonhole her into a larger pantheon of the item girl. And I think she is the only one who fits that category. So that's something I am always thinking about when I do Sridevi. A colleague invited me to Providence to do a tribute to her as part of a film festival, and I did like five songs of her? So some of what *entails choreographing her is like watching the videos and actually trying to emulate what she is doing. All of that to say, when I am doing Sridevi, I am not trying to take the lyrics and the rhythm and do what I would do. It really is about capturing what she does. That's one part of the choreography.*

The other part is ... editing. Like for this reel, I didn't rehearse and then do. I just did over and over again and recorded each time and then spliced together the takes. So one of the things that the digital format allows me to do, is to actually perform the invisible man, and then Anil Kapoor literally fades away. So here the digital is actually the choreography.

RM: The editing is the choreography.

LV/KK: Yeah. The editing is the choreography. Because there is no one take that I wanted the world to see. And that's because I was trying to do the steps from the film in a corridor. And there was a really limited amount of space. And that flinging the body from side to side, couldn't happen in the way that it happens with a camera panning—to catch her close up and also to catch her wide.

RM: And yet I guess it kind of does, because you do work with the depts of the corridor as much as you can ...

LV/KK: As much as ... yes ... so yeah I guess those are some of the things I use. Cause I am really trying to work with her and what she did on screen ... but then with the limits of space as well. I am also very much working inside of drag and drag aesthetics in that my makeup is not actually emulating hers. I know how to do drag makeup, but I don't actually know how to do impersonation makeup. I am working with a wig that I already have. Erm ... I didn't style one to look like her. It somewhat approximates 80s hair. And I happened to have a blue chiffon sari at home. If I didn't have that at home, and my mom had not gifted me hers, I wouldn't have made that video. It wouldn't have been the one I made.

RM: I am really struck by what you've just said, and I don't know if you have thought more about it as a term. But the idea of "approximation" as part of the technologies of the drag-art that you are doing, seems like a very conscious choice. You are very aware that it is LaWhore pretending to be Sridevi. It's not ... how do I get this across in words, as it's such a fine difference? It's not Sridevi in every single dimension

> *of impersonating her. It is an approximation and I wonder if that is a conscious part of your strategy?*
>
> KK/LV: Yeah ... I mean I am not a great dancer.
>
> *(RM and LV/KK laugh)*
>
> LV/KK: *And I know that we can tease out what that means, etc....*
>
> RM: Exactly, and that is a whole other conversation....
>
> LV/KK: Sure, but I have no rigorous dance training and I don't have extended practice that allows me to put movement into my body at the rate at which a professionally trained dancer would, right? So approximation is good enough for me. And I am not mad about it. It allows me to actually make as opposed to get stuck in perfectionism. I've already told myself that I am never going to get there, so let me make what I like as opposed to try and make that perfect thing.
>
> RM: I mean that seems so important as it allows you to explore the possibilities of the craft, the actual movements, the actual act of conjuring this diva, it is also allowing others to almost give themselves permission to approximate in the ways in which they can conjure femininity or they can become feminine, regardless of their own gender identities.
>
> KK/LV: Yeah, and you know by doing Anil Kapoor also, I think I am still approximating him. I am not going to get there. I am not.... I think I am barely succeeding in masculinity let alone femininity. And I'll admit that it's helpful to have the digital editing in terms of obscuring some of the things I am conscious about. Cutting out bits but also being able to use filters. They are really helpful for making me feel good about the work even if I am self-conscious about it.

LaWhore's Work in #KaateNahinKatte

Since that summer of 2020, when I watched LaWhore's Instareel of *Kaate Nahin* on a loop, I have returned to the reel and closely followed the comments on it, started by LaWhore's own:

> Lawhorevagistan: Re-enacting your sexual awakenings. #mrindia #sridevi #anilkapoor #hindisongs #bollywood #iloveyou #kaatenahikatte #auntielookedamazing #bluesari #sareenotsorry #saree #auntiefashion #dragqueen #desidragqueen #lgbt #queer

LaWhore gives us the permission to re-enact our sexual awakenings and takes me straight back to my childhood memories of dancing under the shower in my mother's blue chiffon sari. And the emphasis on "re-enact" seems exactly right. Those of us who experienced the original dance sequence in the 1980s in Sridevi and Kapoor's love-dance will each have a personal memory attached to its repercussions vis-à-vis our own sexual awakenings at the time. Nearly four decades on, its appeal continues to allure us all, regardless of our genders and our sexualities.

The comments, which I have anonymized below, continue to signal the intricate technologies that enable these awakenings and fantasies: "this eyebrow abhinaya is making us all feel things 🔥"; "10/10 mustache and makeup"; and "Just looking at this all my fantasies are fulfilled. 💯". But I was struck, in particular, by this exchange between one particular Insta handle who says "The pansexuals are suffering ❤" to which @lawhorevagistan responds "my work here is done". This brief, fun, insightful, and quippy exchange makes me take seriously the extent of "work" that LaWhore is undertaking at multiple dimensions in this reels: she mobilizes a world-making of critical encounters between queer and non-queer peoples of all genders; she extends a critical commentary on the relationships between gender expressions, embodiments, and corporealities; and she presents an opportunity for self-reflection on cisgenderism and heteronormativity for the cis-het people among us. Khubchandani summarize the "work" that they wish to undertake through LaWhore's drag art and how it enters into dialogue with their gay male interlocutors whom they encountered during their ethnography for *Ishtyle*:

> I want to make sense of how reenactments of Hindi film dance by my gay male interlocutors and their theorizations of these performances evidence the transgressive qualities of film dance. Bollywood diva worship holds liberatory possibilities for those consumers of popular culture who feel constrained by the paradigms of normativity espoused by the very medium. (Khubchandani 2016, 72)

It makes every sense for LaWhore's work to focus on the "liberatory possibilities" for her fellow queer communities. By approximating Sridevi's iconic sensual, sexy, and wayward femininity as a *desi* drag queen, her danced "gestures bring queerness into visibility through a sincere execution of anachronistic, animalistic, vulgar, foreign dance" (Khubchandani 2016, 83). But,

I would argue too that for her non-queer audience, she also visibilizes the instability of our own cisgenderist ideas of gender, particularly femininity (Lennon and Mistler 2016), and the heteropatriarchal conceptualizations of sexual desire that arise out of them. Watching the same queer subject perform every gender and allude and speak to every sexual desire creates a necessary disruption to our dominant, binarized, cisgender, and heteronormative social order that Sridevi and Kapoor absolutely upheld. Where LaWhore and Kareem focus their gaze on us, every single member of their Instareel audience – Sridevi and Kapoor focused their gaze on each other. The world of sexual desire shifts from depictions of dominant cis-heterosexuality to an expansive pansexuality. But, as Khubchandani reminds us, LaWhore's work is about so much more as it spills beyond her work and into their life and builds community:

> Drag is a way for me to play with gender on stage and also off. I bought all these jewelry for LaWhore to wear, and then I also wear it as well. And it just made me comfortable shopping in a different aisle. It has shifted the way I think about gender and fashion ad and joy. And the thing about drag that is most important to me is that it is about community. So, it's not just about me feeling my fantasy on stage, but it's also about creating an experience for the audience as well. And it's that thing that happens between us that I think is the most important and beautiful. (Khubchandani in Queer Everything 2023)

LaWhore's approximation of Sridevi is also a helpful reminder of Sridevi's own cisgender hyperfeminized presentation of Indian femininity in *Mr India*, and is in itself a form of drag that is sanctioned by, and in part serves, the heteropatriarchy. This too reinforces the very instability of gender and reminds us that embodiments of femininity for people of all genders are performative acts, learned, rehearsed, and embodied through repetitions and stylizations (Butler 1990).

> KK/LV: *So to me, this is something I did in my living room and now it's going to appear in an academic book. And it feels funny to be very honest, that this is something that you think matters. So maybe, you could talk about the work that LaWhore does, or you think the reel is doing by living as a digital object.*

RM: One of the things that stands out about this reel, as you have described just, is that it makes you feel good. But I think it makes others feel good too, as we watch the reel. What I am interested to figure out is why and how it is making us feel this good as we watch the reel. It certainly makes me feel good. I can certainly start from that place.

The idea of not rejecting the burden of perfectionism, that leaning into approximation on your part as LaWhore, liberates those of us witnessing and engaging with the reel. It gifts us a sense of relief in knowing there is a way to feel good about ourselves without being perfect in whatever gender identity we move through the world. And then I am thinking about the comment on the reel that says "pansexuals are suffering" to which you respond "I've done my work here"—and I need to get to deeper grips with what this exchange means. But I feel as though it signals that the reel is a place of community building and a space of solidarity and understanding on this digital platform between queer and non-queer folks. Obviously, the ways in which I as a cis-het woman am engaging with the reel is likely to be very different to how a queer person might engage with it. But the work it's doing for me is probably making me question the codes on which the performances of femininities are built. And how they might be built differently for queer and non-queer peoples. And how I think it's creating a space for understanding—even if we have known this theoretically—because you are demonstrating—that these codes of femininity are learned and therefore can be unlearned and relearnt. When I think back to my Ma tying a knot with her hair, that is a particular set of codes of femininity she would have learned and was leaning into. But if I were to watch LaWhore repeating the same gesture, and approximate my Ma's tying of her knot, it would do something different for me. It would expose the learned-ness of gender.

To me it feels like the reel is creating a digital community in which queer and non-queer people can witness that codes of gender are learned, and unlearned, and relearned and reperformed. And that that's a very empowering thing.

KK/LV: I mean I think by doing a particular diva in her way, it also tells us that the chiffonography love of Bollywood films comes from somewhere. That feeling of when you put on a sari and it drapes nicely, that feeling actually comes from somewhere. It's not that the sari is ontologically beautiful or graceful, but that we have learned it somewhere.

> But then it also I think goes further to say that okay, gender is something we learn from somewhere. So, can we make with it, or is it just a thing that we do? Right? Like can we use the sari in the wrong way? Swing around and run around with it? As opposed to merely stand like a good *bhodromohila* in it, poised and respectable. So going back to those wrong kinds of choreographies, I think Sridevi has given us so many possibilities....
>
> RM: Yeah, you are so completely right. And as you say, the history of chiffonography—which I love.
>
> LV/KK: I stole it from RuPaul's Drag Race....
>
> RM: Oh I see! So the chiffonography is historicized in your reel. It's thus not just conjuring Sridevi, it is conjuring all the heroines that have come before her and after, and all the wet sari sequences of Bollywood.
>
> LV/KK: Right ...
>
> RM: And you replicate the wet-sari dance sequence on the reel through using the raindrops filter. So it is so obviously a heightened and mediated version of and commentary on the original—and therefore an approximation at so many levels! As opposed to the thing itself. That it offers us a way of understanding the histories out of which it derives. And at the same time offers us new ways to consider how the sari can be worn and performed differently. How the sari can become deviant. And, likewise, all the other components in the reel can be similarly understood as both a nod to what they are coming out of, while signaling their own distinct futures. And that's both fun and also critically rich in terms of the materialities of the reference points you are using, and also what they can become.

Auntie Does Fun: *Mazaa* as Resistance

When asked what it means to do fun scholarship, Khubchandani reminds us:

> As critical scholars who are pointing out the structures of power that surround us, we often create conditions in which we are not allowed to feel good and the people we write about are not allowed to feel good. Because everything is so bad. And it is bad. But, how do we make space to say

otherwise? How do we acknowledge that people are having fun despite violent conditions around them? (quoted in Queer Everything 2023)

They continue to explain that while, too often, the stories of minoritized peoples focus on serious themes of oppression and violence, "they are also having a great time. And we forget to account for that" (quoted in Queer Everything 2023). Centering *mazaa*, the Hindi/Urdu word meaning fun, as method, Jonathan Shapiro Anjaria and Ulka Anjaria in their special section titled "*Mazaa*: Rethinking Fun, Pleasure and Play in South Asia" for *South Asia: Journal of South Asian Studies* (2020) make a case for the fun, the pleasurable, the joyous as resistive strategies in the face of oppressive regimes and violence:

> Dwelling in mazaa does not mean ignoring inequalities, violence or power, but finding new ways of writing about the forms of life that thrive even in times of crisis. It also means illuminating how pleasure can generate new communities and political possibilities as well as new understandings of the role of the critic in social analysis. (Anjaria and Anjaria 2020, 232)

LaWhore's drag art and the ways in which she informs and meanders in and out of Kareem's scholarship embodies the urgency and vitality of fun art-scholarship.

> *RM: It is undeniable that your drag-art is full of joy and its fun and it gives you the giggles but it also seems to me to be completely grounded in taking on and signaling multiple and intersecting systems of oppressions in terms of the myriad ways in which bodies are policed and monitored. It signals to me the care and attentiveness with which you dance between joy and resistance. So, I would love for you to maybe share as concluding thoughts on understandings, and embodiments and deployments of queer-joy in drag your art-scholarship.*
>
> *LV/KK: Thank you for saying this. You use words like "oppressive systems" or "resistance,"; I think when I am making work I am not thinking about those things. But this is again where I think scholarship is shaping my drag. For instance, I know there are certain things I don't want to replicate. I think my training in critical scholarship has taught me about the kinds of systems of knowledge that shapes the selection of tracks I'll do, it shapes the way I do them. And that instinct*

to choose the kinds of performances and execute them the way I do comes out of a desire to not replicate or reproduce, for lack of a better term, "problematic shit."

So it's not the digital content that is calling out power. And there is a lot of drag that does that. I don't turn to the didactic in that way in my work. I think I am saying this because people might read this and think, "oh let me look at LaWhore's videos" and they won't find the critique there. But what I am also hoping is that they don't find the problematic stuff. All of that said, I am sure I am replicating some norm, right? So, I don't think there is... (long pause)... there isn't a way out.

But while we are on the inside of power structures and systems that constantly confine us, and confine different people differently, I am also very aware that people live with joy and pleasure. And regardless of how oppressed they may be, people in difficult life and institutional conditions find other ways to be, right? And this is something that I think has been articulated most clearly in opening to the "Mazaa" special issue. That the way we want to tell stories of the Global South, minoritized folks, etc. is always through violence. It's the only way that we legitimate stories in art. And I think we need other options. Because people live with other options. And so, I think joy is one word, but silliness is another, play is another, irreverence, camp, excess—like it's actually an expansive world of styles that are in tandem with and also beyond the kind of constrictive life conditions that we live inside of. So it may be a bit more of an ambivalent answer to your question, but it is also the way I make work. I am not sitting there trying to resist. I am just doing, right? We are in a pandemic and I need something to fill time. I am alone in my house for hours. And I make something. And I am not trying to be flippant, or dismissive about the work my work does. But also there is an acknowledgment that creativity is part of everyday living. And to go back to your first question, LaWhore is part of everyday living for me. She is an extension of being part of a difficult world that manages gender, and power, and privilege, and race. And she has to do things differently in person than she can on digital media. She has to do things different in India than she does in the US. There are all these different ways in which she also has to negotiate expectations and contexts and power and privilege.

Yeah, I feel like I am not ending on the joyous note....

> RM: Perhaps, but I actually think ambivalence is really important to acknowledge in such a conversation. Not least because I am really not trying to shape the ending—it really should be shaped by where the conversation has taken us. And I think what you are saying about how so often the burden of articulating violence is placed on minoritized peoples and legitimates their works, that it is a problematic and limiting way of understanding and engaging with their works - it's all so crucial to acknowledge in this *adda*. It is such an important statement that when you are making work, you are not making work to resist. You are simply making work. That work of course maybe read in complex ways. And this is where I think we are exposing the very important stakes in artist-scholar conversations. A scholar like myself is coming into this conversation with the thought "I see the potential of resistance in this work, but is it being made through that lens?" And it's wonderful and so important to hear you say "no, it is not—and I don't dismiss the fact that it may be read that way, but that's not my work's impetus." I think it's joyous to hear you say back to me that actually that's a limiting perspective on the work. That in itself is an invaluable unmaking of my thinking on #KaateNahin that this *adda* has enabled.

Addas Are Inconclusive

How to find a way to wrap up such an enormously transformative and educational and fun and moving *adda* from which I have grown irrevocably? An *adda* that has mobilized across borders and through Zoom a manifestation of touch that is metaphoric; a touch that is affective; a touch that is about touching, moving, impacting, stirring people into a state of awakenedness; into sustaining communities; into building solidarities across social positions.

A touch(ing) that engenders new and emancipatory world-makings.

Here, Dorinne Kondo's conceptualization of "making" as a linking of "structures of power, labor processes, and performances of gendered, national, and racialized subjectivities in historically and culturally specific settings" (2018) is helpful to understand how this chapter's anchoring in an analysis of #KaateNahinKatte and my *adda* with LaWhore have together considered the act of touching others, metaphorically and in generative ways, as an act of (world)-making; an unmaking. This necessary world-making between queer and non-queer subjects unsettles, unravels, and unmakes the internalized and dominant social orders that center cisgenderism and non-queer ways of knowing and moving through the world. And in doing so, it switches on a mode of self-reflexivity for cis-het women like myself to seriously consider our role in this emancipatory world-making, at a moment in time when LGBTQ+ communities are under attack. This necessarily also spills into how we move and write through our scholarly fields in order to de-center the dominant power regimes that shape them.

In the article "On Surviving a Cis Discipline," Rae Rosenburg names "geography as a cis discipline" and reflects on "what can be productively shifted with that charge" (Rosenburg 2023). Rosenburg goes on to articulate the terms that produce a cis discipline breaking them down from this central tenet: "A cis discipline is structured by a nexus of cisnormativity and discursive erasures of trans people" (2023). The charges that Rosenburg lists hold true also for our fields of dance and performance studies. In the article "Shakespearean Performance through a Trans Lens," Alexa Alice Joubin foregrounds "notion of transness" in order to unsettle the "compulsory normativity" of theater stagings of Shakespeare plays and create opportunities to "analyze the transitive social space and characters' resistance or willingness to inhabit that space" (2023, 69). Performance studies scholar Rachel Hann reminds us that trans techniques are processes that can be self-determined, playful, or enforced. Indeed, transgendering exists through and within cisgender coded territories of gender (Hann 2024).

Once we are alerted to our dominant ways of seeing, conceptualizing, and writing performance and we recognize the harms they reproduce, it becomes vital to stop and reconsider everything. This is particularly hard when we occupy, as we all do, positions of privilege while simultaneously experiencing oppression. No matter how alert we think we are to centering equitable practices in our research, our performance practices, and our writing, our internalized and dominant positions are ever present, and we need to constantly remain vigilant to them. To hold the first thought that enters our mind accountable, and to question why we think it, and why we write the way we do seems more urgent now than ever before. If we want to contribute to new and just world-makings, we have to question "the purported neutrality of cisgender subject positions" (Joubin 2023, 65), and "de-center the cisgender perspective that has been passed on as a default position" (Joubin 2023, 83). This is necessary in order to dismantle our own internalized and binarized understandings of the world. Rachel Hann reinforces the relationship between nonbinary thinking and new and just world-making in her article on atmospherics and argues that "a nonbinary approach to stage aesthetics reorientates stage encounters as indeterminate worlding envelopes" (2021). My *adda* with LaWhore signals both the desperate need for such world-makings in this moment in time, and simultaneously makes crystal clear, at least to me, the responsibility of cis and non-queer people in this urgent endeavor. Reflecting on the sustained transphobic attacks that are currently being waged on drag queens, Khubchandani reminds us, for instance, of the significant role of cis-queens in sustaining and nurturing drag art through these trans-hostile times:

> If drag is banned, I am hoping that cis-queens will keep doing drag and hold the scene together, and who can't be punished by these transphobic legislations. But who can keep queer aesthetics alive. And who will make room for queer and trans joy because of their cis privilege.

After all, as Khubchandani reminds us, "being Disney princesses is being cis-queens" (Khubchandani in Queer Everything 2023). Such conscious and cross-positional solidarity mobilizing has to be the only way to cede space to and make space for the flourishing of our trans and queer siblings, their loves and lives.

References

Anjaria, Jonathan Shapiro, and Ulka Anjaria. 2020. "*Mazaa*: Rethinking Fun, Pleasure and Play in South Asia, South Asia." Journal of South Asian Studies 43 (2): 232–242.

Banerjee, Tania. 2021. "Adda: The Secret to Bengali Conviviality." Accessed March 1, 2023. https://www.bbc.com/travel/article/20210812-adda-the-secret-to-bengali-conviviality.

Banerji, Anurima, and Royona Mitra. 2020. "Preface." In Decolonizing Dance Discourses: Conversations across the Field of Dance Studies, edited by Anurima Banerji and Royona Mitra, 40: 4–5. Oak Creek, WI: Dance Studies Association.

Butler, Judith. 1990. Gender Trouble: Feminism and the Subversion of Identity. New York. Routledge.

Chakravarti, Sueep. 2017. "A Brief History of Āddā—the Bengali Fine Art of Discussion." Accessed March 15, 2023. https://qz.com/india/1122129/adda-a-brief-history-of-the-bengali-fine-art-of-discussion.

Dutta, Debolina. 2022. "Adda." In Research Handbook on Law and Literature, edited by Peter Goodrich, Daniela Gandorfer, and Cecilia Gebruers, 147–173. Cheltenham: Elgar Publishing.

Empson, Olivia. 2023. "Drag Storytellers Grapple with Growing Threats by Republicans and Far Right." The Guardian. March 23. Accessed June 1, 2023. <https://www.theguardian.com/world/2023/mar/23/us-drag-storytellers-face-growing-threats.

Hann, Rachel. 2021. "On Atmospherics: Staging Stormzy and Nonbinary Thinking." Ambiances 7: 1–21.

Hann, Rachel. 2024. "Transgendering-assemblages: Sin Wai Kin's Trans Techniques and Acts of Boybanding." *Critical Studies in Fashion & Beauty* 15: 75–97.

India Culture Lab. 2020. "Auntology with Kareem Khubchandani: The Meme Project." Accessed April 1, 2023. https://www.youtube.com/watch?v=WSppRQe3kBs.

Joubin, Alexa Alice. 2023. "Trans as Method: The Sociality of Gender and Shakespeare." Borrowers and Lenders: The Journal of Shakespeare and Appropriation 14 (2): 3–21.

Kedhar, Anusha. 2020. "It Is Time for a Caste Reckoning in Indian 'Classical' Dance." In Decolonizing Dance Discourses: Conversations across the Field of Dance Studies, edited by Anurima Banerji and Royona Mitra, 40: 4–5. Oak Creek, WI: Dance Studies Association.

Khubchandani, Kareem. 2015. "Lessons in Drag: An Interview with LaWhore Vagistan." Theatre Topics 25 (3): 285–294.

Khubchandani, Kareem. 2016. "Snakes on the Dance Floor: Bollywood, Gesture, and Gender." The Velvet Light Trap 77: 69–85.

Khubchandani, Kareem. 2020. Ishtyle: Accenting Gay Indian Nightlife. Ann Arbor: University of Michigan Press.

Khubchandani, Kareem. 2023. Decolonize Drag (Decolonize That!). New York: OR Books.

Kondo, Dorinne. 2018. World-Making: Race, Performance, and the Work of Creativity. Durham, NC: Duke University Press.

Krishnan, Hari. 2019. Celluloid Classicism: Early Tamil Cinema and the Making of Modern Bharatanatyam. Middletown, CT: Wesleyan University Press.

Lennon, Erica, and Brian J. Mistler. 2014. "Cisgenderism." Transgender Studies Quarterly 1 (1–2): 63–64.

Mitra, Royona. 2019. "Costuming Brownnesses in British South Asian Dance." In The Futures of Dance Studies, edited by Janice Ross, Susan Manning, and Rebecca Schneider, 471–488. Madison: University of Wisconsin Press.

O'Shea, Janet. At Home in the World: Bharata Natyam on the Global Stage. Middletown: Wesleyan University Press.

Queer Everything. 2023. "Welcome Professor Vagistan!" Queer Everything. Accessed April 1, 2023. https://www.queereverything.com/listen/episode/7cdbcdce/welcome-professor-vagistan.

Rivera-Servera, Ramon H. 2017. "History in Drag: Latina/o Queer Affective Circuits in Chicago." In Latina/o Midwest Reader, edited by Omar Valerio-Jimenez and Santiago Vaquera-Vasquez, 185–195. Urbana: University of Illinois Press.

Rosenburg, Rae. 2023. "On Surviving a Cis Discipline." Environment and Planning D: Society and Space 41(4): 600–605.

Sen, Debarati. 2011. "Speech Genres and Identity: The Place of Adda in Bengali Cultural Discourse." Journal of Emerging Knowledge on Emerging Markets 3. doi: 10.7885/1946-651X.1062.

Singh, Pratishtha. 2020. "The Micropolitics of an 'Adda' for Women in India: Shaheen Bagh." Astragalo 27: 97–104.

Soneji, Davesh. 2012. Unfinished Gestures: Dvadasis, Memory, and Modernity in South India. Chicago: University of Chicago Press.

Squirrel, Tom. 2023. "British Extremists Are Importing Tactics from the US Hard Right. Their Target? Family Drag Shows." The Guardian. June 22. Accessed June 25, 2023. https://www.theguardian.com/commentisfree/2023/jun/22/british-extremists-us-right-family-drag-shows-children.

Srinivasan, Amrit. 1985. "Reform and Revival: The Devadasi and her Dance." Economic and Political Weekly 20 (44): 1869–1876.

Vagistan, LaWhore. 2020. "How to Be an Auntie." TEDxTufts. Accessed April 15, 2023. https://www.youtube.com/watch?v=Z9IYJlC_VWY.

Afterwords

Against Conclusions

A book has many endings: the promise of what follows as each chapter wraps up; the final word in the final sentence in the final paragraph in the final section; the last item on the reference list; "The End"; and so many more. But, it seems to me that the most limiting of them is the "conclusion," offered invariably in the guise of a succinct summary of key ideas that have been presented in preceding pages, and followed swiftly by a seeming urge to position one's own words as the final and definitive ones on the topic in focus. Conclusions, a mode I have leaned into heavily in my own prior writings, now makes me uncomfortable.

Conclusions try to impose upon our understandably messy and complex humanities research journeys the standards of scientific inquiry, requiring us to provide proofs (or disproofs) of the various hypotheses that we may have been posing along the way. This negates the very real possibility that some hypotheses continue to remain hypotheses. And that as inconclusive hypotheses, they are in and of themselves vital points of reference in all attempts at future knowledge production in the field.

Conclusions reek of arrogance in their attempt to frame the terms and parameters of how ongoing conversations on the topic/s in question can, could, or even should unfold.

Conclusions are thus a way to attempt to control the narrative of our inquiries, even beyond our book's pages.

Conclusions imply the shutting down of conversations, and a troublingly attached ownership of both the conversations that have been had, and their closures.

But, what if there are no closures?
What if there are only openings?

Conclusions signal a particular manifestation of mastery, a scholarly disposition and preoccupation whose questioning and unraveling decolonial scholar Julietta Singh has compellingly argued for (2018). In her book *Unthinking Mastery*, Singh positions her call as an "appeal to begin not simply to repudiate practices of mastery" (Singh 2018, 2) but, thinking with Donna Haraway, also to remain attentive to trouble "where, how, between whom, and toward what futures mastery is engaged" (Singh 2018, 2). Moving against the mastery that is embodied in conclusions offers an opportunity to both write and also read in ways that open up possibilities to "imagining otherwise and dwelling elsewhere, to the relentless exercise of unearthing and envisioning new human forms and conceptualizations of agency" (Singh 2018, 6).

If I have learned anything at all throughout this transformative book-writing journey, as a result of being in prolonged conversations with each of my artists-interlocutors about their dance-making and world-making and their places in the world, it is that there is no closure to such conversations. There are only openings. And that no single person owns the ideas that were generated, and shared, and nurtured collectively.

Our agencies are distributed and coalitional. Every idea generates another. They circulate in tandem. They inform and impact each other. More ideas are born. As dance scholar Anusha Kedhar reminds me in personal communications where we critique the neoliberal demands placed on researchers for originality and indeed mastery:

> I feel like part of the problem is the notion that ideas are wholly original or can be individually owned/attributed. If we can acknowledge that ideas circulate and are shared, people might be less scared that citing others would reduce the value of their scholarship. (Kedhar 2023)

Kedhar and I both realize of course that her observations above are not original in and of themselves, but they helpfully reinforce the need for us as researchers to embrace a healthier and more coalitional acknowledgment that our ideas are always in conversation with, and emerge from, others' ideas and, in that sense, nothing is wholly original.

This book is the result of
    a series of long, interconnected, entwined, and open conversations
        that have opened conversations.

This book is the result of
    connecting thinking and actions and feelings of, and between,
artists and people;
        who do not know each other.

            And yet
they have contributed collectively to its knowledge-making.
This book is born of collectivity.

How to mark this vital process of coalitional and emancipatory world-making in my final gesture on the page?
        What can possibly be its most fitting ending?
                How to make this ending another opening?

            Another beginning?

Feminism, gender and sexuality scholar Srila Roy reminds us in her careful and caring response to a forum of scholars curated to critically engage with her book *Changing the Subject: Feminist and Queer Politics in Neoliberal India* of the need to treat "the book as an opening," and the act of reading the book as one that "extend[s] its scope, and foreground[s] its limits and tensions with a caring, critical gaze" (Roy 2023, 1). This offers for me some reassuring counterpoint to the neoliberal authorial agenda of the conventional "conclusion" that tries to have and own the last word.

It is one way to unthink the mastery of conclusions.

I have been endlessly inspired too by my long *adda* with LaWhore Vagistan/Kareem Khubchandani, as per the previous chapter, in which they revealed their search for alternative, looser, and more creative modalities of writing. In that *adda* I emotionally admitted to never giving myself the permission to loosen up, to have fun, to put silliness at the heart of my rigor as an academic, for fear of not being taken seriously as a racially minoritized immigrant woman scholar in the Global North academy. Taking seriously Khubchandani's call for fun, also echoed by Jonathan Shapiro Anjaria and Ulka Anjaria in their special section titled "*Mazaa*: Rethinking Fun, Pleasure and Play in South Asia" for *South Asia: Journal of South Asian Studies* (2020), I am making here a conscious move against conclusions. In its place I am in search of discovering more joy and pleasure in alternative endings that we can derive from writing and reading creative prose. Inspired by Anjaria and Anjaria to channel *mazaa*, the Hindi/Urdu word for fun, not as an obstacle to academic rigor, but rather to champion its "embodied, unwieldly and seductive properties [that] can generate new ways of knowing, analysing, critiquing and writing" (Anjaria and Anjaria 2020; 232), I thus offer here an **AFTERWORDs**.

For there are many words that (will) come after this book.

And I am really hopeful that they are not mine.

Willing these other words into being, I enter a fictive relationship with my four transnationally situated artist-interlocutors Akila, Diya Naidu, Nahid Siddiqui, and LaWhore Vagistan, and end this book with a short and fictional WhatsApp conversation among them. In this creative choice, I wish to mark and honor a refreshing move in the last decade of dance and performance studies that explores a myriad creative ways to be in community, conversation and even signal coauthorings with our subjects, as demonstrated in the inspiring models put into motion by Kemi Adeyemi (2022), Melissa Blanco Borelli (2016), Imani Kai Johnson (2022), Kareem Khubchandhani (2015), Jacqueline Shea Murphy (2022), and Hershini Bhana Young (2023), among others.

But why a fictive WhatsApp thread? Why not an actual one?

These are valid questions that have been posed to me along the way. I have lots of instinctual reasons for following this fictive route. Firstly, I am reluctant to ask more of my generous and gracious artists, who have given so much to this project already, without being compensated materially for their work. Secondly, based on their words and sharings with me through all my individual conversations with them, I am following my intuition to create an imagined virtual confluence that will allow me to create openings, cracks, and fissures for the futures of such *actual* in-person conversations. If I signal the possibility of their union through this fictional narrative, then perhaps they actually will meet? Thirdly, by approximating my subjects (thank you LaWhore for your wisdom on this in Chapter 4!) through leaning into their words, while clearly signaling all the time that these words do not belong to them, and therefore not pretending to actually be them, I am hoping to complicate and expose the historic tendencies in our fields to speak *for* our subjects. In this I am taking a risk while trying desperately not to reproduce this troubling power dynamic. And I might well fail. But I want to explore the fine lines between what is at stake and for whom in the artist-scholar collaborations that we researchers so heavily rely on. Fourthly, and finally, I have tried to counter any tendency to speak *for* my subjects, by seeking each of their permission to try out my experimental and creative instincts. I have subsequently shared a finalized draft with them, inviting them to edit, amend, delete, add, and finalize this fictive thread however they wish to—such that they really do have the last word on its form and content, while keeping their labour minimal and on their own terms. In this, I have attempted a mode of coauthoring of this book's ending with my artist-interlocutors, without whom it could not, and would not, exist.

I bring this fictional intergenerational gathering of aunties together as their common conduit, and then leave them to their community. On their own terms. I frame them/us as aunties inspired, yet again, by my *adda* with LaWhore, calling us to embrace the aunties we want to become in the world and in our art-making: not afraid to speak truth to power, embracing change, caring, generative, full of love and compassion, and with a healthy distance from, and critique of, harmful forces among us. I see in my interlocutors aunties who are "women, femme, and queer figures adjacent to or at the periphery of a nuclear family formation" (Khubchandani 2022, 223). I see how their performance projects of world-makings align with Critical Aunty Studies' investment "in the ways that political, economic, moral, and cultural projects are mobilized in and through the figure of the aunty" (Khubchandani 2022, 223). Each of my artist-interlocutors, in their respective works, "recall and recalibrate systems of racialization, gender, kinship, violence, and care," and, through the specificities of their "forms, structures, and aesthetics," they make sense of and critique our "lived conditions [in order to] create alternative sociopolitical ecologies" (Khubchandani 2022, 223). They are the good force and good faith aunties we aspire to be. To bring them into conversation seems the logical and joyous step here.

This conversation never actually happened.
　　These words were never exchanged.
　　　　This thread is a figment of my imagination.
　　　　　But my subjects read the thread.
　　　　　　They edited words and added messages and
　　　　　　amended the flow.

　　　　　　They co-authored the ending and
　　　　　　　　closed the loop,
　　　　　　　　　　and (un)made contact
　　　　　　　　　　　with me
　　　　　　　　　　　　on their own terms.

AFTERWORDS

> **THIS INTERGENERATIONAL VIRTUAL *ADDA* NEVER HAPPENED**

> (Not) 27 June 2023

> Royona Mitra created group "Aunties (Un)Making Contact ☺"

> Hello everyone – it has been such a pleasure and an honour to work with your words in this book. So many of them resonate in each other's, and they also diverge in some exciting and important ways. It seems selfish for me to be the sole conduit and home of these insights.
>
> I have been wondering for a while now how best to extend your connections to me and this book to each other. So that it can stand alone, beyond and distinct from myself. And so, I thought it might be fun to connect you all via this WhatsApp thread. What could possibly be more South Asian? What could possibly be more transnational? And, most importantly, what could POSSIBLY be a more auntie move? ☺
>
> I hope my gesture to enable you to make contact (ha!) with each other is generative. I can only imagine all the things you might have to say. Thank you again for trusting me with all your words and feelings and thoughts during this epic journey.
>
> I'll shortly make you all admins on this thread and take my leave. I wish you all meaningful contact-making ☺.
>
> 13:20

> Royona Mitra Left

> (Not) Akila
> Hi! What a great idea – I've been wondering about all the different artists you have been bringing together in your writing and wanting to know more about everyone else and their work. Thank you for connecting us Royona and nice to meet you all! Oh - that was the quickest entrance and exit! ☺
> 14:00

> (Not) Diya Naidu
> Hello everyone and hi and bye Royona! Well this has really blown my mind in the best possible ways. What a pleasure to meet you all. Thank goodness for desi WhatsApp – "(un)making contact since November 2009" ☺.
> 14:10

(Not) LaWhore Vagistan
Hahahaha! Is that how long this app has been around?! Nearly two decades and look at the havoc it has wreaked. ☹ And yes, so great to meet you all.
14:30

(Not) Nahid Siddiqui
Sorry to come late to this party in senior auntie style. ☺ Joyous indeed - what joy to finally connect with everyone. And yes, the allure of WhatsApp University for my generation is indeed terrifying. Where are you all based? Would be so wonderful to meet you in person too someday. I am in Birmingham in the UK, but over the last many years have lived and moved between Pakistan and the UK.
16:00

(Not) Akila
I am in Chennai, and I think Diya is in Bangalore?
16:15

(Not) Diya Naidu
Yes, that's right...
16:20

(Not) LaWhore Vagistan
I live and work in the US – but this auntie has ancestry across South Asia and its diasporas – Sindh, Ghana, Gibraltar. Of multiple homes at once. Kind of why Vagistan is the place that homes me within.
16:30

(Not) Diya Naidu
So true! I cannot get my elderly relatives to stop taking lessons at WhatsApp University – it's really scary! But then, once in a while, it has its joyous reasons for existing. Such as these moments.
16:35

> **(Not) Akila**
> Goodness, we are spread out all over – and Royona is based outside of London, pulling and weaving all our threads together. I can't wait to learn more about each of your work and how it embodies an (un)making of contact. Freeing contact from contact improvisation seems crucial. To think about contact in more expansive ways that comes out of our collective and distinct South Asian embodiments – whatever that means – seems a welcome move.
> 16:40

> **(Not) Diya Naidu**
> Yes, especially as my own work is so often reliant on contact and touch and partnering – and so this expansiveness is necessary. We need more complex layers in our thinking and language as dancers and dance-makers. I mean we all know that not all contact in dance, or indeed life, has to constitute physical touch. But how often do we *actually* think this expansively in our practice?
> 16:50

> **(Not) Nahid Siddiqui**
> Well, quite Diya. The import and imposition of language, such as contact, that means something so specific in western "postmodern" dance, upon dance practices that are derived beyond its linguistic and cultural parameters is not helpful. So I wonder if it also depends on what constitutes our own practice. Contact to me, in dance, is a metaphor for connection, for community, for immersion with the environment, with oneself. In my work it rarely ever involves physical touch – except maybe touching my own skin.
> 17:00

> **(Not) Akila**
> But, the thing is, contact is *also* physical touch! Touch that is denied. Touch that is considered impure. Touch that is harmful. Touch that literally kills. But also touch we must aspire to in order to dismantle the very powers that prevents us from touching.
> 17:15

> **(Not) Diya Naidu**
> So this is exactly my thing. I have been trying to understand how as an Indian society that is so averse to touch, we can move beyond this stigma and come to understanding and embrace the value of human touch. But I come up against a conundrum. Can we move beyond this stigma, without first confronting the power regimes that shape it? And in confronting these power regimes in our dance, could we, inadvertently, end up reinforcing them?
> 17:20

(Not) LaWhore Vagistan
Yes, contact is many, many things and its multiple manifestations can and do co-exist. I remember the summer of 2020 with horror, being in covid lockdown, just myself and Kareem, in our apartment. I would come and go – but Kareem was always present. We both craved hugs, craved touch, craved contact. But we also found joy in community on Zoom and Insta and WhatsApp, in our community gatherings with our queer siblings. Those virtual communities did, in fact, touch and soothe and heal. Sometimes I wonder if we over valorize and romanticize "the real", the in-person, the face-to-face.

We learnt so much from our virtual classrooms in those days. That disabled folks, queer folks, racially minoritized folks, caste-oppressed folks could navigate their learning environments in more empowered ways, much more on their own terms. No longer having to move through physical spaces that were never built or meant for them. They grew. They found new networks and platforms.

Yet, it is also true that while for someone virtual contact-making is a dream, for others it is a nightmare. The terms of such contact-making depends very much on who we are and how we move through the world. How we navigate power determines what kinds of contact we find generative, and the kinds of contact we work hard to avoid, as they harm us.

I am so hopeful that this book is an opening up of these very conversations, and that it will untether all the different ways of understanding and making contact into the dance world.

17:25

(Not) LaWhore Vagistan
Oh gosh, I have written an essay, so sorry! I'm going to sign-off now as Kareem is conjuring me into Sima Aunty from Mumbai. And I really need to go and (un)make some wedding contacts! Until soon – bye all! ☺

17:30

(Not) Diya Naidu
Now THAT'S an auntie I need to see you channel – following you on Insta immediately! Until soon LaWhore – send photos please! ☺

17:35

(Not) Akila
I loved your essay – keep them coming LaWhore! And it's so helpful to read all your thoughts. I can start to get a sense of why Royona brought us all together in this book – the multiplicity of ways in which contact and touch appear and disappear in this book is indeed an opening of this conversation. Nahid – you mentioned how contact to you is community. And in this curated community we now find ourselves on this WhatsApp thread. ☺

17:42

(Not) Nahid Siddiqui

Absolutely dear Akila! The community I seek in my art is both inward—reaching within myself. And also outward—to seek community with my social and ecological companions. Without them, without you all, I am nothing. We are nothing. This soul is forever learning, forever open, forever without borders. Reading all of you and seeing the world through your eyes, makes my heart sing. Filled with gratitude for you all. This WhatsApp chat is a kind of world-making.

Here we are. Dispersed across the world. Connected on an app. Making contact. On our own terms.

17:45

(Not) Diya Naidu

Ok now I am immersed in all your works online! Hello, is it just me? Or is anyone else struck by the electric blue sari on LaWhore in her *Kaate Nahin* Instareel and how it matches almost exactly the electric blue fabric that Nahidji is shrouded in in *Mirror Within?* It is of course the same blue of Sridevi's sari in *Mr India*! Has Royona even realised this? There is a whole book in THIS! ☺

17:53

(Not) LaWhore Vagistan

Good spot Diya! Popping back in briefly to say just IMAGINE if we all turned up to this book launch as multiple manifestations of Sridevi - in our own electric blue chiffons saris? ☺ An intergenerational gathering of *jhatkas* (un)making contact together? ☺

I am trying to imagine what becomes possible when our wayward ideas, and bodies, and voices, and traces make contact with Sridevi's wayward messiness and presence. I am trying to imagine what else is made possible when she is both alone and not; both one and many. And we speak with her, and each other, intimately, on our own terms.

And collectively we unmake contact and choreograph the full complexity and quagmire that is South Asian Touch.

18:00

References

Adeyemi, Kemi. 2022. Feels Right: Black Queer Women and the Politics of Partying in Chicago. Durham, NC: Duke University Press.

Anjaria, Jonathan Shapiro, and Ulka Anjaria. 2022. "*Mazaa*: Rethinking Fun, Pleasure and Play in South Asia, South Asia." Journal of South Asian Studies 43 (2): 232–242.

Blando Borelli, Melissa. 2016. She Is Cuba: A Genealogy of the Mulata Body. Oxford: Oxford University Press.

Johnson, Imani Kai. 2022. Dark Matters in Breaking Cyphers: The Life of Africanist Aesthetics in Global Hip Hop. New York: Oxford University Press.

Kedhar, Anusha. 2023. *Personal communication with the author via WhatsApp.* June 25.

Khubchandani, Kareem. 2015. "Lessons in Drag: An Interview with LaWhore Vagistan." Theatre Topics 25 (3): 285–294.

Khubchandani, Kareem. 2022. "Critical Aunty Studies: An Auntroduction." Text and Performance Quarterly 42 (3): 221–245.

Roy, Srila. 2023. "Dissonant Intimacies: Coloniality and the Failures of South–South Collaboration." The Sociological Review 71(6): 1237–1257.

Shea Murphy, Jacqueline. 2022. Dancing Indigenous Worlds: Choreographies of Relation. Minneapolis: University of Minnesota Press.

Singh, Julietta. 2018. Unthinkng Mastery: Dehumanism and Decolonial Entanglements. Durham and London: Duke University Press.

Young, Hershini Bhana. 2023. Falling, Floating, Flickering. Disability and Differential Movement in African Diasporic Performance. New York: New York University Press.

Notes

Preface

1. Barker claims that the human body responds to a film "haptically, at the tender surface of the body; kinesthetically and muscularly, in the middle dimension of muscles, tendons, and bones that reach toward and through cinematic space; and viscerally, in the murky recesses of the body, where heart, lungs, pulsing fluids, and firing synapses receive, respond to, and reenact the rhythms of cinema" (2009, 3).
2. Scholar of anthropology and South Asian studies Ajantha Subramanian's words are a crucial reminder to anyone who shared my upbringing that, "the history of caste [is] one of transformation, . . . this does not mean that caste has given way to some other form of social classification, such as class. While class is certainly an important form of stratification, continuities of class affiliation, stigmatization, and ascription within the most modern institutional and social spaces reveal the irreducibility of caste to economic differences" (2019, 13).
3. Sujatha Gidla describes the extent of this apartheid reality as a woman "born an untouchable." She writes: "the untouchables, whose special role—whose hereditary duty—is to labor in the fields of others or to do other work that Hindu society considers filthy, are not allowed to live in the village at all. They must live outside the boundaries of the village proper. They are not allowed to enter temples. Not allowed to come near sources of drinking water used by other castes. Not allowed to eat sitting to a caste Hindu or to use the same utensils. There are thousands or other such restrictions and indignities that vary from place to place" (2017, 4).
4. In a published interview with me, the British-Bangladeshi dance-artist and choreographer Akram Khan reveals how, in his first dance piece, *Loose in Flight* in 1999, the repetitive motif of repositioning his elbow to kathak's first position is an echo of his own muscle memory of this very instructional and corrective nature of touch from his teacher Kumudini Lakhia (Khan in Mitra 2017).
5. The government of India recognizes eight "classical" dance forms that are spread across different geographical regions and states. They are: "Bharatanatyam (linked to Tamil Nadu, with influences from Andhra Pradesh and Karnataka), Kuchipudi (from Andhra Pradesh), Odissi (rooted in Odisha), Kathak (connected to Uttar Pradesh, Rajasthan, and West Bengal), Manipuri (from Manipur), Sattriya (originating in Assam), Kathakali, and Mohiniattam (both from Kerala)" (Banerji 2023, 191).
6. Mobilizing "classicized" to this end is also akin to the ways in which race discourse uses the term "minoritized" (verb) over "minority" (noun), to foreground the wielding of power that is exerted onto Black and Global Majority people, which results in their sociocultural dehumanizations and discriminations.

Introduction

1. Rightful critiques proliferate of the increasing metaphorizing of the term "decolonization," following Eve Tuck and K. Wayne Yang's critical intervention (2012). These critiques are aimed at epistemic projects that have mobilized the term as removed from its materialist rooting in modes of resistance by colonized peoples against colonial projects of land, homes, and material dispossessions. One such project guilty of such a metaphoric focus without consideration of its varied, right-wing, and materialist mobilizations across different national contexts is my own involvement in the special issue "Decolonizing Dance Discourses" for *Conversations across the Field of Dance* (2021), coedited with Anurima Banerji. Eighteen months after its publication, reflecting with more nuance, Banerji and I wrote in our Letter to the Editor/Talkback to the special issue that, in fact, the rhetoric of "decolonization" is being mobilized in dangerous ways in India and toward majoritarian politics. Decolonization projects, just like colonization projects, manifest at both material and epistemic dimensions; and to ignore the materialist dimension is reductionist at best, and appropriative at worst. I say this here as a way to necessarily complicate

248 NOTES

the task that was asked of us at the Mellon Dance Studies Seminar in its ask to embody the word "decolonize."
2. I wish to clarify here that I mobilize the phrase "colonized by CI" in an epistemological sense, thinking through ideas of coloniality of knowledge-production and cultural power, while staying fully alert to the very alive material dimensions of colonization on land and resources as integral to ongoing imperialist projects across different parts of the world.
3. In this co-written chapter, Suraj and Michalska, write powerfully about the liberatory potentials of CI when practised in India with and by marginalized communities, placing questions of power asymmetries at the heart of their practice. In doing so, they helpfully point to the gaps in my own former scholarship (Mitra 2021), that did not take this angle into account. I would have liked to have engaged more closely with their chapter in this book if their essay had been published earlier in my book's production timeline, and very much look forward to being in further critical dialogue with them.
4. At the time of researching for the book in conversation with Nahid Siddiqui over Zoom through 2020 and 2021, Siddiqui was living in Pakistan where she had been located for several years. She subsequently relocated back to the UK which is now her permanent home. However, her relationship to her upbringing in Pakistan stays present in her life in the UK.
5. In the last decade, alongside my own, several key and vital publications have positioned new modes of interculturalisms as minoritized subject-driven political and aesthetic movement in theater and dance sectors in the Global North (Knowles 2010; McIvor 2016; McIvor and King 2019; Lei and McIvor 2020). These collective voices have situated the central concerns of power and agency, reclaimed by minoritized artists from the ground up, as integral to the spirit of new interculturalisms, most strongly exemplified in the work on "scalar interculturalism" by Justine Nakase (2019). Nakase's concept provides a helpful and "critical framework that allows us to read intercultural performance on the level of the individual and as it occurs beyond aesthetics" and "extend[s] a politics of scale to cultural production and performance, arguing that performances originating from lower scales (such as the self, the community, and the emergent) have the political potential to challenge or complicate hegemonies emanating from higher scales (such as the national, historical, and global)" (257). In this project, I wish to extend their lines of inquiry by advocating for intersectionality and inter-epistemic knowledge production as central to such interrogations and reclamations of power within the projects of new interculturalism.
6. I use the example of Palestine as at the time of writing, the scale of decimation of Gaza and the loss of Palestinian lives over just two months have been reported as above and beyond the numbers of civilian casualties in all twentieth- and twenty-first-century global wars. This is not to minimize or erase other instances of such destructive unmaking at the hands of ongoing settler-colonial states in other parts of the world, but to use a singular focus that, at the time of writing, is very present in my mind and provides a clear example of the framing of unmaking as only decimation that I am trying to argue against.
7. At a very late stage of this book's production timeline, I am alerted to the intimate ways in which my conceptualization of unmaking – as a method, a politics, and an emancipatory mode - speaks to Black feminist abolitionist criticality, by my friend and dance scholar Arabella Stanger. Without being able to go into the detailed critical dialogue with it as I'd like to, I want to mark and honour here Ruth Wilson Gilmore's essay titled "Abolition Geography and the Problem of Innocence" in its critical signalling that "If unfinished liberation is the still-to-be-achieved work of abolition, then at bottom what is to be abolished isn't the past or its present ghost, but rather the processes of hierarchy, dispossession, and exclusion that congeal in and as group-differentiated vulnerability to premature death" (2017). This does indeed speak closely to me.
8. I wish to acknowledge here performance studies scholar, friend, and colleague Brahma Prakash's suggestion to nuance Sarukkai's analyses via the formal Sanskrit words of *sparsha* and *samyoga* through the everyday colloquialism of the Hindi words *chhuna*, *chhuan*, *chhut*, and *acchut* to demonstrate the interrelationships between language and social practices, and how they reveal the negation of relationality as embedded in Indian societies. I appreciate his editorial eyes, too, on these ideations.
9. Masoom Parmar is a dancer, curator, and arts manager, fueled by his training in bharatanatyam, kathak, and odissi. As a man of Muslim-Zoroastrian heritage, he is invested in questions of identity and belonging, and his middle-class upbringing has inculcated in him a liberal worldview.
10. Anishaa Tavag is a South Indian dancer, editor, writer, and Alexander Technique teacher trainee based in Bangalore. She is invested in questions of collective responsibility and individual reflection in her writing and her choreographic practices. Tavag is conscious of her family's

intergenerational upward social mobility through simultaneous caste privilege, and she tries to reflexively consider her own social positions in everything she does.
11. Hari Krishnan is a US-based choreographer and dancer-scholar who is Professor of Dance at Wesleyan University and also the artistic director of inDANCE. His dance-art and scholarship occupy the interstices between bharatanatyam, contemporary dance, postcoloniality, and queer dance.
12. Mandeep Raikhy is an India-based dance artist, choreographer, pedagogue, and arts administrator who lives in New Delhi. He completed his undergraduate training in London at the Laban Centre in dance-theater and went on to tour with Shobana Jeyasingh Dance Company between 2005 and 2009. He currently teaches at Ambedkar University in New Delhi.
13. I am grateful to my anonymous peer reviews for helping me think through the multiple and formal dimensions of CI that makes it an exclusionary practice for many.
14. Dance scholars Amrit Srinivasan (1985), Janet O'Shea (2007), Davesh Soneji (2012), Sitara Thobani (2017), Hari Krishnan (2019), and Anusha Kedhar (2021) have written about these appropriative erasures in the nationalist reconstruction of bharatanatyam. These same appropriative moves along caste, gender, faith, and class lines are also evident in the formations of kathak, as argued by dance scholar Pallabi Chakravorty (2008) and ethnomusicologist Margaret Walker (2014).

Chapter 1

1. Haja Marie Kanu writes about the way white people take up space on pavements, refusing to cede space to Black and racially minoritized people during encounters that requires negotiating narrow spaces and road safety (2019). Kanu's critical observations about racialized encounters on pavements between white people and Black and racially minoritized people is another dimension of thinking through how different dominant identity positions take up space and move through the world, at the expense of those whom they minoritize in the process, on an everyday basis.

Chapter 2

1. The late Indian choreographer Chandralekha mobilized same-gendered duets between two men and two women in her works, and through these, she teased out and exposed the ways in which these same-gendered duets land upon, are received by, and consumed differently by audiences.

Chapter 3

1. Shakila Taranum Maan is a British Asian filmmaker, theater artist, and activist. She traces her ancestry to a devout Sunni Muslim family in the Punjab region of India who migrated to Kenya in the mid-eighteenth century. Although she identifies as an agnostic, Maan lives with a strong inherited understanding of Sufism as she encountered Rumi's writing through her mother, and remembers attending Sufi gatherings in the UK as a child.
2. For a powerful narration and analysis of Shakila Taranum Maan's life as a feminist and agnostic first-generation British-Pakistani woman and artist, please read her chapter "Gods and Daughters" in an edited anthology titled *Women against Fundamentalism: Stories of Dissent and Solidarity*, edited by Sukhwant Dhaliwal and Nira Yuval-Davis (London: Lawrence & Wishart, 2014).
3. Pandit Birju Maharaj is a renowned kathak danseur and an exponent of the dominant Lucknow Gharana or schools of kathak in India. He taught and led the Kathak Kendra, the premiere national kathak institution in New Delhi, India. After his demise in January 2022, he was named in a series of testimonies on social media for alleged sexual harassment and abuse of many of his young women students.
4. British-Asian dance artists and choreographers Sonia Sabri and Amina Khayyam claim that their respective kathak repertoires are also influenced by Sufism. It is helpful perhaps to understand that Sabri and Khayyam belong to a generation below Siddiqui, and incidentally, that Sabri was also a student of Siddiqui.
5. In a recent interview between Brazilian jiujitsu practitioners scholar Janet O'Shea and dance-artist Akram Khan, Khan too talks about the role of the mirror in dance training and the need to use it as a way of achieving an aesthetic driven by lines. He says that to counter such a surface-based approach to choreography, he finds his martial art training in jiujitsu immensely

generative, as it allows him to focus inward, so as to not remain focused on the ego and the surface alone.
6. In a forthcoming publication titled "Kathak Is Always Already Queer," British-Indian queer dance-artist Jaivant Patel and I write about unsettling of sringara rituals beyond its heteropatriarchal presentations in kathak, through a close analysis of Patel's dance-film *I Am Your Skin* (2021).
7. There are, of course, many noteworthy high-profile UK-based women kathak artists such as Urja Thakore, Amina Khayyam, Vidya Patel, and Sonia Sabri.

Chapter 4

1. While the politics of caste in the appropriative histories and making of Indian dance has been addressed in the scholarship of Amrit Srinivasan, Janet O'Shea, Davesh Soneji, and Hari Krishnan, among others, what is new and significant in this current moment is that the caste critiques are finally being mobilized by caste-oppressed and anti-caste hereditary dance artists, and are consciously politicized.
2. Anurima Banerji, Anusha Kedhar, and I currently are working on a coauthored publication titled "'It's Gender, Not Caste': A Digital Discourse Analysis of Indian 'Classical' Dance and the Negation of Intersectionality" that teases out the relationships between social media and social justice mobilizations in the Indian dance world. We presented a draft of this work at the (Virtual) Ecologies in the Field of Dance conference, organized by the Gesellschaft für Tanzforschung (GTF) in Cologne from October 27 to 29, 2023.
3. I am conscious that the word and action "agitate" is central to the early 20th century Indian lawyer, activist and social reformer Dr Bhimrao Ramji Ambedkar's anti-caste slogan 'educate, agitate, organise' as a means to advocating for uprisings towards caste annihilation.
4. In a forthcoming book chapter titled "Kathak Is Always Already Queer: Jaivant Patel Dance and *I Am Your Skin*" (2021), British Asian queer dance-artist Jaivant Patel and I argue how the presence of hairy arms in depictions of femininities in the works of queer artists of all genders disrupts and queers normative expectations of South Asian femininity and its toxic normalization of hairless womanhood.

Index

For the benefit of digital users, indexed terms that span two pages (e.g., 52–53) may, on occasion, appear on only one of those pages.

Figures are indicated by an italic *f* following the page number.

abhinaya, 216–17
ableism, 30–31, 72–73, 159, 190
al-Adawiyya, Rabi'a, 172
addas
    caste, class, gender and, 187–89
    Chakravarti, S., on, 187
    contact and, 59, 184–85
    COVID-19 pandemic and, 190–93
    Dutta on, 186, 188, 189–90
    as inconclusive, 230–32
    with Khubchandani/Vagistan, 194–204, 212–16, 217–23, 225–27, 228–32, 237–38
    LGBTQ+ rights, 186
    as method, 184–85
    Sen on, 187
    Singh on, 188–89
Adeyemi, Kemi, 237–38
Adivasi dance performances, 45–47
agitate, 250n.3
Ahmed, Sara, 15
Akila, 22–23, 55–56, 66
    on caste-oppressed people, 68
    Chandralekha and, 84–85
    dance, activism and, 68–72
    on "honor killings," 74–76, 80–81
    See also Theenda Theenda
Alexander Technique, 16–17
Ambedkar, B. R., 56–57, 65
Anatomy of Touch, 16–17
Anderson, Benedict, 51–52
Anjaria, Jonathan Shapiro, 228, 237
Anjaria, Ulka, 228, 237
Arundale, Rukmini Devi, 40
aunties, 216–17, 237–38
Aurat March, 2018, 177–78

Bakshi, Sandeep, 10–11
Bala, Sruti, 10–11
Banerjee, Tania, 187–88
Banerji, Anurima, 45, 50

Banissy, Michael, 16–17
Basu, Priyanka, 177–78
bharatanatyam, 40–41, 42–43, 44–45, 49, 50, 69, 117, 118–19
biopolitics, 85–86, 87
blackface, 221
#BlackLivesMatter, 192
Black subjectivity, 34
Bollywood, 195, 212, 217, 221, 224, 226, 227
"Bollywood Divas 101," 221
Borelli, Melissa Blanco, 237–38
Brackens, Diedrick, 136
Bradley, Rizvana, 34
Brahminical patriarchy, 66–67, 72, 79, 80–81, 155, 158–59
Brahminism and Brahminical practices, 22–23, 42, 45–46, 47, 50, 51–52
    bharatanatyam and, 40–41, 42–43
    caste purity and, 56–57, 65, 73, 79–80, 100–1
    choreopower of, 67–68, 85–86, 88, 91, 99–101
    kathak and, 40, 42–43, 155
    Theenda Theenda on, 65, 67–68, 85–86, 88, 91, 98–99, 100–1
    untouchability and, 49, 50–51, 79–80, 104–5
Butler, Judith, 85–86

camp, 216–17, 229
caste
    Akila on, 68
    Ambedkar on system, 56–57, 65
    choreography, 85–86
    endogamy, 66, 72, 78, 85–86
    gender, class and, 187–89
    gender, sex and, 78–81, 106
    inter-caste contact, 56–57, 65, 67–68, 92–93, 94
    inter-caste intimacies, 22–23, 55–57, 65, 66–67, 71, 72, 73, 74–81, 98–99, 100–1
    Naidu on, 117–18

caste (cont.)
    Theenda Theenda on, 56–57, 65, 70, 72, 74–99
    touch and, 19–20, 29, 42–43, 56–57, 74–99
    untouchability and, 17, 79–80
    upright spine and, 84–85
casteism, 20–21, 42–43, 214
caste politics, 39, 40, 46–47, 86
caste purity, 56–57, 65, 73, 79–81, 100–1
caste supremacy, 20, 21, 22–23, 35–36, 42–43, 66–67
    caste purity and, 65
    endogamy and, 85–86
    female sexuality and, 80
    "honor killings" and, 80–81
    Theenda Theenda challenging, 66–68, 98–99
Chakravarti, Sudeep, 187
Chakravarti, Uma, 78, 80–81
Chaleff, Rebecca, 2–3, 33–34
Chandiran, 65, 66, 67–68, 72–73, 76, 86, 87, 88–92, 93–99, 95f, 96f, 100
Chandralekha, 69, 84–85
Chaodhry, Nighat, 149
Chatterjea, Ananya, 43–44
Chettur, Padmini, 69, 70
chiffonography, 226–27
chhuna, 18. *See also chhuan, chhut*
choreopower, of Brahminism, 67–68, 85–86, 88, 91, 99–101
Chow, Broderick, 6
CI. *See* contact improvisation
cisgender and cis discipline, 231–32
classicized, xxii
colorism, 39, 73
consent, 106–7, 125, 127–28
contact
    adda and, 59, 184–85
    choreographic touch and, 2–3, 6–7
    etymology of, 16
    inter-caste, 56–57, 65, 67–68, 80, 92–93, 94
    samyoga, 17–18, 24, 38–39, 65
    touch and, 16, 17–18, 19, 22–23, 24–25, 34, 35–36, 42, 65, 92–93, 178–79, 214
    unmaking, 16–39, 40–55
contact improvisation (CI), 17
    choreographic touch and, 30
    closed-skinned and, 108–9
    colorism in India and, 39
    gender and, 108–9
    in Global North dance discourse, 1–3
    Holland and Houston-Jones on, 33–34
    Khan, A., on, 37–39
    liberation and, 29, 30–32

    Naidu on, 36–37, 38–39, 108–9, 111, 116, 128–29
    Paxton and, 29–30, 32–34, 35, 110–11, 116
    power and, 30–31, 33, 34–36
    race and, 38–39
    Raikhy on, 36
    Suraj and Michalska, 2–3, 248n.3
    The Silk Route and, 110–11
    touch and, 2, 26, 29, 30, 31–32, 36–37, 49, 108, 116, 213–14
    whiteness of, 33–34, 35, 38–39, 110–11
Cooper, Brittany, 6–7
Cooper Albright, Ann, 2–3, 33–34
Covid-19 pandemic, 28–29, 56, 190–93, 212, 213, 215, 229
Crenshaw, Kimberlé, 6–7

#DalitLivesMatter, 192
Dalit masculinity, 78–79
dance studies, 26–28
Dave, Ranjana, 159
decolonization, 1–2, 5, 247–48n.1
Decolonize Drag (Khubchandani), 194, 199–200
DeFrantz, Thomas F., 12, 217
Digital Touching, 59. *See also* #KaateNahinKatte
disability, 10–11, 30–31, 72–73, 215
Dixit, Madhuri, 212
drag artists and drag performances, 184–86, 194, 222, 224–25, 228, 231–32
Dutta, Debolina, 186, 188, 189–90
Dymoke, Katy, 16, 30–31

ecofeminism, 167, 173–75, 178–80
Egert, Gerko, 27, 85–86
Empson, Olivia, 185–86
endogamy, 66, 72, 78, 85–86
English Vinglish, 218
environmentalism, feminism and, 155–61, 173, 178–79

feminism, 84–85, 106–7, 110–11, 128–29
    ecofeminism, 167, 173–75, 178–80
    environmentalism and, 155–61, 173, 178–79
    intersectional, 220
    in *Mirror Within*, 172–79
    Pakistani, 175–78
Ferri, Giuliana, 170–71
Field, Tiffany, 16–17
Firmino-Castillo, María Regina, 144–45, 159, 178–79
Floyd, George, 192
Friedlander, Shems, 156–57

Gardener, Sally, 40
Gaza, 7, 248n.6
Gazdar, Haris, 21
Geeta, V., 78
gender
   caste, class and, 187–89
   caste, sex and, 78–81, 106
   CI and, 108–9
   cisgender, 231–32
   gender-based violence, 66–67, 106, 177–78
   #KaateNahinKatte and, 226
   race and, 36, 39, 132, 133–34
   sexuality and, 121–22, 127–28, 135, 136–39
   touch and, 25–26, 30, 36–37
   transgender, 231–32
Gilmore, Ruth Wilson, 248n.7
Global North dance discourse, 2–3, 16
Glucklich, Ariel, 18–19
Goldman, Danielle, 2–3, 33–34
Gopal, Priyamvada, 5
Graybill, Rhiannon, 107
gurus, dancers and, 50–51
guru-shishya dance training model, 158–59
Guru, Gopal, 19–20
Gutierrez, Miguel, 31

Hammond, Claudia, 16–17
Hands and Face Project, 137–39
Hann, Rachel, 10–11, 231–32
Haraway, Donna, 235
Ha Young Hwang, 28
Hennessy, Keith, 2–3, 33–34
heteropatriarchy, 158–59, 169, 175, 178–80, 224–25
Hinduism, 45
holding dance, 26–27
Holland, Fred, 2–3, 33–34
"honor killings," 56–57, 65, 66–67, 70–71, 72, 73–76, 80–81, 89–90, 98
Houston-Jones, Ishmael, 2–3, 33–34
Hussain, Ghulam, 21, 148, 173
Hussain, Rukhsar, 172
Hussein, Nesreen, 10–11

inclusion, 10–11
Ingold, Tim, 10–11
inter-caste contact, 56–57, 65, 67–68, 80, 92–93, 94
inter-caste intimacies, 22–23, 55–57, 65, 66–67, 71, 72, 73, 74–81, 98–99, 100–1
interculturalism and intercultural encounters, 5, 107–8, 109, 248n.5
intersectionality, 5, 6–7, 17, 31, 33, 35–36, 150–51, 173–74, 220, 221

Ishtyle, 212, 224

Jaaware, Aniket, 19–20, 22, 24–25
Jabeen, Neelam, 174–75
Jafa, Navina, 44, 52
Jeyasingh, Shobana, 36
Johnson, Imani Kai, 237–38
Joubin, Alexa Alice, 231
Jungle Book Revisited, 23–24

#KaateNahinKatte, 205f, 207f, 208f, 209f, 211f, 219–20
   Instagram comments on, 223–24
   Kapoor and, 59, 204–16, 222, 223, 224–25
   LaWhore's work in, 223–27
   Mr India and, 59, 184–85, 193, 204, 206, 212, 217, 225
   Sridevi and, 59, 204–23, 224–25, 227
Kalavantulu women, 41–42
Kapoor, Anil, 59, 204–16, 222, 223, 224–25
kathak, 49, 58–59, 118–19
   Brahminism and, 40, 42–43, 155
   Mirror Within and, 161–72
   Siddiqui and, 140, 143, 145–47, 148, 150–54, 155–61, 173, 178–80
   space in, 42–43
   Sufism and, 155–61
   touch in training, 49–50
Kedhar, Anusha, 235
Kermani, Sheema, 148, 177–78
Khan, Akram, 22–24, 25–26, 36, 37–39, 42–43, 49–50, 56, 201, 202
Khan, Nadia, 149–50
Khan, Saad, 150
Khan, Saroj, 217
Khan, Sophia, 149
Khubchandani, Kareem, 15, 184–85, 194, 205f, 207f, 237–38
   addas with, 194–204, 212–16, 217–23, 225–27, 228–32, 237–38
   on aunties, 216–17
   Decolonize Drag by, 194, 199–200
   on drag art, 224–25, 231–32
   on *mazaa,* scholarship and, 227–30, 237
   on trans rights, 231–32
   See also #KaateNahinKatte; Vagistan, LaWhore
Kings, A. E., 173–74
Kondo, Dorinne, 10–11, 29, 230–31
Krishnan, Hari, 21–23, 36, 42–43, 249n.11
Kshiti S.V., 216–17
Kuchipudi, 41–42
Kwan, SanSan, 57–58, 107–8, 109, 120–21, 128–29, 130, 136–37

Law, John, 10–11, 12–13
Lepecki, Andre, 53
Levesque, Julian, 173
LGBTQ+ communities and rights, 185–86, 230–31
Loick, Daniel, 106–7
Ludhra, Geeta, 170–72

Maan, Shakila, 58–59, 143–44, 145–47, 151–52, 161–62, 163–64, 167, 249n.1. *See also* Mirror Within
Madhushree, 66, 70–71, 89, 98
Maharaj, Pandit Birju, 40, 148, 249n.3
Manning, Erin, 17–18
Maybee, Julie E., 10–11
mazaa, 227–30, 237
McAllister-Viel, Tara, 28
mess, 12–13
#MeToo movement, 158–59
Michalska, Adrianna, 2–3
Mills, Liz, 28
Mirror Within, 58–59, 145–47, 163*f*, 165*f*, 168*f*
    feminisms within, 172–79
    kathak and, 161–72
    as *nichod*, 160–72
Mr India, 59, 184–85, 193, 204, 206, 212, 217, 225
Mohyeddin, Zia, 149
mujras, 150
Murali, Sharanya, 106
Murphy, Jacqueline Shea, 113, 144, 237–38

Naidu, Diya, 24, 49, 55–56, 105, 109–11, 112*f*, 135*f*
    bharatanatyam training of, 117, 118–19
    biography of, choreographing intimacies and, 116–21
    on caste, 117–18
    on CI, 36–37, 38–39, 108–9, 111, 116, 128–29
    on normalizing touch, 104–6, 108, 110–11, 113
    Raham by, 121–22
    See also Rorschach Touch
Narayan, Vivek V., 85–86
Nash, Jennifer C., 6–7
Nereyeth, Dayita, 112*f*, 128–29, 133–36
new interculturalism, 5
nichod, 160–72
Novack, Cynthia J., 29–30

October 7 attacks, in Israel, 7
Oden, Chelsea, 71
O'Shea, Janet, 44–45, 127

Padukone, Deepika, 218, 220
Paik, Shailaja, 79, 80
Palestinian genocide in Gaza, 7–8, 248n.6
Panigrahi, Priyabrata, 127, 128–30, 133–34, 135–36, 135*f*
Parmar, Masoom, 21–22, 24–25, 39, 49–50, 112*f*, 123–24, 129–30, 133–34, 135–36, 135*f*, 248n.9
Pasha, Nihal, 128*f*
Patel, Shaista, 20–21
patriarchy, 58–59, 84–85, 106, 145–46, 150–51, 175, 178–79
    Brahminical, 66–67, 72, 79, 80–81, 155, 158–59
    heteropatriarchy, 158–59, 169, 175, 178–80, 224–25
Paxton, Steve, 1–2, 29–30, 32–34, 35, 110–11, 116
Pillai, Nrithya, 40–41, 50, 158–59, 192–93
Ponikiewska, Asha, 128–29, 128*f*, 132–34, 132*f*, 136
postcolonial ecofeminism, 174
Prakash, Brahma, 47, 56, 85–86, 87
Purkayastha, Prarthana, 26–27

Qudosi, Shireen, 160
queerness, 136, 137–39, 224–25
queer world-making, 12

race, 36, 38–39, 132, 133–34
Raham, 121–22
Raikhy, Mandeep, 21–23, 36, 42–43, 249n.12
Ray, Tridip, 78
Red Dress Wali Ladki, The, 119
Reed, Sara, 28
remaking, 10–11
Rivera-Servera, Ramon, 218
Rorschach Touch, 57–58, 112*f*, 128*f*, 132*f*, 135*f*
    audience intimacy in, 103–4, 123–24
    choreographing intimacy in, 120–21
    on gender and sexuality, 121–22, 127–28, 135, 136–39
    interculturalism and, 107–8, 109
    intersecting regimes of power and, 111–16
    Kwan and, 107–8, 109, 120–21, 128–29, 130, 136–37
    love as method, loss and harm as residue in, 121–36
    race and gender in, 132, 133–34
    The Silk Route and, 109–11
    touch-gifts in, 103–9, 137–39
    touch in, 103–5, 106, 107–8, 111–16, 122, 124–25, 127–28, 129

INDEX

Rosenburg, Rae, 231
Roy, Srila, 237
Rumi, Jalalu'ddin, 152–53, 155–57, 167, 169, 172

Salgol, Rubina, 178
Sama, 156–57
samyoga (contact), 17–18, 24, 38–39, 65
Sarco-Thomas, Malaika, 27
Sarkar, Tanika, 78
Sarkar-Munsi, Urmimala, 52
Sarukkai, Sundar, 17–20, 22, 26, 38–39, 50–51, 57–58, 104–5, 107–8, 113
savarna spine, 66, 67–68, 85–86, 99–101
Saviliagno, Marta, 10–11
Scene Unseen, 140–43, 167, 178–79
Schimmel, Annemarie, 156, 172
Seker, Mehmet, 156
Sen, Debarati, 187
Sengupta, Tirna, 45–47
sexuality, gender and, 121–22, 127–28, 135, 136–39
sexual violence, 106–7, 158–59, 177–78
sex workers, 188
Shapiro, Sherry Badger, 71
Shiva, Vandana, 173–74
Showgirls of Pakistan, 150
Shri, 84–85
Siddiqui, Nahid, 22–23, 55–56, 163*f*, 165*f*, 168*f*, 193
  anti-patriarchal choreography of, 58–59, 145–46
  biography of, dance in Pakistan and, 147–54
  environmentalism and feminism of, 155–61, 178–79
  kathak and, 140, 143, 145–47, 148, 150–54, 155–61, 173, 178–80
  Scene Unseen by, 140–43, 167, 178–79
  Sufism of, 58–59, 145–47, 152–53, 155–61, 162, 163–64, 171–72, 173, 178–79
  A Thousand Borrowed Eyes on, 143–44, 145–46, 163–64, 167, 169, 178–79
  See also *Mirror Within*
Silent Burn Project, The, 193
Silk Route, The, 109–11
Singh, Pratistha, 188–90, 235
Smith, Margaret, 172
Smith, TK, 136
solo dance, in classicized Indian dance forms, 40–41, 42–44–, 47, 49, 50–53
sparsha (touch), 17, 18, 24, 65
Spivak, Gayatri, 10–11
Squirrel, Tom, 185

Sridevi, 59, 204–23, 224–25, 227
sringara, 168, 169, 178–79
Stanger, Arabella, 31
Stories of Thumris, 151–52
Subrahmanyam, Padma, 44–45, 52
Sufism, 58–59, 145–47, 152–53, 155–61, 162, 163–64, 171–73, 178–79
Sunalini, K. K., 74
Suraj, Guru, 2–3

Tamalapakula, Sowjanya, 78–79, 80
Tamil Nadu, 56–57, 65, 66–67, 70–71, 72–73, 74, 75, 89
Tarah, Munjulika, 192–93
tattakali, 49, 50–51
Tavag, Anishaa, 21–23, 24, 39, 49, 127, 128–30, 132–36, 132*f*, 248–49n.10
Thakore, Yashoda, 41–42
Thappattam, 68, 70, 75–76
Theatre, Dance and Performance Training, 28–29
Theenda Theenda, 146–47
  as activism, 71–72
  on Brahminical patriarchy, 66–67, 72, 80–81
  on Brahminism, 65, 67–68, 85–86, 88, 91, 98–99, 100–1
  on caste and caste oppression, 56–57, 65, 70, 72, 74–99
  on caste politics, 86
  on caste supremacy, 66–68, 98–99
  Chandiran in, 65, 66, 67–68, 72–73, 76, 86, 87, 88–92, 93–99, 95*f*, 96*f*, 100
  on "honor killings," 56–57, 65, 66–67, 72, 74–75, 89–90, 98
  on inter-caste contact and intimacies, 56–57, 65, 66–68, 71, 72, 74–81, 92–93, 94, 98–99, 100–1
  spine in, 84–86, 87, 88, 90–91, 93–94, 100–1
  therapeutic touch, social touch and, 72–73
  on touch, caste justice and, 81–99
  on touch, inter-caste intimacies, and caste violence, 74–81
  touch and contact in duet interactions of, 92–93
Thousand Borrowed Eyes, A, 143–44, 145–46, 163–64, 167, 169, 178–79
touch
  in bharatanatyam classroom, 49
  Black subjectivity and, 34
  caste and, 19–20, 29, 42–43, 56–57, 74–99
  choreographic, 2–3, 6–7, 30
  CI and, 2, 26, 29, 30, 31–32, 36–37, 49, 108, 116, 213–14

touch (cont.)
　contact and, 16, 17–18, 19, 22–23, 24–25, 34, 35–36, 42, 65, 92–93, 178–79, 214
　Covid-19 pandemic and, 213
　in dance studies, 26–27
　gender and, 25–26, 30, 36–37
　in human development, 16–17
　in kathak training, 49–50
　Naidu on normalizing, 104–6, 108, 110–11, 113
　in *Rorschach Touch*, 103–5, 106, 107–8, 111–16, 122, 124–25, 127–28, 129
　sparsha, 17, 18, 24, 65
　in theater, 36
　in *Theenda Theenda*, 72–73, 74–99
　therapeutic and social, 72–73
　untouchability and, 17, 18–20, 49, 50–51, 105
Touchdown Dance, 30–31
touch-gifts, 103–9
"Touch Test, The," 16–17
transgender and trans people, 231–32

unmaking
　manifesto, 4
　as method, politics, and emancipatory mode, 5–14

unmaking contact, 16–26
　in dance/studies, 26–39
　in South Asian dance/studies, 40–55
untouchability, 20, 21, 80
　Brahminism and, 49, 50–51, 79–80, 104–5
　touch and, 17, 18–20, 49, 50–51, 105

Vagistan, LaWhore, 15, 55–56, 193, 208f, 209f, 211f
　addas with, 194–204, 212–16, 217–23, 225–27, 228–32, 237–38
　on Auntie Sridevi, 216–23
　Ishtyle by, 212, 224
　See also #KaateNahinKatte
Vatsyayan, Kapila, 44, 45, 52

wahdah (unity), 58–59
Warren, Asher, 28–29
Wellcome Collection, 16–17
Welton, Martin, 28–29
whiteness, 33–34, 35, 38–39, 110–11, 132
worlding, 10–11
"Wrong" Contact Manifesto (Holland and Houston-Jones), 33–34

Yohalem, Hannah, 2–3, 33–34
Young, Hershini Bhana, 237–38

Zoom, 190–93, 230

The manufacturer's authorised representative in the EU for product safety is Oxford
University Press España S.A. of El Parque Empresarial San Fernando de Henares,
Avenida de Castilla, 2 – 28830 Madrid (www.oup.es/en or product.safety@oup.com).
OUP España S.A. also acts as importer into Spain of products made by the manufacturer.

Printed in the USA/Agawam, MA
August 8, 2025

891696.009